EMERGING ISSUES IN REHABILITATION COUNSELING

Perspectives on the New Millennium

By

PHILLIP D. RUMRILL, JR., Ph.D., CRC

Department of Educational Foundations and Special Services
Center for Disability Studies
Kent State University
Kent, Ohio

JAMES L. BELLINI

Department of Counseling and Human Services
Syracuse University
Syracuse, New York

LYNN C. KOCH

Department of Educational Foundations and Special Services
Center for Disability Studies
Kent State University
Kent, Ohio

With Invited Contributions

Charles C Thomas
PUBLISHER • LTD.
SPRINGFIELD • ILLINOIS • U.S.A.

Published and Distributed Throughout the World by

CHARLES C THOMAS • PUBLISHER, LTD.
2600 South First Street
Springfield, Illinois 62704

©2001 by CHARLES C THOMAS • PUBLISHER, LTD.

ISBN 0-398-07233-7 (cloth)
ISBN 0-398-07234-5 (paper)

Library of Congress Catalog Card Number: 2001041452

Printed in the United States of America
CR-R-3

Library of Congress Cataloging-in-Publication Data

Rumrill, Phillip D.
  Emerging issues in rehabilitation counseling : perspectives on the
new millennium / by Phillip D. Rumrill, James L. Bellini, Lynn C.
Koch.
      p. cm.
  Includes bibliographical references and index.
  ISBN 0-398-07233-7 (cloth) -- ISBN 0-398-07234-5 (pbk.)
  1. Rehabilitation counseling. 2. Vocational rehabilitation.
I. Bellini, James L. II. Koch, Lynn C. III. Title.

HD7255.5 .R86 2001
362'.0425--dc21

                                                          2001041452

EMERGING ISSUES IN REHABILITATION COUNSELING

For Nathan......**PDR**

For Diana, Jessica, and Vanessa......**JLB**

For Erlyn and Amanda......**LCK**

CONTRIBUTORS

JAMES L. BELLINI, PH.D., CRC
Syracuse University
Syracuse, New York

JOHN BRICOUT, PH.D.
Washington University
St. Louis, Missouri

PAUL M. DEUTSCH, PH.D., CRC
Paul M. Deutsch & Associates
Oviedo, Florida

PATRICK L. DUNN, PH.D., CRC
University of Alabama
Tuscaloosa, Alabama

CAROLYN E. HAWLEY, M.S., CRC
Virginia Commonwealth University
Richmond, Virginia

JULIE KITCHEN, B.S., CDMS, CCM, CLCP
Paul M. Deutsch & Associates
Oviedo, Florida

LYNN C. KOCH, PH.D., CRC
Kent State University
Kent, Ohio

BRIAN T. MCMAHON, PH.D., CRC
Virginia Commonwealth University
Richmond, Virginia

MARY A. MERZ, PH.D., CRC
Maryville University
St. Louis, Missouri

CHRISTINE A. REID, PH.D., CRC, CLCP
Virginia Commonwealth University
Richmond, Virginia

PHILLIP D. RUMRILL, JR. PH.D., CRC
Kent State University
Kent, Ohio

LINDA R. SHAW, PH.D., CRC
University of Florida
Gainesville, Florida

PREFACE

This book was developed as a text for introductory and field-based courses in graduate-level rehabilitation counselor education programs. It also offers practicing rehabilitation counselors, administrators, and educators in-depth discussions of contemporary issues affecting the profession of rehabilitation counseling and its consumers. In developing the structure and organization for this book, we identified topics in our field that have been the subject of considerable change and/or controversy over the past ten to fifteen years. We then invited authors to examine the current status of each topic, framed around the most likely directions that the rehabilitation process will take in the New Millenium.

The book is divided into seven chapters, each of which includes its own list of references. The first chapter addresses new developments in graduate-level rehabilitation education, presented within the context of society's growing and varying demand for qualified rehabilitation practitioners. Chapter 2 presents an in-depth analysis of the vocational rehabilitation (VR) program's changing consumer population, centered on the order of selection mandate in the Rehabilitation Act which requires VR agencies to prioritize services for people with the most significant disabilities. In Chapter 3, life care planning is described as an emerging rehabilitation intervention for people with catastrophic disabilities.

Chapters 4, 5, and 6, respectively, deal with client assessment strategies in the Americans with Disabilities Act (ADA) era, job development and placement strategies for a changing American labor market, and the need for improved postemployment services to help people with disabilities advance in their careers. The final chapter examines the history, current status, and future directions of private-sector rehabilitation, a fast-growing segment of the health care and rehabilitation industries.

Taken in aggregate, these chapters are intended to illuminate important contemporary issues that have broad implicatons for the future of rehabilitation counseling. The authors' perspectives are meant to serve as the basis for discussion and dialogue concerning those topic areas, as well as to provide an overview of what is being researched and written about in the current rehabilitation literature. Rehabiliation counseling is a dynamic, high-growth profession whose leaders and consumers have worked closely together to maintain a reputation steeped in responsiveness, responsibility, client advocacy, and empowerment of people with disabilities. It is our hope that this book will represent a meaningful reference vis-a-vis the policies that govern our field and the practices that underlie it.

PHILLIP D. RUMRILL, JR., PH.D., CRC
JAMES L. BELLINI, PH.D., CRC
LYNN C. KOCH, PH.D., CRC

ACKNOWLEDGMENTS

We would like to express our sincere gratitude to the people who made this project possible and successful. We begin by thanking our mentors and friends around the United States whose work has inspired our teaching, research, and writing: Dr. Jason Andrew of the University of Arkansas, Dr. David Andrews of Keene State College, Mr. Brandon Arterbury of the Arizona Rehabiliation Services Administration, Dr. Norman Berven of the University of Wisconsin, Dr. Brian Bolton of the University of Arkansas, Ms. Eva Cardenas of the Arizona Rehabilitation Services Administration, Dr. Fong Chan of the University of Wisconsin, Dr. Daniel Cook of the University of Arkansas, Dr. George Denny of the University of Arkansas, Dr. Suzanne Gordon of the University of Arkansas, Dr. David Hill of Keene State College, Dr. Ruth Lynch of the University of Wisconsin, Dr. Brian McMahon of Virginia Commonwealth University, Dr. Richard Roessler of the University of Arkansas, Dr. Kay Schriner of the University of Arkansas, Dr. Edna Szymanski of the University of Maryland, Dr. Kenneth Thomas of the University of Wisconsin, Dr. Inez Tucker of the University of Arizona, and Dr. Paul Wehman of Virginia Commonwealth University.

Our gratitude also goes to the outstanding authors who contributed chapters to this text: Dr. John Bricout of Washington University, Dr. Paul Deutsch of Paul M. Deutsch and Associates, Dr. Patrick Dunn of the University of Alabama, Ms. Carolyn Hawley of Virginia Commonwealth University, Ms. Julie Kitchen of Paul M. Deutsch and Assciates, Dr. Brian McMahon of Virginia Commonwealth University, Dr. Mary A. Merz of Maryville University, Dr. Christine Reid of Virginia Commonwealth University, and Dr. Linda Shaw of the University of Florida. Their perspectives provide compelling insight into the emerging trends and future directions of rehabilitation counseling as this profession moves into the twenty-first century.

For their clerical and editorial assistance, we are indebted to Ms. Mary Hennessey, Mr. David Martin, Ms. Deborah Minton, Ms. Amy Pittman, and Ms. Kristi Shearer, all of Kent State University. Special thanks go to Mr. Michael Payne Thomas of Charles C Thomas Publisher for his support and encouragement throughout this project.

CONTENTS

EMERGING ISSUES IN
REHABILITATION COUNSELING

Chapter 1

REHABILITATION COUNSELING AND EDUCATION: CAREER COUNSELING SUGGESTIONS FOR THE FUTURE

Brian T. McMahon, Carolyn E. Hawley, Christine A. Reid,
and Linda R. Shaw

INTRODUCTION

The purpose of this chapter is to describe how students can best prepare for careers in rehabilitation counseling, and discuss occupations that hold promise for rehabilitation counselors in the twenty-first century. Career opportunities for rehabilitation counselors in nontraditional settings are rapidly expanding, and students must able to activate the same career counseling principles they teach clients if they are to take full advantage of those opportunities. We begin this chapter with an overview of the current status of the counseling profession. Then, we identify counseling specialties in which there is a growth in employment opportunities. We follow this section with suggestions regarding how rehabilitation counselors can use their unique skills and specialized knowledge to access these opportunities. Our chapter concludes with a discussion regarding how Rehabilitation Counselor Education Programs can go about preparing students for diversified professional experiences in nontraditional settings.

CURRENT STATUS OF THE COUNSELING PROFESSION

According to the *Occupational Outlook Handbook* (JIST Works, 1998), there are about 250,000 counselors in the United States. Counselors are employed in health care facilities; job training, career development, and vocational rehabilitation (VR) centers; social agencies; correctional institutions; residential care facilities; community organizations; drug and alcohol rehabilitation programs; health maintenance organizations; insurance companies; group and private practices; and federal, state, and local government agencies. Job growth for counselors through 2006 is expected to be average, but above average for specialists in mental health, employment, and rehabilitation counseling. Job opportunities for school counselors are on the decline. However, in the wake of the Littleton catastrophe, school counselors are expected to rebound strongly from their projected decline.

The demand for counselors is difficult to estimate. Currently, average utilization within mental health organizations suggests that the nation needs only 70 behavioral-health practitioners per 100,000 United States citizens. There are currently 113 practitioners per 100,000 citizens, suggesting an oversupply. Epidemiological norms, however, suggest that the nation actually needs 250 practitioners per 100,000 citizens. Counselors, psychiatrists, psychologists, and social workers are addressing this need with the latter group currently providing more than 50 percent of all services (American Psychology Association, 1998).

Although the counseling profession's credentialing bodies have steadfastly advocated for a master's degree as the minimally acceptable academic criterion to practice, only six in ten counselors have graduate degrees (JIST Works, 1998). As a group, counselors do not tend to identify themselves as a single, united profession. Only one in five belongs to the American Counseling Association. Many others hold memberships in organizations representing their own counseling specialties.

Students enrolled in graduate counseling programs typically come from undergraduate degree programs in psychology, sociology, rehabilitation services, social work, or related fields. Approximately 133 universities have graduate counseling programs accredited by the Commission on Accreditation of Counseling and Related Educational Programs (CACREP). These programs collectively graduate an unknown number of counselors in the following specialty areas: career, community, gerontological, mental health, school, student affairs, and marriage and family counseling. In comparison, the Council on Rehabilitation Education (CORE) accredits approximately 85 graduate programs. These programs graduate approximately 700 rehabilitation counselors per year (JIST Works, 1998).

Following the completion of the Master of Science (MS) or Master of Arts (MA) degree, about 5 percent of graduates will pursue doctoral studies to become psychologists, counselor educators, researchers, or administrators. Forty-seven states have some form of counselor licensing credential. The National Board for Certified Counselors (NBCC) and the Commission on Rehabilitation Counselor Certification (CRCC) provide national certifications to approximately 24,000 and 15,000 individuals, respectively. Median salaries are just under $40,000 per year; fewer than 10 percent of all counselors earn over $60,000 per year (JIST Works, 1998).

The questions we are addressing in this chapter are: 1) How will we prepare rehabilitation counselors in the century ahead? and, of even greater importance, 2) What exactly should they be prepared to do?

THE OBVIOUS: COUNSELING SPECIALTIES OF PROMISE

The *Occupational Outlook Handbook* (JIST Works, 1998) identifies professions that are obviously related to rehabilitation counseling such as student affair workers, teachers, personnel workers and managers, human services workers, social workers, psychologists, psychiatrists, psychiatric nurses, clergy, occupational therapists, training and development specialists, and equal employment opportunity coordinators. Might it be wise for rehabilitation counseling graduates to include consideration of such related areas when developing their own career paths? Are there additional areas of emphasis that might further expand, or even explode, the range of opportunities for our graduates?

The New Addictions

The term addiction is most readily associated with alcohol and drug abuse. Clearly these issues have been and will continue to be a major concern for many counselors. However, several addictions are receiving wider recognition and are beginning to command both the attention and energy of practicing counselors. Examples include addictions involving excessive work (Robinson, 1998), sexual behavior (Carnes, 1989), and the Internet (Young, 1998). One exciting area of research involves the simultaneous study of multiple addictions and compulsive disorders as manifestations of a common impairment, known as *reward deficiency syndrome* (Blum, Cull, Braverman, & Comings, 1996).

Compulsive gambling is expected to emerge as a major individual and societal problem in the twenty-first century. The broad expansion of gambling across the United States and Canada prompted a comprehensive meta-analysis of gambling prevalence rates by the Harvard Medical School Division on Addictions (Shaffer, Hall, & Bilt, 1997). Composite estimates are that 1.60 percent of adults, 3.88 percent of youth, and 4.67 percent of college students meet the diagnostic criteria for compulsive gambling (level 3 gamblers). Problem gambling exists among an additional 3.85 percent of adults, 9.45 percent of youth, and 15.01 percent of college students. Gambling disorders are increasing in prevalence among adults, and are significantly more prevalent among males and persons with concurrent psychiatric problems. In 1999, a two year, $5 million study was completed by the National Gambling Impact Study Commission. The report of that study describes potential economic benefits of the gambling explosion, while acknowledging social costs such as pathological gambling, crime, and other maladies. The commission called for an explicit moratorium on gambling expansion while further research is conducted.

Incarceration as a Growth Industry

As sad as it may appear, corrections is the largest growing segment of government in nearly every state, far outspending the higher education system in most. Almost two million people will sleep in prison tonight, and the inmate population is growing at 8 percent per year. Two new 1,000-bed facilities must be built each week just to keep up with the demand. The privatization of prisons is operational in 15 states, and 35 states have provisions that permit privatization. The private prison business alone (now housing 5% of all inmates) is a $600 million dollar per year business and is growing at an annual rate of 30 percent (Grugal, 1996). Prison counselor and psychologist jobs will flourish, as will managers of prison industries. Some have quipped that due to managed care, prison is the only place one can receive treatment for substance abuse today. It may be a bad joke, but nonetheless, it does reflect a source of employment opportunity for substance abuse counselors.

The situation is similar for persons with mental illness. Steadman and Cocozza (1993). concluded that "ten to fifteen percent of prison populations has a major DSM-III-R thought disorder or mood disorder and needs the services usually associated with severe or chronic mental illness" (p. 6) Teplin (1990) has estimated that the prison population has two to three times the rate of mental illness as does the general population. A more important implication for the future of counselors, however, is the clear reality that most inmates eventually return to the community. This means that vocational counselors and parole officers with a working knowledge of mental illness will be in extraordinary demand (Veysey, 1994).

The Graying of America

The graying of America has been well documented. A full 35 percent of the U.S. population will be 55 years of age or more by the year 2050. Rapid advances in medicine and technology have resulted in a steady increase in the number of people with disabilities living past retirement age. Moreover, older workers are deferring retirement to later in life than ever before, and many seek to supplement their pensions with part-time employment (Shafer, Choppa, & Siefker, 1993).

Census data (U.S. Department of Commerce, 1995) projects that the proportion of individuals in advanced old age (85 and over) will skyrocket, doubling in size from 1995 to 2030, and increasing fourfold by the year 2050. This age cohort experiences the most problems with functional disability. Vanderheiden (1990) describes the difficulty in pinpointing the exact number of individuals with disabilities or limitations due to aging, but he provides an estimate of somewhere between 12 percent to 20 percent of the population, many with multiple disabilities.

Nearly 500,000 Americans with developmental disabilities live with caregivers who are 60 or older. As these aging caregivers die or become unable to provide assistance, serious demands will be placed upon home-based support services programs in most states (Wright & King, 1999). Without question, those Rehabilitation Counselor Education (RCE) programs that actively support the integrated study of the phenomenon of aging and disability will be rewarded.

Multicultural Counseling

Census data suggests that minority populations will account for most of the U.S. population growth during the next century (Cornman & Kingson, 1996). Asians are projected to represent the fastest growing population in the United States over the next 50 years, accounting for 16.5 percent of the total growth in the U.S. population (Campbell, 1996). Hispanics represent the second fastest growing population, with projections that they will account for 44 percent of the growth in the nation's population. Over the next 50 years, it is also anticipated that "the black population will grow at more than twice the white population's annual rate of change" (U.S. Department of Commerce, 1995, p. 14).

Because the dramatic swing in the racial makeup of the U.S. population has already begun, the counseling literature and practice standards reflect the importance of developing multicultural competencies (Altarriba & Bauer, 1998; Arredondo, 1999; Smart, 1998; Weinrach & Thomas, 1998). Counselors with excellent skills in multicultural counseling will be in great demand in order to improve the effectiveness of services to the growing minority population. Additionally, there exists a need to address adjustment issues likely to accompany the social and political upheaval that tends to occur with rapidly changing demographics (McDaniel, 1995).

Life Care Planning

Life care planning is a systematic methodology for identifying and quantifying the multidimensional, disability-related needs of an individual. In a highly competitive health care industry, the life care plan will ultimately come to be regarded as the ultimate discharge plan for health care facilities. These plans also will be useful as educational tools for case managers who need to anticipate and articulate future needs for consumers, family members, claims adjusters, and other stakeholders. Life care plans are also useful to assist insurers with accurate reserve setting as well as in the development of structured settlements and special needs trusts (Reid, Deutsch, Kitchen, & Aznavoorian, 1999). These applications are also cited by Weed (1999), who would add mediation, divorce, and family financial planning to the menu of uses for life care planning methodology.

The Globalization of Rehabilitation

Worldwide there are more than 500 million people with disabilities. Most face a daily battle for even their most basic human rights. They experience daily discrimination and exclusion from equality of opportunity, particularly among women who receive less than one-fifth of rehabilitation resources worldwide. The United Nations' authority on international disability issues (Lindqvist, 1999), predicts that the number of people with disabilities is likely to increase radically over the next 25 years in both developed and developing countries. Global economic development will mean longer life expectancy, lower mortality rates for children with congenital conditions, more traffic, industrial development, hazardous wastes, overcrowding, and violence. Many governments are rethinking their disability policies and will look to the United States to square their commitments to equal rights with the fiscal demands that these commitments will pose on their budgets.

APPLYING CAREER COUNSELING PRINCIPLES

With a new century upon us, rehabilitation counseling is, like most other professions, engaging in strategic planning, redefining or reengineering itself, or at least taking inventory of its present status and future possibilities. For reasons stated above, the profession is likely to undergo substantial changes in the century ahead. Perhaps even this view of rehabilitation counseling, however, is still too narrow. Perhaps the profession has yet to exercise its full potential, applying its knowledge base in the nontraditional marketplace, seizing opportunities discovered by others as a result of adventure, innovation, or happenstance.

The authors maintain that rehabilitation counseling should be true to its history and tradition by emphasizing the basic elements of the profession that distinguish it from others: disability, counseling, and vocational rehabilitation. At the same time, however, it is crucial that we recognize the professional's unique ability to adapt these elements to other social, business, and rehabilitation-related problems in a whole host of settings, geographic locations, and populations. How, then, can we begin to identify those new applications and opportunities? The authors believe that the answer is rooted in two principles that have their roots in career counseling. Specifically, our profession will better served if we can: 1) expand the range of occupations considered before committing to a specific career path, and 2) identify and apply transferable skills when expanding the range of jobs considered.

The remainder of this section is a guided tour of what happens to rehabilitation counselor education when it is subjected to its own principles, that is, when we practice what we preach. If these principles are good enough for our clients, they should also have value when applied to our own profession. This chapter is an attempt to share this challenge with the reader—to apply rehabilitation counseling's best tools to our own current problems.

The Less than Obvious: Applying Transferable Skills Analysis to Our Profession

Rehabilitation counselors have access to some powerful tools for career exploration. Imagine the trained rehabilitation counselor as a client who, for whatever reason, can no longer continue in our profession. If a transferable skills analysis (TSA) were performed upon this generic rehabilitation counselor, hundreds of related occupations to which our clients' skills could readily transfer would be identified. Table 1-I provides precisely such a listing, and includes a few selected examples of occupations that provide high growth potential and high wages. As for any client, actually entering such an occupation might require additional training, work experience, or even formal education. But the undisputed fact remains: The skills that we provide in our rehabilitation counseling education (RCE) programs are transferable to many attractive occupations.

Next, one could perform a similar analysis using more specific knowledge and skills domains in isolation of other factors. Consider, for example, personal adjustment counseling skills, vocational evaluation skills, job placement skills, advocacy skills, or case management skills. To what occupations might these competencies be transferable? Findings include such diverse occupations as financial aid counselor, loan officer, advertising manager, foreign student adviser, grant coordinator, psychometrist, revenue agent, equal employment opportunity officer, admissions evaluator, investigator, eligibility worker, benefits manager, and customer service representative (examples only).

Table 1.I. OCCUPATIONS TO WHICH REHABILITATION COUNSELING
SKILLS ARE TRANSFERABLE

Transferability Level	*Job Title*	*DOT Code*
5	Conciliator	169.207-010
6	Human Resource Advisor	166.267-046
6	Economist	050.067-010
6	Job Development Specialist	166.267-034
8	Labor Relations Manager	166.167.034
8	Director of Compliance	188.117-046
8	Risk and Insurance Manager	186.117-066
8	Director of Outpatient Rehabilitation Services	187.117-058
8	Utilization Coordinator	169.167-018
8	Industrial Arts Teacher	091.122-010
8	Recruiter	166.267-026
8	Compensation Manager	166.167-022
8	Job Analyst	166.267-018
8	Director of Vocational Training	097.167-010
8	Director of Employment Services	188.117-030
8	General Claims Agent	186.117-030
8	Apprenticeship Consultant	188.117-010
8	Director of Placement	166.167-018
8	Manager of Procurement Services	162.167-022
8	Safety Manager	012.167-058
8	Technical Training Coordinator	166.167-054
8	Director, Council on Aging	188.117-058
8	Estate Planner	186.167-010
8	Warden	188.167-018
8	In-service Coordinator	079.127-010
9	Employment Interviewer	166.267-010
9	Lobbyist	165.017-010
9	Claim Examiner	168.267-014
9	Arbitrator	169.107-010
9	Personnel Recruiter	166.267-038
9	Retirement Officer	166.267-030
9	Occupational Analyst	166.067-010
9	Employee Relations Specialist	166.267-042
9	Veterans Contact Representative	187.167-198
9	Prisoner Classification Interviewer	166.267-022
9	Credit Counselor	160.207-010
9	Hospital Insurance Representative	166.267-014

Beyond the construct of TSA, this approach is consistent with several other career counseling concepts that are widely accepted today. These include portable skills, career resilience (Szymanski, 1999), career portfolios, career transition, career planning for the life span (Koch & Johnston-Rodriguez, 1997), planned happenstance, and the advantages of open-mindedness (Mitchell, Levin, & Krumboltz, 1999).

IMPLICATIONS FOR REHABILITATION COUNSELOR EDUCATION

The authors are not suggesting that RCE programs are the only place where these skills can be acquired or improved. However, they may be as good as or better than the alternatives. For many years, rehabilitation counseling has struggled to define itself as a profession, as evidenced by an extraordinary number of roles and functions studies. Defining the profession has been difficult because of its diversity and the overlap that exists with other helping professions (Leahy, Chan, Taylor, Wood, & Downey, 1998; Rubin, Chan, & McMahon, 1997). Nevertheless, rehabilitation counseling leadership finalized a Scope of Practice Statement, which defines the core competencies of rehabilitation counselors. Published by the Commission on Rehabilitation Counselor Certification, this document is endorsed by all major professional rehabilitation counseling organizations and credentialing bodies. Now that core competencies have been so clearly defined, a logical next step for the profession might be to seek new applications of those competencies in nontraditional settings, especially if society, technology, and the political climate suggest these new directions.

Returning to rehabilitation counselor education, Hershenson and McKenna (1998) describe the dilemma that is introduced by expanding the profession into new directions:

How to incorporate new content into the curriculum without losing continuity of identity, deleting material that will violate accreditation standards, or disrupting programmatic research efforts. Perhaps these issues can be resolved by a two-pronged approach, simultaneously (a) teaching a more narrowly defined core body of professional knowledge, skills, and attitudes; and (b) training entering practitioners in contextual vigilance and in flexibility and adaptability to change. Of these two, the latter is more difficult to achieve (p. 285).

The next question becomes, "What if our RCE programs actively recruited and embraced students who wanted to develop skills that could be transferred into these occupations of opportunity?" Certainly this is what occurs in law school or MBA programs. Students study law and business with career applications in mind that may be poorly developed or highly personal. RCE students may understand this better than the educators. Many students, and often the better students, sometimes gravitate to seemingly unrelated occupations in which their RCE skills are still applied or even featured. This is not "occupational drift," "error variance," or "accident theory" at work. These are well-informed young people who understood the power of expanding their own view of the world of work and applying the concept of transferable skills.

The authors have educated graduates who work today as primary managers, human resource professionals, software developers, publishers, sports agents, risk managers, diversity specialists, outplacement specialists, corporate recruiters, expert witnesses, strategy consultants to trial attorneys, injury prevention specialists, legislative assistants, politicians, mediators, arbitrators, process observers, group facilitators, insurance adjusters, political activists, behavior analysts, and job analysts. A cursory check of RCE colleagues reveals additional jobs in which the incumbents identified their graduate education as helpful. These include careers in real estate, financial planning, hospital administration, test development, pharmaceutical sales, human resources, outplacement, and health care marketing. Other alumni have job titles such as fishing guide, relocation specialist, counselor for injured athletes, domestic violence specialist, director of services for students with disabilities in higher education, developer of rehabilitation technology, neuropsychology technician, stock broker, prevention specialist, director of recreation and other therapeutic interventions for children, systems analyst, vocational consultant regarding marital dissolution, intelligence officer, designer of clothing for persons with disabilities, and wine maker. Relevance to rehabilitation counseling is obviously quite variable.

Many articles have appeared which examine the characteristics of rehabilitation students and alumni (e.g., Emener, Tannenbaum, &

Cady, 1989). How many have addressed truly difficult questions, including those to which we may not want answers? What are the levels of unmet expectations among our graduates? How much competition exists for quality jobs? With 16 million students in American colleges and universities, with 40 percent of all college-age Americans now attending college, with half of all Americans having some exposure to higher education, and with 1,600 public institutions of higher learning, why do some RCE programs find quality applicants so difficult to identify? How might a limited view of who we are and what we do serve to divide us from the rest of the world of human services and other viable areas of employment?

Some rehabilitation educators feel that rehabilitation counseling has been well served by featuring its narrow distinctions from related health and human service professions, such as social work, psychology, or any of a myriad of counseling specializations. Is this the best we can do? Consider this alternative: What if getting the M.S. degree was like getting a business or law degree? In this scenario, the student learns a set of core principles and the curriculum illustrates how these might be applied to solving a vast array of problems. RCE programs could immediately attract more students who seek a generic exposure to skills and ideas that may equip them for any number of professional endeavors. When they complete their degrees and go on to careers outside the mainstream of rehabilitation counseling, they would bring with them an understanding of multipotentiality (including their own), effective listening, disability awareness, advocacy, multiculturalism, career development, accommodations, altering environments to fit people–and the power of these tools and ideas.

Green (1997) provides examples of three professionals (nurse, engineer, and attorney) who transferred their skills and knowledge successfully from their occupations of origin. In her article entitled "Traditional Degrees, Nontraditional Jobs: A Degree is Not a Life Sentence," she advises "You have skills; it's up to you to translate those skills into something marketable. Be creative in figuring out ways to transfer your knowledge, interests, and experience into another field" (p. 15).

Counselor Education as Cross-Training

How can the skills and experiences developed in RCE programs enhance the personal and professional development of people who are already deeply committed to other professions? Chiappone (1992) describes another demographic reality: intense competition in the now 30- to 60-year-old age group for supervisory positions. Ambitious persons from all professions are cross-training to achieve advancement. Look around campus and you will see physicians cross-training in business and public health, attorneys cross-training in accountancy, teachers cross-training in administration, allied health professionals cross-training in different allied health professions, and engineers cross-training in everything. According to the Nierenberg Group (1998), workplace success is based on five business skills, the highest three of which are interpersonal communications, self-motivation, and conflict resolution (rated as important by 90 to 95% of respondents). In this context, how appealing would certificate programs be, including a two- to three-course sequence in such areas as basic listening and attending, cultural diversity, career counseling, disability awareness, team building, leadership development, and addictionology?

Job Placement Education as Cross-Training

Many rehabilitation and career counselors have redirected their efforts from consumer-oriented services toward employer-oriented services. They have developed significant relationships with employers, and in that context have become valuable resources to them in a variety of areas. Are there currently employed professionals in business and industry who might benefit from limited coursework in job placement, return-to-work programs, disability management, nondiscrimination and affirmative action, injury prevention, welfare-to-work, accommodations and ergonomics, ADA implementation, and making goods and services accessible to customers with disabilities?

Case Management Education as Cross-Training

In the near future, employment opportunities for case managers in the worker compensation arena will become compressed. Growth will occur in health care, but at a slower rate. The expansion of managed care (and especially the competition therein) will level off. Reforms in laws, policies, and regulations will likely have the effect of reducing conflicts between stakeholders (e.g., worker and employer). By extension, this may mean less need for case management, because opportunities for case managers tend to be created by conflict. Still, there exists a number of established professionals within business and industry who could benefit from coursework in case management, life care planning, disability evaluation, confidentiality of medical information, utilization of community resources, benefit systems, cost benefit analysis, rehabilitation planning, and program evaluation.

THE IMPORTANCE OF DIVERSIFYING SOURCES
OF REIMBURSEMENT

As faculty members in Colleges and Schools of Allied Health Professions, the authors have occasion from time to time to compare our situation with that of our sister professions. Many feel that rehabilitation counseling was the "big loser" in the mid-1970s. At that time, due in part to the fragmentation brought about by multiple professional organizations, the profession did not establish itself as a reimbursable medical specialization. Consequently, rehabilitation counseling was not able to directly tap into the larger funding sources; that is, group health insurance and medical assistance. Our colleagues in physical therapy, occupational therapy, psychology, and speech therapy soared past us in terms of numbers, salaries, status, and working conditions. Their educational programs became ever more specialized, and foundations such as rehabilitation philosophy, interdisciplinary team functioning, cultural diversity, and case management were rarely expressly addressed.

In the meantime, rehabilitation counselors found employment where they could—state and federal VR programs, insurance rehabilitation, mental health counseling, school-to-work transition, substance abuse counseling, case management, supervision and administration, job placement, employer consultation, employee assistance programs, and the like. Recently the worm has turned. Hit hard by changes in Medicare reimbursement mandated by the Balanced Budget Act of 1997 (i.e., $1,500 cap on restorative rehabilitation services), employers have announced personnel cuts of 10 to 60 percent for reimbursable therapists (Saphir, 1999). National hospital and skilled nursing companies, rehabilitation hospitals, and outpatient rehabilitation facilities are laying off therapists by the thousands, while others are implementing broad-based salary reductions. Although rehabilitation counseling is inherently more diversified than any reimbursable discipline, it behooves us to be more forward-looking than our colleagues.

History has taught us that future funding for rehabilitation endeavors cannot be separated from legislative opportunities. At every turn, there exist enormous opportunities as well as threats. For example, the Community Renewal Act currently under consideration in the House of Representatives calls for an investment of billions of dollars in drug and alcohol prevention and treatment. Regrettably, these monies could be routed through religious organizations that would be exempt from credentialing standards in the hiring of "counselors." Additionally, the bill promotes a view of chemical dependency as a moral failure as opposed to a legitimate medical condition.

The apparently successful assault on welfare benefits will soon be followed by an assault on disability benefits vis-à-vis the Work Incentives Improvement Act. Rehabilitation counselors will play a major role in that arena. The infusion of capital available for return-to-work programs from the Social Security Administration will be multiples of anything we have observed to date in the public and private sectors combined. These new sources of revenue will be directed at one-stop career centers, placement-oriented providers, and employer and VR service delivery networks (Sampson & Reardon, 1998). Who can mobilize faster to beat us out of yet another extraordinary opportunity? Can occupational therapists do this even faster than nurses are monopolizing case management at our expense? Can employer networks mobilize even faster than social workers cordoned off mental health and welfare-to-work? Will our multiple professional organizations continue to compete and obsess over affiliation issues and letterhead while these important issues are resolved to our exclusion?

SUMMARY

The degree of occupational inheritance in rehabilitation counseling appears to be very small. Why is it that the children of rehabilitation counselors do not pursue similar career paths, a common practice in other reputable professions? One may assume that, at a minimum, rehabilitation counselors are likely to communicate a number of "life lessons" that they have come to embrace (e.g., the value, dignity, and multipotentiality of all citizens including persons with disabilities). What follows from this is the multipotentiality of well-trained rehabilitation counselors who, if they practice what they preach, will apply their own power tools (such as transferable skills analysis) to the advancement of their own profession. Perhaps then rehabilitation counselors will rediscover a profession that will be actively encouraged even for their own children.

REFERENCES

Altarriba, J., & Bauer, L. M. (1998). Counseling the Hispanic client: Cuban Americans, Mexican Americans, and Puerto Ricans. *Journal of Counseling and Development, 76,* 389-395.

American Psychology Association Research Office. (1998). Psychologists, social workers, and psychiatrists: Too many or not enough? *APA Monitor,* September, p. 21.

Arredondo, P. (1999). Multicultural counseling competencies as tools to address oppression and racism. *Journal of Counseling and Development, 77,* 102-108.

Blum, K., Cull, J., Braverman, E., & Comings, D. (1996). Reward deficiency syndrome. *American Scientist, 84,* 132-145.

Campbell, P. R. (1996). *Population projections for states by age, sex, race, and Hispanic origin: 1995 to 2025.* U.S. Bureau of the Census, Population Division, PPL-47.

Carnes, P. J. (1989). *Contrary to love: Helping the sexual addict.* Minneapolis, MN: Compcare Publications.

Chiappone, J. M. (1992). The career development professional of the 1990s: A training model. In H. D. Lea & Z. B. Leibowitz (Eds.), *Adult career development: Concepts, issues, and practices* (pp. 364-379). Alexandria, VA: National Career Development Association.

Cornman, J. M., & Kingson, E. R. (1996). Trends, issues, perspectives, and values for the aging of the baby boom cohorts. *Gerontology, 36,* 15-26.

Emener, W. G., Tannenbaum, S. L., & Cady, B. A. (1989). Rehabilitation counselor education students' career goal aspirations and development: An empirical investigation. *Rehabilitation Education, 4,* 121-137.

Green, K. (1997). Traditional degrees, nontraditional jobs: A degree is not a life sentence. *Occupational Outlook Quarterly, 41*(1), 13-19.

Grugal, R. (1996). Prison operator thrives in crime crackdown. *Investor's Business Daily,* March 4.

Hershenson, D. B., & McKenna, M. A. (1998). Trends affecting rehabilitation counselor education. *Rehabilitation Education, 12,* 277-288.

JIST Works, Inc. (1998). *The enhanced occupational outlook handbook,* 2nd ed. Indianapolis, IN: Author.

Koch, L., & Johnston-Rodriguez, S. (1997). The career portfolio: A vocational rehabilitation tool for assessment, planning, and placement. *Journal of Job Placement, 13*(1), 19-22.

Leahy, M., Chan, F., Taylor, D., Wood, C., & Downey, C. (1998). Evolving knowl-
edge and skill factors for practice in private sector rehabilitation. *The Rehabilitation Professional, 6*, 34-48.

Lindqvist, B. (1999). *World disability report.* Geneva, Switzerland: International
Disability Foundation.

McDaniel, A. (1995). The dynamic racial composition of the United States. *Dedalus, 124*, 179-199.

Menand, L. (1996). How to make a Ph.D. matter. *New York Times.* September 22,
1996.

Mitchell, K. E., Levin, A. S., & Krumboltz, J. D. (1999). Planned happenstance:
Constructing unexpected career opportunities. *Journal of Counseling and Development, 77*, 115-124.

Nierenberg Group. (1998). Important skills. *HR Factfinder*, December, p. 8.

Reid, P., Deutsch, P., Kitchen, J., & Aznavoorian, K. (1999). Life care planning. In F.
Chan & M. Leahy (Eds.), *Healthcare and disability case management* (pp. 415-453).
Lake Zurich, IL: Vocational Consultants Press.

Robinson, B. E. (1998). *Chained to the desk: A guidebook for workaholics, their partners
and children, and the clinicians who treat them.* New York: NYU Press.

Rubin, S., Chan, F., & McMahon, B. T. (1997). Research directions related to rehabilitation practice: A Delphi study. *Journal of Rehabilitation, 64*, 19-26.

Sampson, J. P., & Reardon, R. C. (1998). Maximizing staff resources in meeting the
needs of job seekers in one-stop centers. *Journal of Employment Counseling, 35*, 50-
68.

Saphir, A. (1999). How far they have fallen. *Week in Healthcare*, April 12, 12-13.

Shafer, K., Choppa, A. J., & Siefker, J. M. (1993). Vocational rehabilitation of older
displaced workers. *Journal of Rehabilitation, 59*(3), 35-39.

Shaffer, H. J., Hall, M. N. & Bilt, J. V. (1997). *Estimating the prevalence of disordered gambling behavior in the United States and Canada: A meta-analysis.* Boston: Harvard
Medical School Division on Addictions.

Smart, J. F. (1998). Multicultural rehabilitation education: Issues of implementation.
Rehabilitation Education, 12, 129-136.

Steadman, J., & Cocozza, J. (1993). *Mental illness in America's prisons.* Seattle, WA: The
National Coalition for Mental and Substance Abuse Health Care in the Justice
System.

Szymanski, E. N. (1999). Disability, job stress, the changing nature of careers, and
the career resilience portfolio. *Rehabilitation Counseling Bulletin, 42*, 279-289.

Teplin, L. A. (1990). The prevalence of severe mental disorder among male urban
jail detainees: Comparison with the Epidemiologic Catchment Area Program.
American Journal of Public Health, 80, 663-669.

U.S. Department of Commerce, Bureau of the Census. (1995). *Population projections
of the United States by age, sex, race, and Hispanic origin: 1995 to 2050.* Washington,
DC: Author.

Vanderheiden, G. C. (1990). Thirty-something million: Should they be exceptions? *Human Factors, 32*(4), 383-396.

Veysey, B. (1994). *Challenges for the future.* In National Institute of Corrections: Topics in community corrections (pp. 3-10). Longmont, CO: National Institute of Corrections.

Weed, R. O. (1999). Life care planning: Past, present, and future. In R. O. Weed (Ed.), *Life care planning and case management handbook* (pp. 1-14). Boca Raton, FL: CRC Press.

Weinrach, S. G., & Thomas, K. R. (1998). Diversity-sensitive counseling today: A postmodern clash of values. *Journal of Counseling and Development, 76,* 115-122.

Wright, B., & King, M. (1999). Developmental disabilities and aging. National Conference of State Legislatures. *Legisbrief, 7*(15).

Young, K. S. (1998). *Caught in the net: How to recognize the signs of internet addiction and a winning strategy for recovery.* New York: John Wiley and Sons.

Chapter 2

IMPLEMENTATION AND EVALUATION OF THE ORDER OF SELECTION MANDATE IN STATE VOCATIONAL REHABILITATION AGENCIES

JAMES L. BELLINI

INTRODUCTION

Order of selection is the cornerstone of the long-standing federal policy initiative to serve individuals with the most significant[1] disabilities in the state-federal vocational rehabilitation (VR) program. The order of selection provision was included in the 1973 Rehabilitation Act to ensure that individuals with significant disabilities are not denied participation in the VR program because of the cost and complexity of their service needs (Barrett et al., 1978; Eleventh Institute on Rehabilitation Issues, 1974; United States General Accounting Office [USGAO], 1991). State VR agencies are required to implement an order of selection procedure to provide priority services to individuals with the most significant disabilities when the agency

---

Note: The views expressed in this chapter are those of the author. No official endorsement by the U.S. Department of Education or the Rehabilitation Services Administration is intended or should be inferred.

1. Terminology used in the Rehabilitation Act has been revised on several occasions. The original legislation (P.L. 93-112) used the term "individual with most severe handicaps" to identify the target population for priority service. In the 1992 Amendments to the Rehabilitation Act, the term was changed to "individual with the most severe disabilities." In the 1998 Amendments to the Rehabilitation Act the term was changed again, to "individual with the most significant disabilities." Throughout this chapter I will conform to contemporary terminology and refer to "individuals with the most significant disabilities" when discussing the target population for priority VR service.

determines, on the basis of projected fiscal and personnel resources, that it will be unable to serve all eligible applicants (*Federal Register*, May 14, 1996).

Despite a continuing commitment in federal disability policy to serving individuals with significant disabilities, the order of selection mandate remains controversial (Bellini, 1997; Schriner, 1996; USGAO, 1991). Implementation of the order of selection provision may result in denial of needed VR services for persons with disabilities who qualify for the VR program but who do not qualify for priority services as individuals with most significant disabilities. Conversely, individuals who have more significant disabilities and require more extensive VR services to achieve their employment goals are given higher priority within order of selection plans and may therefore be more likely to receive the services they need to become employed. Clearly, if the VR program were more adequately funded to meet the rehabilitation needs of all individuals with disabilities, the order of selection provision would be unnecessary. As social policy, the necessity of order of selection is rooted in inadequate funding of the state-federal VR program. Thus, the most fundamental controversy spawned by the order of selection policy pertains to who among the millions of Americans with disabilities are to be provided VR services when agency resources are inadequate to serve all eligible persons with disabilities.

The purpose of this chapter is to discuss the implementation of the order of selection mandate in state VR agencies. The following sections will complete the review: (a) legislative history of the mandate and evaluation of policy implementation; (b) equity concepts as they apply to the order of selection policy; (c) current status of policy implementation in state VR agencies; (d) review of the empirical literature on order of selection; and (e) summary and conclusions.

ORDER OF SELECTION: LEGISLATIVE HISTORY AND POLICY IMPLEMENTATION

The Rehabilitation Act of 1973

Order of selection was first mandated in the 1973 Rehabilitation Act (P.L. 93-112) and has remained a key provision in all subsequent

Amendments to the Act. During congressional hearings held in 1972, numerous persons with significant disabilities provided testimony that they had been denied needed VR services due to the severity of their disabilities (Barrett et al., 1978; Urban Institute, 1974). Congress became convinced that individuals with significant disabilities, for whom VR services are intended in principle, should not be denied needed services because of erroneous assumptions about the cost or complexity of their rehabilitation needs or about their ability to benefit from VR services and achieve successful employment outcomes.

Barrett et al. (1978) noted that there was considerable discussion in the congressional hearings on the Rehabilitation Act pertaining to the definition of individual with significant disabilities and the ramifications of various definitions. Problems with defining the key term revolved around the relationship among three alternative criteria for determining the degree of severity: 1) impairment categories, or the cause of the disability; 2) functional limitation, or the effect of the disability in terms of capacity; and 3) case difficulty, or the effect of the disability in terms of services needed to achieve a successful outcome (Barrett et al., 1978).

All three criteria were included in the federal definition of individual with significant disabilities. Thus, individual with significant disabilities was defined in the Rehabilitation Act (P.L. 93-112) and subsequent regulations on the basis of medical diagnostic categories (e.g., autism, cerebral palsy, mental illness, heart disease) or limitation in functional capacity in one or more key life areas (i.e., mobility, communication, self care, self-direction, interpersonal skills, work tolerance, and work skills) coupled with the need for multiple services over extended time as these relate to employability (Barrett et al., 1978).

Implementation of Order of Selection: A Sluggish Beginning

Despite the fact that the mandate to serve individuals with most significant disabilities required immediate changes in the operations of state VR agencies (Barrett et al., 1978), the implementation of the mandate proceeded slowly for the first two decades following the passage of the Rehabilitation Act. Specifically, from the passage of the Act in 1973 to 1991, more than half of the state VR agencies never used an order of selection procedure to prioritize services, and only nine states had "extended experience"–defined as at least two consecutive years experience–in implementing the mandate (USGAO, 1991). At the same time, state VR agencies reported a gradual increase in the proportion of persons with significant disabilities served, from 45 percent in 1976 to 68 percent of the total in 1989 (USGAO, 1991). Reasons for the sluggish implementation of order of selection included: 1) ambiguity with regard to the statutory definition of individual with significant disabilities; 2) the lack of a statutory definition of individual with the most significant disabilities; and 3) the fact that the provision, as established in the Rehabilitation Act and subsequent regulations, was a weak mandate that failed to provide state VR agencies with necessary incentives.

Ambiguity in regard to the statutory definition.

The inclusion of all three previously mentioned criteria in the federal definition of individual with significant disabilities contributed to confusion for state VR agencies attempting to implement the provision, because the three criteria may not be strongly correlated in every case. In many cases, medical diagnoses (e.g., mental retardation, renal disease) are not useful either in determining the specific nature or severity of functional limitations or the service needs of the individual with disability (Nagi, 1991). Thus, each criterion potentially resulted in a somewhat different target population for priority service, depending on the nature of the impairment (or medical diagnosis) and its impact on the person's functioning (Koshel & Granger, 1978; Urban Institute, 1974).

The ambiguity of the federal definition sparked considerable debate in the rehabilitation profession during the 1970s and 1980s regarding the relationships among impairments, functional limitations, and service needs, as well as interest in the development of psychometric instruments to assess and quantify functional limitations (Frey, 1984; Koshel & Granger, 1978; Rehabilitation Services Administration [RSA], 1978). As a result of this debate, a broad consensus emerged among citizens with disabilities and rehabilitationists that identification of functional limitations in key life areas is the most appropriate approach to defining significant disability (Barrett et al., 1978; Coalition of Citizens with Disabilities, 1991; Nagi, 1991; RSA, 1992).

Current RSA guidelines to state VR agencies strongly emphasize the functional approach to identifying persons with most significant disabilities.

The absence of a statutory definition of individual with the most significant disabilities.

The definition of individual with the most significant disabilities is the most important issue affecting implementation of order of selection, with, potentially, the broadest ramifications for who will be served under the mandate. Despite the fact that the Rehabilitation Act specifically requires priority VR services to individuals with the most significant disabilities, legislation and regulations define only the term individual with significant disabilities (RSA, 1992). RSA acknowledged the difficulty of operationally defining this key term, stating that, in the event that an agency is unable to distinguish between individuals with the *most* significant disabilities and individuals with significant disabilities, the agency may serve individuals with significant disabilities on a first-applied, first-served basis (RSA, 1992). Not surprisingly, many state VR agencies also refrained from defining individual with the most significant disabilities. Instead, most agencies dichotomized disability into severe and non-severe categories and served individuals in the severe category first (RSA, 1992).

As will be discussed later in this chapter, recent Amendments to the Rehabilitation Act reflect a stronger commitment to the mandate to serve persons with the most significant disabilities. There is little doubt, however, that the lack of a federal definition of individual with the most significant disabilities, coupled with inadequate guidance from RSA to the state VR agencies, limited the impact of the mandate during its first two decades of implementation.

Order of selection: A weak mandate.

The state-federal VR program is best described as a partnership between the federal office (i.e., RSA) and state VR agencies (Rubin & Roessler, 2000). Consistent with this notion of a state-federal partnership, during the early years of order of selection implementation state VR agencies retained considerable discretion in interpreting what the legislative mandate should mean. In the years following the passage of P.L. 93-112, most state agencies did not extensively modify their organizations, leaving it to the counselor to implement the order of selection mandate in eligibility decisions and service delivery (Barrett et al., 1978).

Coupled with the considerable discretion afforded the state VR agencies in interpreting the federal policy, RSA until recently also provided few incentives to facilitate implementation of the mandate. Although legislation required state agencies to implement an order of selection procedure when the agency determined that it would be unable to serve all eligible applicants, many states simply affirmed their ability to serve all eligible applicants and thereby avoided implementing the mandate (USGAO, 1991). Until very recently, federal guidelines did not require state VR agencies to explain how, given their fiscal and personnel resources, they were able to adequately serve all eligible applicants.

Another factor that has weakened the impact of the order of selection mandate is the reluctance of state VR administrators to implement it despite flat or decreasing funding levels, coupled with increasing demand for VR services (USGAO, 1991). Some state administrators argued that, in implementing priority services to individuals with the *most* significant disabilities, agencies would be forced to choose between serving a small number of high-cost consumers with the most significant disabilities and serving many more consumers with less significant disabilities who, presumably, would achieve more successful vocational outcomes at much lower cost to the agency (USGAO, 1991). Thus, their reluctance to implement order of selection was associated with concerns over higher costs and reduced program benefits related to serving individuals with more significant disabilities, thereby resulting (as the argument goes) in an erosion of the favorable cost/benefit ratio for VR (Eleventh Institute on Rehabilitation Issues, 1974; USGAO, 1991). Given that a favorable cost/benefit ratio for VR has been a potent argument in favor of securing funding from both state and federal governments (Rubin & Roessler, 2000), the reluctance of state VR administrators is understandable.

The USGAO Report and the Acceleration of Order of Selection Implementation

In 1991, the USGAO (the investigative office of Congress) published a comprehensive evaluation of order of selection implementation that was highly critical of RSA. In this report, the USGAO examined how some states were implementing order of selection, whether these states were implementing federal guidelines consistently, and why other states were not implementing the mandate. Among their findings, the USGAO reported that few states were using order of selection to prioritize services to persons with the most significant disabilities, but those states that were implementing the mandate appeared to be doing so in a manner consistent with the existing guidelines. VR administrators in states that used the provision reported that it was an effective mechanism for ensuring the participation of individuals with significant disabilities. Also, some agencies maintained that they did not implement the mandate because they were able to serve all eligible applicants, yet they employed caseload management techniques such as reducing outreach efforts and waiting lists to limit applicants when resources were not available to serve additional clients (USGAO, 1991). The USGAO report concluded that RSA had not provided state agencies with adequate guidance to implement the order of selection mandate. Subsequent federal legislation indicates that the USGAO report was a watershed in the brief history of the mandate.

In response to the USGAO report, RSA promulgated a new manual to the state agencies for implementing order of selection (RSA, 1992). This manual included detailed regulations governing when and how order of selection is to be implemented, and a model order of selection plan to help guide state agency planning.

The 1992 Amendments to the Rehabilitation Act reflected a continuing emphasis on serving individuals with significant disabilities, and it included several provisions that addressed issues identified in the 1991 USGAO report. For example, the 1992 Amendments required that state VR agencies determine applicant eligibility in a timely manner, and document in the state plan the nature and scope of outreach efforts to individuals with significant disabilities and other underserved groups. Moreover, state agencies that affirmed their ability to serve all eligible applicants were required to document how this would be accomplished given available resources (*Federal Register*, 1993).

Following the USGAO report and the 1992 Amendments, the implementation of order of selection procedures by state VR agencies increased substantially. RSA (1996) reported that, as of April 1, 1996, thirty of the 57 VR agencies (excluding the agencies that serve only persons with blindness and visual impairments) were operating under an order of selection provision. The same number of state agencies were providing VR services on a priority basis in 1999 (RSA, 1999).

The proportion of individuals with significant disabilities served by state VR agencies has also increased steadily over the past 15 years, reaching 73 percent of the total population in 1993 (RSA, 1995). However, the proportion of individuals with significant disabilities served varies widely from state to state, from a high of 96.9 percent (Illinois) to a low of 27 percent (Hawaii). Among the ten state agencies that, in fiscal year 1993, served the highest proportion of individuals with significant disabilities, only Florida (ranked tenth nationally) was not operating under order of selection (RSA, 1995). These data suggest that order of selection is an effective mechanism for ensuring that individuals with significant disabilities are served in state VR agencies.

The increased utilization of order of selection in recent years is directly related to more explicit guidelines issued by RSA and the corresponding reduction of the discretion afforded the state agencies in interpreting the meaning of the mandate. Moreover, the clarity and precision of the recent federal guidelines enhance the fairness, or equity, in how state VR agencies implement order of selection procedures.

EQUITY AND ORDER OF SELECTION POLICY

Equity, or fairness, is a central theme in public policy (Stone, 1988), and has become an increasingly important theme in rehabilitation policy (Bellini, 1997; Gatens-Robinson & Rubin, 1995; Schriner, Rumrill, & Parlin, 1995). Equity in the distribution of VR services is the policy goal of the mandate to serve individuals with the most significant disabilities. Equity concepts are applied in policy analysis to understand and resolve distributive problems, particularly as related to the fair distribution of scarce resources (Stone, 1988; Young, 1994). Equity concepts provide analytical tools to understand the principles underlying the order of selection policy, key issues in implementing the mandate, and how the implementation of the mandate should be evaluated (Bellini, 1997).

Justice is based on the application of an appropriate principle as the basis for distributing resources. Moreover, there are typically several defensible but competing views of the single policy goal of equity (Stone, 1988). For example, interested parties may differ as to 1) who are the recipients and what are the most defensible ways of defining them, 2) what resources are being distributed and what are the various ways of defining them, and 3) what are the social processes by which distribution is determined. Challenges to any particular equity solution may be based on the redefinition of any (or all) of these dimensions. Moreover, the paradox inherent in distributive problems is that equity for some people may mean inequality for others, but still be acceptable because the process by which goods are distributed is regarded as fair (Stone, 1988).

In order of selection, the item to be distributed—VR services—is clear. The recipients and how to define them (i.e., how to define individuals with the most significant disabilities), and the process by which the target population is identified (i.e., how agencies and counselors operationalize the definition in the VR eligibility process) have been the principal dimensions of controversy. Differing attitudes of VR agency administrators and counselors toward the mandate, and differences in implementation of the mandate by state agencies, are rooted in the application of potentially incompatible equity standards and result in different approaches to defining who has the greatest claim to VR agency resources.

Equity Standards and Vocational Rehabilitation

Young (1994) noted that society often allocates scarce and indivisible resources (e.g., VR services) by appealing to some notion of priority among claimants. Priority asserts that the person with the greatest claim to the available resources (according to relevant criteria) should receive them. The resources available for the VR program have never been sufficient to serve all potentially eligible individuals with disabilities (Berkowitz, 1987). Hence, throughout its history, state VR agencies have implemented a priority system, based on a standard of equity, to select appropriate applicants for services. Over time, it is the relevant criteria for selection, or equity standard, which has changed.

The fair opportunity standard of equity figures prominently in American disability and rehabilitation policy, and it is fundamental to the order of selection policy (Bellini, 1997). The fair opportunity rule requires that persons not be denied social benefits on the basis of undeserved or uncontrollable disadvantaging characteristics (e.g., disability). For these individuals to have fair social opportunities, the disadvantages they have received in the lottery of life must be counterbalanced (Gatens-Robinson & Rubin, 1995). Rehabilitation policies reflect two primary strategies for implementing the fair opportunity rule: 1) an impairment-based strategy, in which a share of social resources is allocated to different disability groups based on similarity of impairment; and 2) a specialized services approach in which people with disabilities are provided specialized services to ameliorate the disadvantages associated with disability (Schriner et al., 1995). The Developmental Disabilities Services and Facilities Construction (DDSFC) Act of 1970 (P.L. 91-5176) created the Administration on Developmental Disabilities and supported the development of an array of community services for persons with developmental disabilities (Rubin & Roessler, 2000). This reflects an impairment-based strategy for social policy because the DDSFC Act mandates funding and other vital governmental resources specifically for persons with developmental disabilities (i.e., persons whose disabilities manifest prior to age 22). Numerous state and federal laws address the needs of specific disability groups and therefore reflect an impairment based strategy for disability and rehabilitation policy.

The state-federal VR program represents the clearest example of the specialized services approach to disability and rehabilitation policy. The fundamental purpose of the state-federal VR program is to assist persons with disabilities to secure and maintain employment. To meet this goal, eligible persons with disabilities are provided specialized services that are consistent with their rehabilitation needs, and VR agency resources are allocated to all qualifying persons with disabilities regardless of their specific impairments rather than to particular groups based on similarity of impairment. The state-federal VR program reflects the fundamental policy assumption that fair opportunity to achieve employment is best provided to persons with disabilities by specialized services rather than the generic career counseling and employment services that are typically available to American citizens from state employment offices.

Whereas the impairment-based and specialized services strategies for implementing the fair opportunity rule are primarily directed to allocation of state and federal resources (e.g., funding and services) to persons with disabilities, the Americans with Disabilities Act (ADA) of 1990 represents an extension of the fair opportunity rule into the private sphere. The ADA mandates accommodation for disability by local and state governments, public services, and private employers, so that persons with disabilities are not denied access to the same social benefits and opportunities that other American citizens enjoy.

A utilitarian standard of equity was also highly influential from the start of the VR program and it is closely related to the fundamental VR program goal of promoting the employment of people with disabilities (Berkowitz, 1987; Obermann, 1965). Historically, the VR program served the larger policy objective of enhancing the human capital and economic competitiveness of the nation through retraining individuals who had been injured in industrial accidents (Berkowitz, 1987; Schriner et al., 1995). Given this larger policy objective and the minimal resources devoted to VR, it is understandable that the application of the fair opportunity rule in VR policy was modified (and some might say superseded) by a utilitarian approach which viewed equity as a function of maximizing program benefits and returns by allocating resources to individuals perceived as most able to achieve successful vocational outcomes (Berkowitz, 1987; Rubin & Roessler, 2000). In this case, fairness is conceived as the most efficient use of scarce resources (i.e., VR services) and is reflected in the traditional cost/benefit argument for VR (Gatens-Robinson & Rubin, 1995). Hence, individuals who were perceived as most able to benefit from VR services in terms of employment were provided services, and individuals perceived as unable to benefit because of significant disability were often not provided needed services.

A third potential standard of equity–the equal share standard–would require the allocation of equal shares of resources (e.g., VR services and/or funding) to all VR consumers. Given adequate funding, the equal share rule would likely result in access to VR services by the greatest number of persons with disabilities (Gatens-Robinson & Rubin, 1995). The equal share standard is appealing to American sensibilities and appears to be the equity solution promoted in states that are currently experimenting with voucher systems of service provision. Although states differ in how they implement this service innovation, the basic idea is that VR consumers receive vouchers for a given amount of service funds and are empowered to spend these funds on whatever services they choose. However appealing as a principle for promoting consumer choice, the equal share standard has limitations in regard to the VR goal of allocating services to persons with disabilities who need them most. First, it is well known that differences among disabilities result in major differences in the amount and cost of VR services required for successful employment (Gatens-Robinson & Rubin, 1995). Given these differences among disabilities, justice inheres in each VR consumer receiving the resources he or she requires to become employed, rather than an equal share of resources. Secondly, reasonable application of the equal share principle of justice would require substantially higher federal and state funding of the VR program than is currently provided to ensure that all eligible persons with disabilities are adequately served. It is precisely the underfunding of the VR program that has resulted in the federal policy to serve persons with the most significant disabilities first based on the fair opportunity standard.

Fair Opportunity: The Equity Standard for Order of Selection

Order of selection policy represents a realignment of equity standards in the state-federal VR program, by reducing (but not eliminating) the latitude of agencies to select individuals based on perceived probability of benefit, and by underscoring the fair opportunity rule. As noted previously, the order of selection provision was included in the Rehabilitation Act because Congress became convinced that many individuals with significant disabilities, for whom VR services were intended in principle (based on the fair opportunity standard), could potentially benefit from the provision of VR services in terms of employment, yet were not being provided the necessary services (Barrett et al., 1978). Accordingly, the utilitarian standard of equity was judged by Congress to be an insufficient rationale for denying VR program benefits to a large segment of the potential target population and was inconsistent with fair opportunity.

Order of selection was intended as a remedy for the perceived unfairness in how VR services were being allocated and called for priority services to individuals with the most significant disabilities who could potentially benefit in terms of employment. Priority services are provided to counterbalance the greater disadvantages associated with significant disability and to enable these individuals to have fair social opportunities. Hence, the realignment of equity standards in order of selection—from utilitarianism to fair opportunity—entailed a redefinition of who among the large target population for VR has the greatest claim to the available resources.

The tension between the two equity standards—fair opportunity and the utilitarian approach—was a source of controversy in regard to order of selection and influenced the quality of order of selection implementation. As the USGAO report noted, some VR administrators may be reluctant to implement order of selection because they assume a reduction of program benefits associated with serving individuals with more significant disabilities. Alternately, VR administrators in states that implement an order of selection procedure reported that the mandate helps focus needed resources on individuals with significant disabilities (USGAO, 1991).

IMPLEMENTATION OF ORDER OF SELECTION IN STATE VR AGENCIES

Current RSA Guidelines for Order of Selection

Recent regulations promulgated by RSA (*Federal Register*, May 14, 1996) provided new guidelines to state VR agencies related to factors that should and should not be considered in establishing an order of selection plan. These new regulations serve as the guidelines by which counselors make their determinations of applicants' eligibility for priority service as individuals with the most significant disabilities.

As is common practice for government agencies, the issuance of new regulations follows the solicitation of comments from interested parties (in this case, organizations of persons with disabilities, persons with disabilities and their advocates, state VR administrators, rehabilitation researchers and educators) and the subsequent analysis of these suggestions by RSA administrators in light of the language and intent of the Rehabilitation Act. Thus, the published rules and regulations highlight the intent of Congress and contain a discussion of key issues raised by commentors related to the implementation of order of selection policy and its relation to other federal policies for persons with disabilities.

These federal guidelines have the force of law and in some cases represent a reversal of policy on specific issues. For example, RSA guidelines published in 1992 stated that, if state VR agencies were unable to distinguish "individuals with the most significant disabilities" from "individuals with significant disabilities," then they may elect to serve individuals with significant disabilities on a first-applied, first-served basis (RSA, 1992). The 1996 regulations to the Rehabilitation Act as amended reverse this policy and require that all individuals with most significant disabilities must be served before persons in lower priority categories are served (*Federal Register*, May 14, 1996). Whereas prior to 1996 state VR agencies were permitted but not required to develop specific criteria for priority categories in their order of selection plans, the 1996 federal regulations establish this as a statutory requirement for state agencies. Together these two provisions require state VR agencies to define the key term individual with the most significant disabilities and establish criteria for priority categories.

Also, prior to the issuance of the 1996 regulations RSA and many state agencies interpreted existing guidelines to permit the provision of "no cost" rehabilitation services (i.e, counseling/guidance, diagnosis/evaluation, and placement services that are provided by agency counselors at no extra cost to the agency) to persons with less significant disabilities while simultaneously providing more extensive services to persons with significant disabilities within the order of selection plan (RSA, 1992). The 1996 regulations reversed this policy and require state agencies operating on the basis of order of selection to serve persons with the most significant disabilities first. If, for example, a state VR agency has established three categories for serving eligible individuals (e.g., individuals with the most significant disabilities, individuals with significant disabilities, and individuals with nonsignificant disabilities), the agency must provide all needed services to persons in the highest priority category before providing any services to individuals in lower priority categories (*Federal Register*, May 14, 1996).

Further, the 1996 regulations state that the federal definition of "individual with significant disabilities" is insufficient for the purpose of establishing priority services for individuals with the most significant disabilities. State agencies must refine at least one of the three criteria (i.e., limitations in functional capacity in major life areas, need for multiple services, and need for services over extended time) to identify this subgroup. The goal of refining the statutory criteria is to enable counselors to link "the nature and depth of the individual's functional limitations with the need for multiple and complex services that require an extended time for completion" (Federal Register, May 14, 1996, p. 24395).

A state agency may refine the first criterion by requiring that the individual demonstrate limitations in functional capacity in three (or two, or four) major life areas (i.e., mobility, communication, self-care, self direction, interpersonal skills, work tolerance, work skills). Federal regulations provide relatively detailed definitions of the seven functional capacity groupings specified in the Rehabilitation Act.

1. *Mobility* means an individual's access to his or her environment either through his or her own ability or through the assistance of others. To meet the criteria for impairment in mobility the individual:
   a. has no independent mobility; or
   b. is unable to make use of available modes of transportation; or
   c. is unable to climb one flight of stairs or walk 100 yards without a pause; or
   d. requires customized rehabilitation technology for an employment outcome.
2. *Communication* means the individual's ability to express himself or herself through speech and/or the ability to receive communication and/or process communication. To meet the criteria for impairment in communication the individual:
   a. cannot communicate independently; or
   b. is unable to make use of available modes of communication; or
   c. requires customized rehabilitation technology; or
   d. is unable to exhibit appropriate communication due to cognitive dysfunctional mental illness.
3. *Self-care* means the ability to conduct the essential activities of daily living unassisted by another person. To meet the criteria for impairment in self-care, the individual requires supervision or personal assistance service with the essential activities of daily living.

4. *Self-direction* means the capacity to organize, structure, and manage activities in a manner that best serves the rehabilitation objectives of the individual. To meet the criteria for impairment in self-direction the individual:
   a. requires ongoing prompts or assistance to understand and remember instructions; or
   b. requires ongoing prompts or assistance in the area of concentration or persistence to stay on task; or
   c. requires customized rehabilitation technology to accommodate the lack of concentration or to remember instructions or to understand instructions.
5. *Interpersonal skill* means the ability of the individual to interact in a socially acceptable manner with coworkers, supervisors, peers, and the general public. To meet criteria for impairment in interpersonal skills the individual:
   a. does not accept instructions and respond appropriately to criticism from supervisors; or
   b. does not get along with coworkers or peers without distracting them or exhibiting behavioral extremes; or
   c. does not maintain socially acceptable behavior.
6. *Work tolerance* means the ability to carry out work tasks in an efficient and effective manner over a sustained period of time. To meet the criteria for impairment in work tolerance the individual:
   a. requires customized rehabilitation technology to perform work activities; or
   b. requires individualized accommodation or intervention to perform work activities.
7. *Work skills* means the specific job skills required to carry out work functions. To meet the criteria for impairment in work skills the individual must have a limited capacity to acquire work skills. (RSA, 1999)

Alternately, for the purpose of defining individual with the most significant disabilities, the agency may refine the functional capacity criterion by specifying the degree or number of particular functional limitations within a given major life area or areas, such as five specific functional limitations. An example of specific functional limitations within the life area of self-direction may include:

(1) purposeless shifting from one activity to another; (2) inability to follow through with and complete assignments; (3) problems related to time management; (4) making decisions impulsively without consideration for previous plans or experience; (5) limitations in gathering, organizing, and analyzing information; (6) difficulties in adapting to changing work requirements; and (7) inability to monitor work performance and to adjust behaviors and activities. (*Federal Register*, May 14, 1996, p. 24395)

A state agency may choose to refine the second criterion (i.e., need for multiple services) by specifying a minimum number of services required by the individual, or may refine the third criterion (i.e., extended time) by specifying the period of time at the upper end of the range required for individuals with the most significant disabilities to achieve an employment outcome after eliminating exceptional cases. State agencies may also choose alternate methods of refining these criteria as long as these methods are consistent with RSA regulations. As will be demonstrated in an analysis of current state plans, states more often refine the functional capacity criterion than the other two criteria.

RSA regulations (*Federal Register*, May 14, 1996) also specify a number of factors that cannot be used in determining priority service for eligible persons with disabilities.

An order of selection may not be based on any other factors including

(i) Any duration of residency requirement, provided the individual is present in the State;

(ii) Type of disability;

(iii) Age, gender, race, color, creed, or national origin;

(iv) Source of referral;

(v) Type of expected employment outcome;

(vi) The need for specific services or anticipated cost of services required by an individual; or

(vii) The income level of an individual or an individual's family. (p. 24402)

The purpose of these restrictions is to ensure that the implementation of order of selection is equitable for all individuals who qualify for priority service based exclusively on those criteria specified in the Rehabilitation Act and used to place individuals in particular categories. As a matter of social policy, it is understood that fairness or equity as related to order of selection policy requires consistency in its implementation. For example, the prohibition against using the need for specific services or anticipated cost of services as a criterion for an order of selection is intended to prevent a state VR agency from giving priority to persons who require short-term and less costly services over persons who require long-term and more costly services. Also, this provision prevents a state VR agency from giving priority to individuals with certain service needs, such as the need for physical restoration services over individuals who have other service needs, such as the need for vocational training (*Federal Register*, May 14, 1996). In general, these guidelines build upon the fundamental rehabilitation principles that rehabilitation services should be 1) comprehensive in scope, and 2) tailored to meet the unique rehabilitation needs of individuals with disabilities. These principles are central for the implementation of order of selection in state VR agencies.

Federal regulations also specify that

> socioeconomic factors, such as levels of educational achievement or length of unemployment or underemployment, and personality traits, such as levels of self-esteem, however, cannot be used in establishing an order of selection because these factors are not measures of severity of disability or even measures of disability. (p. 24395)

Again, the purpose of these guidelines is to ensure that order of selection criteria do not inadvertently favor some individuals with certain disadvantaging, *non-disability-specific* characteristics over other individuals who have significant disabilities but who may not have other disadvantaging characteristics. For example, individuals whose disabilities were acquired at birth or during the developmental years (e.g., autism or mental retardation) may on average have lower educational achievement than individuals who acquired their disabilities in adulthood or after having completed higher levels of education. Thus, the prohibition against using the educational level of the applicant as an explicit criterion for order of selection is intended to ensure that the selection process is equitable for all persons with significant disabilities and does not favor some individuals over others based on mitigating, non-disability-specific factors. Similarly, using a factor such as a history of repeated failures in employment as an explicit criterion of priority service would have the effect of excluding youth who have very significant disabilities but may have little or no employment history from the highest priority category.

Content Analysis of Current State VR Agency Order of Selection Plans

For the purpose of identifying commonalities and differences among state VR agencies in implementing the order of selection provision, Table 2.I presents the number and types of categories as well as the specific criteria used for determining eligibility for priority services by each state VR agency that implemented order of selection in fiscal year 2000. Only general state VR agency plans are included. State VR agencies that exclusively serve persons with blindness or visual impairments are not included in the table because these plans use criteria that are highly specific to functional capacities and limitations associated with blindness. Therefore, these plans are not comparable to state plans for VR agencies that serve the entire population of persons with a wide range of impairments and disabilities.

As Table 2.I indicates, the thirty order of selection plans have many similarities but also have significant differences. As required by RSA, all of these plans have at least three categories: most significant, significant, and nonsignificant. Also, applicants' eligibility for priority services depends on which category they are placed in following the comprehensive case study. Also, as specified in federal regulations, all the state plans use functional criteria–i.e., functional capacity in major life areas–coupled with the need for multiple services over extended time as the basis for eligibility for priority services.

As noted previously, recent federal guidelines require state VR agencies to establish additional criteria as the basis for defining individual with the most significant disabilities. Moreover, these criteria cannot conflict with existing statutory regulations. As Table 2.I indicates, all of the state plans use additional criteria, but the plans differ in the specific standards used. Most states adhere to the basic functional criteria and identify applicants with the greatest need for services as those whose impairments result in limitations in multiple life areas. There is also variation among state VR agencies in 1) the number of priority categories used to define individuals with the most significant disabilities and 2) the definitions of key terms used as criteria. For example, the number of priority categories specified in order of selection plans varies from a minimum of three to a maximum of seven.

TABLE 2.I. ORDER OF SELECTION PLANS IN VR AGENCIES FOR
FISCAL YEAR 2000 (GENERAL OR COMBINED AGENCIES ONLY).

State	Number/Type of Categories	Specific Criteria for Determining Eligibility for Priority Services
AZ	3: most significant	limited functional capacity in 3 life areas and requires multiple services/extended time
	significant	limited functional capacity in 3 life areas and requires multiple services/extended time
	nonsignificant	meets standard VR program elegibility
AR	4: most significant	* limited functional capacity in 2 life areas and requires major, multiple services/extended time
	significant	* limited functional capacity in 1 life areas and requires major, multiple services/extended time
	nonsignificant (2)	meets standard VR program elegibility

* Defines multiple services as needing 2 or more major services–physical or psychological restoration, training, counseling, guidance, placement. Support services such as transportation and maintenance are not considered to be major services.

CAL	Priority for service is based on higher scores (more significant limitations) on the "significance scale," a counselor rated measure of 10 functional capacity areas and 3 components for each area: frequency, extent, and environment.	
COL	3: most significant	*limited functional capacity in 3 life areas and requires multiple services over extended time
	significant	*limited functional capacity in 1 life area and requires multiple services over extended time
	nonsignificant	meets standard VR program elegibility

* Defines multiple services as 2 or more "core" services–physical or psychological restoration, training, counseling, guidance, placement. Defines extended time as needing a minimum of 5 months to complete rehabilitation program.

CONN	3: most significant	limited functional capacity in 3 life areas, requires multiple services over extended time or requires significant, ongoing disability-related support services on the job following closure from time-limited services
	significant	limited functional capacity in 1 life area, requires multiple services over extended time
	nonsignificant	meets standard VR eligibility criteria

FL	3: most significant	*limited functional capacity in 2 life areas and requires major multiple services/extended time
	significant	*limited functional capacity in 1 life area and requires major, multiple services/extended time
	nonsignificant	meets standard VR elegibility criteria

* Defines "major" services as two or more services in addition to assessment, guidance and counseling, and job placement services. Defines extended time as needing a minimum of 6 months to complete rehabilitation program.

GA	7: most significant (2)	limited functional capacity in 2 life areas and requires multiple primary services over extended time
	significant (4)	limited functional capacity in 1 life area and requires multiple services over extended time
	nonsignificant	meets standard VR eligibility criteria

IL	3: most significant (2)	*limited functional capacity in 2 life areas and requires multiple services over extended time
	significant	*limited functional capacity in 1 life area and requires multiple services over extended time
	nonsignificant	meets standard VR eligibility criteria

* Defines multiple services as "core" VR services: counseling and guidance, physical restoration, training, and placement as listed in the consumer's IPE extended time as needing a minimum of 6 months to complete rehabilitation program.

IA	3: most significant	limited functional capacity in 3 life areas and requires multiple services over extended time
	significant	limited functional capacity in 1 or more life areas and requires multiple services over extended time
	nonsignificant	meets standard VR eligibility criteria

KS	3: most significant	limited functional capacity in 4 life areas and requires multiple services over extended time
	significant	limited functional capacity in 1 life area and requires multiple services over extended time
	nonsignificant	meets standard VR eligibility criteria

KY	6: most significant	*limited functional capacity in 4 life areas and requires multiple services over extended time
	significant (3)	limited functional capacity in 3 life areas and requires multiple services over extended time
		limited functional capacity in 2 life areas and requires multiple services over extended time
		limited functional capacity in 1 life area and requires multiple services over extended time
	nonsignificant (2)	meets standard VR eligibility criteria and has permanent functional limitations
		meets standard VR eligibility criteria

* Most significant status also requires the need for "intensive long-term support to facilitate performance of work activities on or off the job. Intensive long-term support may include (but is not limited to): personal attendant care, complex rehabilitation services, job coaching, or other long-term intervention during the person's work life.

LA	3: most significant	*limited functional capacity in 4 life areas, and requires multiple services over extended time and/or long-term support services after placement to maintain employment
	significant	limited functional capacity in 3 life areas and requires multiple services over extended time
	nonsignificant	meets standard VR eligibility criteria

* Defines extended time as needing a minimum of 6 months to complete rehabilitation program.

MA	3: most significant	limited functional capacity in 2 life areas, and requires multiple services/extended time
	significant	limited functional capacity in 1 life area and requires multiple services/extended time
	nonsignificant	meets standard VR eligibility criteria

MD	3: most significant	limited functional capacity in 2 life areas, and requires multiple services/extended time
	significant	limited functional capacity in 1 life area and requires multiple services/extended time
	nonsignificant	meets standard VR eligibility criteria

ME	3: most significant	limited functional capacity in 2 life areas, and requires multiple services/extended time
	significant	limited functional capacity in 1 life area and requires multiple services/extended time
	nonsignificant	meets standard VR eligibility criteria

MN	3: most significant	limited functional capacity in 3 life areas, and requires multiple services/extended time
	significant (2)	limited functional capacity in 2 life areas and requires multiple services/extended time
		limited functional capacity in 1 life area and requires multiple services/extended time
	nonsignificant	meets standard VR eligibility criteria

MS	3: most significant	limited functional capacity in 2 life areas, and requires multiple services/extended time
	significant	limited functional capacity in 1 life area and requires multiple services/extended time
	nonsignificant	meets standard VR eligibility criteria

NE	3: most significant	limited functional capacity in 1 life area, requires multiple services over extended time **and** for whom competitive employment has not occurred, or whose competitive employment has been intermittent or interrupted as a result of significant physical or mental impairment
	significant	limited functional capacity in 1 life area and requires multiple services over extended time
	nonsignificant	meets standard VR eligibility criteria
NJ	3: most significant	limited functional capacity in 2 life areas, and requires multiple services/extended time
	significant	limited functional capacity in 1 life area and requires multiple services/extended time
	nonsignificant	meets standard VR eligibility criteria
NM	3: most significant	limited functional capacity in 2 life areas, and requires multiple services/extended time
	significant	limited functional capacity in 1 life area and requires multiple services/extended time
	nonsignificant	meets standard VR eligibility criteria
ND	3: most significant	limited functional capacity in 2 life areas, and requires multiple services/extended time
	significant	limited functional capacity in 1 life area and requires multiple services/extended time
	nonsignificant	meets standard VR eligibility criteria
OH	3: most significant	limited functional capacity in 2 life areas, and requires multiple services/extended time
	significant	*limited functional capacity in 1 life area and requires multiple services/extended time
	nonsignificant	meets standard VR eligibility criteria

* Individuals who are determined eligible for SSDI or SSI on basis of disability are presumed to meet OH criteria for significant status but not for most significant status.

OK	4: most significant	limited functional capacity in 3 life areas, and requires multiple services/extended time
	significant (2)	limited functional capacity in 2 life areas and requires multiple services/extended time
		limited functional capacity in 1 life area and requires multiple services/extended time
	nonsignificant	meets standard VR eligibility criteria
PA	3: most significant	limited functional capacity in 3 life areas, and requires multiple services/extended time
	significant	limited functional capacity in 1 life area and requires multiple services/extended time
	nonsignificant	meets standard VR eligibility criteria

RI	3: most significant	limited functional capacity in 3 life areas, and requires multiple services/extended time
	significant	*limited functional capacity in 1 life area and requires multiple services/extended time
	nonsignificant	meets standard VR eligibility criteria
TN	4: most significant	*limited functional capacity in 2 life areas, and 2 or more major services/extended time
	significant	*limited functional capacity in 1 life area and requires 2 or more services/extended time
	nonsignificant	*meets standard eligibility criteria and required 2 or more major services over extended time meets standard VR eligibility criteria

* Defines major services as all services except transportation, maintenance, and routine counseling and guidance that should be provided in every case. Defines extended time as needing a minimum of 6 months to complete rehabilitation program.

VI	3: most significant	limited functional capacity in 3 life areas, and requires multiple services/extended time
	significant	limited functional capacity in 1 life area and requires multiple services/extended time
	nonsignificant	meets standard VR eligibility criteria
VT	3: most significant	*limited functional capacity in 2 life areas, and requires at least 1 primary service to address functional losses associated with disability and multiple services/extended time
	significant	*limited functional capacity in 1 life area and requires multiple services/extended time
	nonsignificant	meets standard VR eligibility criteria

* "Primary services" include (but are not limited to) physical restoration, training, and work-site modificaion. Multiple services are defined as routine services (e.g., counseling, guidance, and placement) plus at least one other service. Extended time is defined as needing at least 6 months to complete the rehabilitation program.

| WI | 7: most significant (1) | Significant limitations of functional capacity in 3 or more life areas and requires mulitple services over extended time. |
| | significant (2) | Significant limitations of functional capacity in 2 or more life areas and requires mulitple services over extended time.
Significant limitations of functional capacity in 1 or more life area and requires mulitple services over extended time. |

	nonsignificant (4)	Significant limitations of functional capacity in 4 or more life areas and must lack either or both requirements for multiple VR services or extended time to complete IPE.
		Significant limitations of functional capacity in 1 to 3 life areas and must lack either or both requirements for multiple VR services or extended time to complete IPE.
		Nonsignificant limitations of functional capacity in at least 4 life areas and may or may not require multiple services over extended time.
		Nonsignificant limitations of functional capacity in 1 to 3 life areas and may or may not require multiple services over extended time.
WV	4: most significant	*limited functional capacity in 2 life areas, and requires multiple services over extended time
	significant	*limited functional capacity in 1 life area and requires multiple services over extended time
	significant (2)	meets standard VR eligibility criteria and has permanent functional limitations
	significant	meets standard VR eligibility criteria but does not have permanent functional limitations

* Multiple services are defined as 2 or more "core" services: physical or mental restoration, training, counseling and guidance, placement, rehabilitation technology. Extended time is defined as needing at least 9 months to complete rehabilitation program.

State agencies define individual with the most significant disabilities as having limitations in functional capacity in two, three, or four major life areas. Some states, however, utilize additional functional criteria. For example, California places individuals in service priority categories based on scores on the "significance scale," a counselor rating instrument that addresses ten functional capacity areas, the frequency and extent of functional limitation in each capacity area, and the environment in which limitations are experienced within each capacity area. The Connecticut VR agency requires that individuals in the highest priority category have limitations in functional capacity in three major life areas and need "significant on-going disability-related services on the job following closure from time-limited services." Both the Kentucky and Louisiana agencies assign priority status to applicants who have limited functional capacity in four major life areas, require multiple services over extended time, and/or need long-term support services following placement to maintain employment. The

Kentucky plan further defines long-term support services as "including (but not limited to): personal attendant care, complex rehabilitation services, job coaching, or other long-term intervention during the person's work life."

The Nebraska agency assigns priority status to persons who have limited functional capacity in one life area, need multiple services over extended time, and for whom competitive employment has not occurred, or whose competitive employment has been intermittent or interrupted as a result of significant physical or mental impairment. The Tennessee agency assigns priority status to persons with limited functional capacity in two life areas who require two or more major services over extended time. The Vermont agency takes a similar approach and requires at least one primary service to address the functional losses associated with disability for placement in the highest priority category.

Most state VR agencies reference the need for "multiple services over extended time" as criteria for the most significant category, but some agencies also specify the need for "core" or "major" services. There is also variation among the state VR agency definitions of multiple, core, primary, and/or major services, and extended time. Most state agencies do not specify definitions for these key criteria. A few state agencies define multiple services as two or more "major" services (e.g., Arkansas, Colorado, Illinois, West Virginia) and classify physical or mental restoration, rehabilitation technology, training, counseling/guidance, assessment, and placement as major or core services. In these states, major or core services are distinguished from secondary services (e.g., transportation, maintenance, or child care) that may facilitate the achievement of the employment goal but are not tied directly to the remediation of functional limitations associated with disability. By contrast, the Florida and Vermont agencies define counseling/guidance, assessment, and placement as routine services that are provided in every case. The Florida agency defines multiple services as two or more services *in addition to* routine services. The Vermont VR agency defines multiple services as routine services plus at least one primary service (including but not limited to physical restoration, training, and worksite modification).

Finally, most state VR agencies do not explicitly define "extended time" as a criterion for priority services. However, the Colorado agency defines extended time as needing a minimum of five months to complete the rehabilitation program, whereas the Florida, Illinois, Louisiana, Tennessee, and Vermont agencies specify six months to completion, and West Virginia uses a criterion of nine months for "extended time."

Overall, there is a high degree of uniformity in the criteria used by state VR agencies for the purpose of establishing service priority, and these criteria closely parallel RSA guidelines for order of selection. However, some states establish more rigorous standards for placement in the highest priority categories, usually by requiring that the disability have a broader, more serious functional impact in multiple life areas. Some VR agencies also refine the service needs criterion of the federal definition of "individual with significant disability" to identify those persons who require more intensive services to achieve employment.

EMPIRICAL RESEARCH ON ORDER OF SELECTION IMPLEMENTATION

Progress in meeting the mandate to serve individuals with the most significant disabilities is ultimately evaluated in terms of equity. Two criteria for applying and evaluating a priority system in relation to a given distributive problem are: 1) consistency, that distinctions according to type should be made in a consistent manner, or made in the same way independently of the other claimants present and how much they receive; and 2) impartiality, that claimants of the same type should be treated equally, and claimants of different types should be treated differently (Young, 1994). Consistency and impartiality serve as useful organizing constructs for evaluating the quality of order of selection implementation in state VR agencies.

Consistency as an indicator of equity pertains to the issue of VR program participation by individuals with the most significant disabilities and is directly applicable to the evaluation of counselors' implementation of order of selection guidelines in the eligibility decision phase of the VR process. Progress in meeting the order of selection mandate depends on consistency among counselors in identifying individuals with the most significant disabilities for priority services. Impartiality as an indicator of equity in order of selection implementation is germane to the service delivery phase of the VR process.

Progress in meeting the order of selection mandate depends on impartiality by counselors in allocating VR agency resources to persons with the most significant disabilities (i.e., claimants of the same type).

Research on Participation

In the evaluation of order of selection implementation, distinctions according to type refer to counselors' decisions regarding the significance of applicants' disabilities, based on documentation of functional limitations in key life areas and service needs (RSA, 1992). Therefore, consistency in eligibility decisions means that individuals identified as more significantly disabled would have more significant functional limitations and service needs than individuals identified as less (or not) significantly disabled. The most direct approach to evaluating consistency in counselors' decisions and equity in access to VR services for persons with the most significant disabilities is to compare applicants' measured functional limitations in key life areas and service needs in relation to counselors' eligibility decisions both within and across state agencies. In the absence of standardized data on applicants' functional limitations and service needs, other criteria known to be indicative of disability significance are substituted (e.g., Social Security Disability status).

An alternate approach to evaluating consistency in order of selection implementation is to compare the participation of distinct disability groups in state VR agencies. Given the traditional VR focus on serving individuals with a wide range of primary disabilities, it is assumed that consistent application of the eligibility criteria for significant disability would also continue the pattern of equitable representation for individuals with a variety of primary disabilities (e.g., orthopedic, psychiatric, mental retardation). However, a finding that some disability groups are more likely to be determined eligible for priority services than other groups (i.e., unequal representation) would not necessarily mean that counselors make inconsistent decisions. Unequal representation could be warranted if it was a consequence of greater inherent severity of the functional limitations and service needs associated with specific impairments (e.g., severe mental retardation).

The few studies that have examined equity issues demonstrate these various approaches to operationalizing significant disability. These studies also illustrate that the measurement of significant disability presents the greatest difficulties in evaluating the quality of order of selection implementation. Most importantly, conclusions about equity in VR participation are not warranted in the absence of standard data on key severity variables.

The USGAO (1991) study was motivated by concern that counselors in states operating under the order of selection mandate may be systematically altering their classifications of applicants to justify providing services. Hence, the study examined the consistency of counselors in making judgments about applicants' disability significance and compared individuals classified as significantly disabled and non-significantly disabled in states that were operating under an order of selection plan and states that were serving all eligible applicants. The USGAO used the following five factors thought to be indicative of significance of disability as the basis for comparing order of selection and non-order of selection states: 1) competitively employed at application; 2) institutionalized at application; 3) receiving services at a rehabilitation facility; 4) receiving Social Security Disability Insurance or Supplementary Security Income; and 5) with a primary disability of mental illness or mental retardation. It was reasoned that, if counselors were making consistent eligibility decisions, then comparable percentages of individuals with these five characteristics would be classified as significantly disabled and non-significantly disabled in the two types of states. On the other hand, if counselors in state agencies using an order of selection procedure were systematically altering their classification criteria to justify services, then differences between the two types of states in the percentages of persons with the five severity characteristics would likely be found. The results confirmed that the differences were minimal in the two types of states for each of the five client characteristics analyzed. The USGAO (1991) concluded that counselors appeared to apply severity criteria consistently in state VR agencies that used the order of selection provision.

Andrews et al. (1992) reported that, between 1977 and 1984, individuals with physical disabilities were slightly more likely to be identified as significantly disabled than individuals with psychiatric disabilities. They suggested that the reliance on recency of hospitalization as a criterion of significant disability for individuals with psychiatric disabilities results in inequitable representation for this group, and recommended the development of alternate criteria to reflect the higher incidence of individuals with significant psychiatric disabilities who are served in community rather than institutional settings.

Salkever (1994) examined a large national sample of individuals with developmental disabilities drawn from the 1990 National Consumer Survey of People with Developmental Disabilities and Their Families and from RSA national data. A primary purpose of the study was to determine the likelihood that an individual with particular developmental disabilities (e.g., autism, cerebral palsy, mental retardation) and need for substantial or some assistance in the seven major life areas had received VR services. Salkever (1994) reported that, in fiscal years 1990-1992, persons with a primary disability of mental retardation were approximately 12 percent *less* likely to receive VR services than individuals with other developmental disabilities. Also, for the total sample of individuals with developmental disabilities, the severity of individuals' activity limitations was negatively correlated with probability of receiving VR services. Salkever (1996) reported that, regardless of the nature of the primary developmental disability, individuals who required substantial assistance in the major life activity of making decisions was approximately 17 percent *less* likely to receive VR services in 1990-1992, and persons who required substantial assistance in self-care and learning were 13 percent and 11 percent *less* likely to receive VR services, respectively, than persons who did not require substantial assistance in these areas.

These results are surprising because developmental disabilities in general and mental retardation in particular are known to have profound effects on individuals' life functioning, and it is therefore assumed that priority for VR services based on functional criteria would likely result in a larger proportion of persons with developmental disabilities being served in state VR agencies. The results pertaining to the specific functional capacities of persons with developmental disabilities and probability of being served in state VR are more disturbing, because RSA regulations define individual with significant disabilities primarily in terms of significant functional (or activity) limitations. Hence, one would expect that severity of activity limitations would be positively associated with likelihood of receiving VR services under an order of selection procedure rather than negatively correlated as reported by Salkever (1994).

Although the results reported by Salkever (1994) are compelling, they are by no means conclusive as an evaluation of order of selection implementation. First, the sample of persons with developmental disabilities was not limited to states whose VR agencies were operating under an order of selection plan. The interpretation of these results therefore pertains to all state VR agencies, not just those that were explicitly serving persons with the most significant disabilities first. Secondly, data on participation in state VR were drawn from the years 1990-1992, and this is the time period that preceded the promulgation of stricter federal guidelines related to order of selection and the acceleration of implementation of the mandate in state agencies.

Bellini, Bolton, and Neath (1996) investigated the consistency of counselor eligibility decisions in one state VR agency (Arkansas) that was implementing an order of selection procedure to prioritize services to persons with significant disabilities. These authors used a standardized assessment instrument of applicants' functional capacities—the Functional Assessment Inventory [FAI] (Crewe & Athelstan, 1984)—to document counselors' selection decisions. Agency data for the years 1992-1994 were analyzed. Following the clinical case study, but prior to making the eligibility decision, counselors rated the vocationally relevant functional limitations of VR applicants along the seven FAI dimensions which correspond relatively closely to the seven major life areas specified in federal regulations. The consistency of counselor eligibility decisions was then evaluated in relation to the profiles of applicants' functional limitations and additional case difficulty factors (e.g., education, work status at referral, Social Security Disability status).

Bellini et al. (1996) reported that individuals who were determined eligible for VR and identified as significantly disabled had considerably greater counselor-rated functional limitations in key life areas than individuals who 1) were not accepted for VR services for reasons specified as "no disabling condition" or "no vocational impediment to employment" and 2) were eligible for VR services as a person with disability with an impediment to employment but were identified as nonsignificantly disabled. Counselors' eligibility decisions (or, the selection categories in which applicants were placed following the clinical case study) were highly consistent with their quantitative ratings of applicants' functional capacities. Bellini et al. reported that 44 percent of the variation in counselors' decisions was explained by applicants' documented functional limitations and case difficulty factors.

This study is noteworthy because it was the first to explore the relationship between applicant functional limitations that were documented by the counselor and quantified using a standardized instrument and subsequent counselor decision making. Bellini et al. (1996) concluded that: 1) the results constituted modest support for the validity of counselors' decisions about applicants' severity of disability in an agency implementing the order of selection mandate, and 2) the FAI, along with a measure of social disadvantages (i.e., the Scale of Social Disadvantage; Bellini, Bolton, & Neath, 1995), provides a solid quantitative foundation for state agency research, documentation, and evaluation in the area of eligibility determination. However, the generalizability of this study as applied to evaluating the quality of order of selection implementation is limited because data were drawn from one VR agency only.

Research on Service Delivery

The evaluation of equity in service delivery, or impartiality in the allocation of agency resources, is also complex. Fair opportunity means that those applicants with the greatest needs (i.e., individuals with the most significant disabilities) should receive the largest share of agency resources. However, how "largest share" is defined will determine what approach is used to evaluate equity in service delivery. Indicators of agency resource allocation may include the number, type, and intensity of services provided, the length of time in services or in service planning, service costs, as well as indicators of counselor efforts which may not be reflected elsewhere (RSA, 1992). Also, evaluation typically involves comparison of service delivery for different groups with distinct rehabilitation needs.

Alternately, a fundamental principle of VR service delivery is that services are tailored to meet the individual's rehabilitation needs (Rubin & Roessler, 2000). Hence, in the case of the individual consumer, equity would entail that the person received all the service he or she needed to become employed, and group comparisons do not address the appropriateness of services for a given individual.

The same ambiguities that plague evaluation of equity in participation also make evaluation of equity in service delivery challenging. The lack of standardized data on participants' severity factors and the relationship of these to service needs makes comparisons within and across VR agencies problematic and permits only the most tentative conclusions. However, in the absence of these key data, one approach to evaluating equity is to compare the total services and costs of these services to distinct disability groups (e.g., individuals with orthopedic disabilities, psychiatric disabilities, visual impairments).

The USGAO (1993) examined the VR services provided to a national sample composed of consumers with significant and non-significant disabilities and classified by primary disability type. The USGAO reported small differences on total services received for individuals identified as having significant (M=3.8) and nonsignificant (M=3.4) disabilities, but larger differences on total costs of services for these two groups (M=$1,798 for individuals with significant disabilities and M=$1,175 for persons with nonsignificant disabilities). Also, small differences were reported for total services received by individuals in seven disability groups (e.g., orthopedic, psychiatric), but large differences were found in the costs of services to these groups. For example, individuals with visual impairments received 3.8 total services at an average cost of $2,401 per case, whereas individuals with mental illness and substance abuse primary disabilities received on average 3.8 and 4.0 services at average cost of $1,224 and $975, respectively. These latter results, however, do not compare persons with significant and nonsignificant disabilities within these seven disability groups; nor do the group comparisons address the appropriateness of services for a given individual. Both caveats limit the applicability of the USGAO (1993) results to the equity issue of service provision to persons with most significant disabilities.

Bellini, Bolton, and Neath (1997) examined VR services provided to consumers whose cases were closed as successfully rehabilitated (status 26) and not rehabilitated (status 28) during the years 1992 to 1995 in one state agency (Arkansas) that was operating under an order of selection plan. Service intensity was operationalized as 1) total services provided, 2) time in rehabilitation, and 3) total agency costs associated with the case. Profiles of discrete services and the three service intensity variables were examined for five primary disability groups: orthopedic, chronic-medical, psychiatric, mental retardation, and learning disability. Bellini et al. (1997) reported that differences in total services and time in rehabilitation for the five groups were minimal. However, differences in average total agency expenditures for the five groups were substantial, ranging from an average of $1,250 for individuals with a psychiatric primary disability to $2,190 for persons with a primary disability of mental retardation. Bellini et al. also reported low correlations among the measures of service intensity. They concluded that, although the RSA definition of individual with significant disabilities suggests substantial overlap between the need for multiple services and the need for services over an extended time, the empirical data indicates that the overlap between these measures of service intensity is actually minimal.

SUMMARY AND CONCLUSIONS

Order of selection, the mandate to serve persons with the most significant disabilities in the state-federal VR program, was first included in the 1973 Rehabilitation Act to ensure that persons with disabilities with the greatest rehabilitation needs would be a priority for state VR agencies. However, several problems plagued the implementation of the mandate during the first two decades, including 1) ambiguity regarding the federal definition of individual with significant disabilities, 2) the lack of a statutory definition of individual with the most significant disabilities, and 3) lack of guidance from the federal office to the state VR agencies. As a result of these difficulties, most states did not implement an order of selection procedure, and some states that did use the provision served persons with significant disabilities on a first-applied, first-served basis.

The 1992 Amendments to the Rehabilitation Act and subsequent federal regulations strengthened the commitment to serve individuals with the most significant disabilities in the state-federal VR program. State VR agencies that implement an order of selection plan are now required to define individual with most significant disabilities for the purpose of establishing priority categories and provide all needed services to persons in the highest priority category before individuals in lower priority categories are served. Moreover, state VR agencies that affirm the ability to serve all eligible applicants are required to specify how they will accomplish this.

As a result of detailed guidelines issued by the federal office, more state VR agencies are now implementing order of selection procedures than ever before. Also, there is a relatively high degree of consistency among the state VR agencies in how they define the target population. Most agencies choose to refine the functional capacity criterion of the federal definition and define individual with the most significant disabilities as having limited functional capacity in multiple life areas (two, three, or four areas) and requiring multiple services over extended time.

Recent RSA data suggest that state VR agencies are serving greater numbers of individuals with significant disabilities. However, it is difficult to determine whether state agencies and counselors are implementing order of selection provisions in an appropriate manner. In other words, do the empirical data indicate genuine progress in serving individuals with the most significant disabilities? The research findings on the implementation of order of selection reviewed in this chapter do not provide a clear, unambiguous answer to this question.

Consistency in applying the fair opportunity standard in order of selection means that counselors select individuals with the most significant disabilities for priority service. The investigations by USGAO (1993) and Bellini et al. (1996) suggest that rehabilitation counselors classify individuals with reasonable consistency into significant and nonsignificant categories for the purpose of establishing priority for service. The study by Salkever (1994), limited to persons with developmental disabilities, indicates that order of selection had not resulted in greater access to VR services by this population. However, these projects used data drawn from the early 1990s, that is, prior to the issuance of stricter federal guidelines for order of selection implementation. Thus, these studies have limited relevance for the current status of policy implementation. Research in this area has also been hindered by the different definitions and selection procedures used in the state VR agencies. The recent federal guidelines have resulted in greater consistency in state order of selection plans, and should permit more effective comparisons of order of selection implementation on the national level.

Research on VR service delivery has been similarly ambiguous. As noted previously, impartiality in applying the fair opportunity standard in VR service provision means that persons with different primary disabilities but the same classification (i.e., as an individual with the most significant disabilities) should receive a comparable share of resources. The studies by USGAO (1993) and Bellini et al. (1997) indicate minimal differences in the number of VR services that persons with different primary disabilities receive, but large differences in the average amount of service funds allocated to disability groups. These results may suggest problems in allocating agency resources in an impartial manner if it is determined that persons with some primary disabilities are more likely to receive the services they need than persons with other primary disabilities. In the case of the individual consumer, however, equity requires that the person receive all the services he or she needs to become employed, and group comparisons do not address the appropriateness of services for a given individual.

The evaluation of the quality of order of selection implementation requires more careful research on the functional characteristics of VR applicants, delivery of services by the VR agency, and employment outcomes achieved by persons with the most significant disabilities. Routine collection of standard, quantified data on applicants' severity of disability would enable agency administrators, program planners, legislators, and advocacy groups working at the local, state, and federal levels to evaluate the quality of order of selection implementation. In the absence of these key data on the severity indicators of VR participants, conclusions about equity issues such as the consistency of counselors' eligibility decisions and impartiality in allocation of agency resources will remain tentative.

REFERENCES

Andrews, H., Barker, J., Pittman, J., Mars, L., Struening, E., & LaRocca, N. (1992). National trends in vocational rehabilitation: A comparison of individuals with physical disabilities and individuals with psychiatric disabilities. *Journal of Rehabilitation, 58*(1), 7-16.

Barrett, L., Collignon, F., Dodson, R., Langlois, S., Rogers, J., & Shea, S. (1978). *Implementing the Rehabilitation Act of 1973: The vocational rehabilitation program response.* Berkeley, CA: Berkeley Planning Associates.

Bellini, J. (1997). Equity and the Order of Selection mandate: Critical issues in implementation and evaluation. *Journal of Disability Policy Studies, 9*(1), 107-124.

Bellini, J., Bolton, B., & Neath, J. (1995). The development of a Scale of Social Disadvantage for vocational rehabilitation. *Journal of Rehabilitation Administration, 19*(2), 107-118.

Bellini, J., Bolton, B., & Neath, J. (1996). Diagnostic determinants of rehabilitation counselor eligibility decisions. *Journal of Rehabilitation Administration, 20*(2), 93-106.

Bellini, J., Bolton, B., & Neath, J. (1997). Operationalizing multiple services over extended time as a measure of service intensity. *Journal of Rehabilitation Administration, 22*(1), 47-64.

Berkowitz, E. (1987). *Disabled policy: America's programs for the handicapped.* New York: Cambridge University Press.

Coalition of Citizens with Disabilities. (1991). *Draft recommendations for reauthorization of the Rehabilitation Act.* Washington, DC: Author.

Crewe, N., & Athelstan, G. (1984). *Functional Assessment Inventory manual.* Minneapolis: University of Minnesota.

Eleventh Institute on Rehabilitation Issues. (1974). *Rehabilitation of the significantly disabled.* Dunbar, WV: West Virginia Research and Training Center.

Federal Register. (1993, July 16). Vol. 58, No. 135. Proposed rules: The state vocational rehabilitation services program.

Federal Register. (1996, May 14). Vol. 61, No. 94. Rules and regulations: The state vocational rehabilitation services program.

Frey, W. (1984). Functional assessment in the 1980s: A conceptual enigma, a technical challenge. In A. S. Halpern & M. J. Fuhrer (Eds.), *Functional assessment in rehabilitation.* Baltimore, MD: Paul H. Brookes.

Gatens-Robinson, E., & Rubin, S. (1995). Societal values and ethical commitments that influence rehabilitation service delivery behavior. In S. Rubin & R. Roessler (Eds.), *Foundations of the vocational rehabilitation process* (4th ed.; pp. 157-174). Austin, TX: Pro-Ed.

Koshel, J., & Granger, C. (1978). Rehabilitation terminology: Who is severely disabled? *Rehabilitation Literature, 39*(4), 102-106.

Nagi, S. (1991). Disability concepts revisited: Implications for prevention. In A. M. Pope & A. R. Tarlov (Eds.), *Disability in America: Toward a national agenda for prevention.* Washington, DC: National Academy Press.

National Institute on Disability and Rehabilitation Research. (1992). *Digest of data on persons with disabilities.* Washington, DC: Office of Special Education and Rehabilitative Services, United States Department of Education.

Obermann, C. E. (1965). *A history of vocational rehabilitation in America.* Minneapolis, MN: T. S. Denison & Company, Inc.

Rehabilitation Services Administration. (1978). *Rehabilitation brief: Who is severely handicapped? The need for a workable definition.* Washington, DC: United States Department of Education, Rehabilitation Services Administration.

Rehabilitation Services Administration. (1992). *Order of selection for services guidance, Chapter G2501.* Washington, DC: United States Department of Education, Rehabilitation Services Administration.

Rehabilitation Services Administration. (1995). *Information memorandum: Caseload statistics, state vocational rehabilitation agencies, fiscal year 1993.* Washington, DC: United States Department of Education, Rehabilitation Services Administration.

Rehabilitation Services Administration. (1996). *Commissioner's memorandum: State VR agencies on an order of selection as of April 1, 1996.* Washington, DC: United States Department of Education, Rehabilitation Services Administration.

Rehabilitation Services Administration. (1999). *State vocational rehabilitation agency order of selection plans for fiscal year 2000.* Washington, DC: United States Department of Education, Rehabilitation Services Administration.

Rubin, S., & Roessler, R. (2000). *Foundations of the vocational rehabilitation process* (5th ed.) Austin, TX: Pro-Ed.

Salkever, D. (1994). Access to vocational rehabilitation services for people with severe disabilities: Analysis of the 1990 Developmental Disabilities National Consumer Survey. *Journal of Disability Policy Studies, 5*(2), 45-64.

Schriner, K. (1996). The Rehabilitation Act Amendments of 1992: Initiatives and issues. *Journal of Applied Rehabilitation Counseling, 27*(1), 37-41.

Schriner, K. F., Rumrill, P., & Parlin, R. (1995). Rethinking disability policy: Equity in the ADA era and the meaning of specialized services for people with disabilities. *Journal of Health and Human Services Administration, 17*(4), 478-500.

Stone, D. (1988). *Policy paradox and political reason.* Philadelphia: Temple University Press.

United States General Accounting Office. (1991). *Vocational rehabilitation: Clearer guidance could help focus services on those with severe disabilities.* Gaithersburg, MD: Author.

United States General Accounting Office. (1993). *Vocational rehabilitation: Evidence for federal program's effectiveness is mixed.* Gaithersburg, MD: Author.

Urban Institute. (1974). *Report of the Comprehensive Service Needs Study.* Washington, DC: United States Department of Health, Education, and Welfare.

Young, P. (1994). *Equity: In theory and practice.* Princeton, NJ: Sage.

Chapter 3

LIFE CARE PLANNING: AN EMERGING REHABILITATION INTERVENTION

CHRISTINE A. REID, PAUL M. DEUTSCH, AND JULIE KITCHEN

INTRODUCTION

What can rehabilitation counselors do to empower catastrophically injured individuals, maximizing their quality of life, minimizing disability-related complications, and minimizing costs of needed services? Rehabilitation counselors can learn to apply life care planning (LCP) techniques, and put themselves on the "cutting edge" of practice in a rapidly increasing number of rehabilitation environments.

LCP is a systematic methodology for identifying, quantifying, and clearly communicating the multidimensional disability-related needs of an individual. A life care plan is a document that summarizes those needs and provides a "roadmap" for consumers and rehabilitation counselors to follow when addressing client needs in a comprehensive yet cost-effective manner. Through the use of LCP methodology, rehabilitation counselors can maximize beneficial outcomes for individuals with disabilities while minimizing costs. Costs are controlled through both a proactive approach to preventing complications and a systematic approach to curtailing duplication of services. At the same time, service effectiveness is enhanced by careful consideration of a multitude of factors that interact to affect rehabilitation and quality of life outcomes (Reid, Deutsch, Kitchen, & Aznavoorian, 1999).

Note: Portions of this chapter were adapted from "Life Care Planning," by C. Reid, P. Deutsch, J. Kitchen, & K. Aznavoorian (1999), in F. Chan & M. Leahy (Eds.), *Healthcare and Disability Case Management* (pp. 415-453), Lake Zurich, IL: Vocational Consultants Press. Adapted with permission.

HISTORY AND DEVELOPMENT OF LIFE CARE PLANNING

Life care planning is an outgrowth of research begun in the late 1970s and was first addressed extensively in the publication *Damages in Tort Actions* (Deutsch & Raffa, 1982). The need for LCP methodology was identified through the following:

1. It was recognized that individuals with disabilities and their families (especially in pediatric cases) needed a concise summary of a plan that could be taken away from an evaluation and used as a guideline for future reference.
2. It was important to have a means for communication among all parties involved in a litigated injury case regarding the precise needs dictated by the onset of a disability. The life care plan became a tool to communicate this information in a clear, concise, and precise fashion.
3. Catastrophic case management dictated the need for proactive planning, rather than simple reaction to circumstances dictating the client's immediate needs.
4. Life care planning was designed to break the effects of disability into the most basic components, thereby allowing complex concerns to be more carefully assessed with a view toward prevention of problems rather than "management by chaos."
5. Life care planning methodology was developed to take into consideration the injury or disability; the needs, goals, interests, and preferences of the individual; the needs of the family; and the realities of the geographical region in which the individual and family reside.

In 1987, the Rehabilitation Training Institute (RTI) was founded in Orlando, Florida as a national, postgraduate institute to 1) encourage the development of life care planning, and 2) facilitate its use in case management of catastrophic disability and impairment claims (RTI, 1997).

Recently, the Commission on Disability Examiner Certification (CDEC) implemented a national certification process in the area of life care planning (CDEC, 1996). Although such certification is not currently required for practice in many settings, it remains to be seen whether certification will increase in importance, especially in forensic situations.

Applications of Life Care Planning

In its early stages, the foremost application of LCP was through the consultation process. Consultation, primarily with insurance carriers and attorneys involved in injury litigation, developed into an important area of practice for rehabilitation professionals. The demands generated by participants in the litigation process significantly influenced LCP and enhanced its credibility and acceptance, both within and outside the courtroom. Currently, qualified life care planners are recognized in court as expert witnesses with knowledge and skills in rehabilitation and case management that are not generally available through traditional medical testimony. Their skills and expertise are utilized in an increasing number of applications outside the courtroom, as well.

LCP has become an integral part of the rehabilitation case management process for individuals with catastrophic injuries. Increasingly, both service providers and funding sources are recognizing the importance of advanced planning rather than attempting to manage disability through spur-of-the-moment reactions to series of crises. Weed (1995) has discussed the importance of LCP as a managed care tool; Weed and Riddick (1992) have examined its use as a case management tool.

Life care plans comprehensively address quality-of-life issues, long-term needs of the individual and his or her family, potential complications of medical conditions, and nonmedical issues (e.g., transportation, architectural renovations for home care). These plans can facilitate the person's transition from a rehabilitation facility to life outside that facility. Deutsch (1990) described the value of life care plans for individuals being discharged from one level of care to another or to the home community. He observed that an effective discharge plan (i.e., life care plan) should provide continuity between and among service providers at different levels of care, as well as serve as a basis for guiding the overall rehabilitation plan. The life care plan should empower the individual with a disability by promoting self-awareness and by providing specific information pertinent to both short- and long-term planning. As Deutsch noted, important aspects of the life care planner's role include identifying funds available for needed services and working to ascertain alternative income sources.

The Rehabilitation Professional's Role as Educator

After development of the life care plan, the rehabilitation professional's first and foremost role is as a teacher who must be prepared to educate all parties concerned so that effective and well-informed decisions can be made regarding how to meet the person's future needs. The life care plan should serve as an educational tool to communicate complex issues in an understandable manner. Judges and juries need to be educated regarding the disability-related needs of an individual, to be able to make informed decisions. A life care planner should not tell jury members how much money to award a plaintiff, but should instead educate the jury about the expected costs associated with that injury so that the jurors can make their own appropriate decisions. Deutsch (1990) addressed ways to effectively communicate with judges and juries in *A Guide to Rehabilitation Testimony: The Expert's Role as an Educator.*

Catastrophically injured individuals and their families need to understand what services will be needed at what times throughout the life span, at what costs and from what resources, and what might be the consequences of not obtaining those services. In the absence of this understanding, there is a great risk of families spending most of the money from an insurance settlement without making provisions for the person's increased service needs later in life.

LIFE CARE PLANNING METHODOLOGY

The most critical aspect of LCP is the development of a consistent methodology for analyzing the needs dictated by the onset of a disability (Deutsch, 1995). This methodology takes into consideration individual, family, and geographic needs of the person. The goal is to meet an individual's rehabilitation and long-term disability-related needs, to prevent further injury, and to make feasible the best possible quality of life.

Principle of Consistency

The hallmark of effective LCP is a consistent approach to gathering information, considering the implications of that information, and presenting it in an understandable format. Life care planners should not develop "luxury" plans including the most expensive options possible when hired by a plaintiff, nor search for ways to provide the barest minimum of services regardless of individual needs when hired by an insurance company. The most respected life care planners follow a consistent approach to plan development with each and every case; their plans are based upon the demonstrated needs of each individual for whom a plan is created. To these planners, it does not matter whether they are hired by plaintiff or defense in a litigated case, by an insurance company to assist with case management and reserve setting, or by any other party to develop a life care plan – the plan that is developed will be tailored to the actual needs of the individual with a disability, which should not vary depending on the nature of the referral source.

Basic Tenets of Life Care Planning

A distinction should be made between actual life care plan development and the structuring of a plan constrained by specific financial limitations. Life care plans are based upon the actual needs of an individual, not on the projected resources available. In some catastrophic injury cases, the individual's actual needs may exceed the resources that become available to meet those needs. However, it is important even in those cases to identify the discrepancy between needs and resource availability, and to educate the parties involved about potential implications of not meeting the identified needs. McCoy (1996) suggested that if life care planners are asked to generate a plan to best utilize a specific amount of funding, a different name should be used for the plan, such as "Medical/Equipment Cost Projections Analysis."

Proactive, not Reactive.

Life care plans should be developed and implemented in a preventative manner that minimizes the occurrence of complications. The recommendations must be clearly related to evaluation data that identify specific individual needs, and they must be expected to benefit the individual. If an individual is not expected to benefit from a given service or piece of equipment, such a recommendation should not be made. On the other hand, if a recommendation is expected to benefit the individual, the expected benefit should be considered in developing the rest of the plan. For example, if an individual with paraplegia but no history of decubiti (pressure sores) is provided appropriate wheelchair cushioning and training regarding pressure release, skin inspection, and other methods to prevent the development of decubiti, that individual's life care plan should not include provisions for four surgeries per year to treat frequent and serious decubiti.

Benefits of Maximizing Potential.

In addition to individual quality of life benefits, there can be financial benefits to maximizing rehabilitation outcomes through the provision of timely and appropriate services. For example, consider the costs over a lifetime for two different twenty-four-year-old individuals with a C5-6 spinal cord injury. One individual can turn himself over at night or can tolerate six hours without being turned. The other individual cannot. The difference in expected costs over the lifetime for these two individuals is approximately two million dollars.

Multidimensionality

Each recommendation, driven by a specific deficit or dysfunction, will affect other recommendations both directly and indirectly. Some directly affected items may force recommendation changes by limiting time available for other items, for example. Multiple disabilities and multiple service providers might dictate multiple similar recommendations, thereby resulting in service overlaps or duplications.

Consider the Entire Costs

Not only life care plan developers, but also people implementing the plans need to consider the entire cost of selecting a given service option or piece of equipment. For equipment, the overall costs take into account the costs of maintenance and frequency of need for replacement. Some issues related to the entire costs of hiring service providers are discussed by Thomas and Kitchen (1996), who compared the costs of hiring a personal care attendant through an agency with the cost of an attendant employed through private hire. When total costs (including employer social security and Medicare matches, state unemployment taxes, fringe benefits, payroll expenses, background checks, appropriate supervision, etc.) of a private hire are considered, the appeal of hiring through an agency increases greatly.

In a life care plan the entire costs provided do not include two important categories: potential complications and future technology. The costs associated with both of these cannot be accurately predicted. The degree to which complications will be experienced or future technology will be developed to meet a given individual's needs cannot be known. Therefore, those costs are not included in life care plans. However, it is important for life care planners and case managers to inform decision makers that there is potential for development of complications, as well as for invention of future technology, which could have on impact on lifetime costs even though that impact is not considered in the plan.

Psychological Considerations

Psychological factors have a significant impact on the quality of life for individuals with catastrophic injuries. Not only medical and physical/functional needs, but also psychological needs must be addressed in LCP. Having choices and exercising control over one's environment are especially important for individuals with catastrophic injuries that interfere with mobility and physical function. In some ways, for example, installation of an environmental control unit is a psychological intervention. If an individual with tetraplegia has a personal care attendant available to turn the channels on a television set or to dial a telephone, a naive observer might question the need for a voice-activated system to operate those items. However, the psychological importance of restoring as much choice and independent control over one's environment as possible should not be underestimated. Choices can be made available in other ways, as well. To use another example, instead of just running through a standard physical therapy routine in a given order, a physical therapist could ask the client, "Would you rather work on your legs or your arms first today?"

Psychological interventions should take into consideration the current demonstrated needs of the individual and his or her family, as well as future adjustments anticipated over the life span. For an adult who is injured, adjustments are expected during life changes such as retirement. For children with disabilities, appropriate short-term psychological goals should be established for different developmental stages.

Disability Interacts with Aging

Not only psychological aspects, but also physical aspects of function will normally vary with age. However, when disability interacts with the aging process, some body parts "wear out" faster than they would for an individual without a disability. For example, an individual who uses a manual wheelchair during young adulthood may be expected to require a power wheelchair later in life. That person"s shoulders, which were not designed to be weight-bearing joints, will likely lose function over time faster than they would for an individual who doesn't use a wheelchair.

Process of LCP Development

Life care planning is a process that results in individualized plans tailored to the needs of a specific person. It is important that the life care planner conduct an on-site interview with the catastrophically injured individual and, whenever possible, his or her family. Recommendations must be made within the context of individual, family, disability, and regional factors.

A comprehensive review of all available medical, psychological, and rehabilitation-related information is required. School records for children and work histories for adults should also be reviewed. The life care planner must be aware of all medical and rehabilitative aspects of the case, and determine what other evaluations may be needed to identify the individual's disability-related needs. Communication and consultation with the other members of the rehabilitation team are essential. Specific questions may be needed for each specialist, to ascertain and integrate the projected evaluations, treatment recommendations, and therapeutic modalities needed in each area.

Areas analyzed within the development of a life care plan include projected health-related professional evaluations, projected therapeutic modalities, diagnostic testing and educational assessments, wheelchair needs, wheelchair accessories and maintenance, orthopedic equipment needs, orthotic or prosthetic requirements, disability-related home furnishings and accessories, aids for independent function, drug and medical supply needs, home care or facility-based care needs, projected and routine future medical care, projected future surgical treatment or other aggressive medical care, transportation needs, required architectural renovations, leisure time and recreational equipment requirements, and specific vocational rehabilitation needs.

Recommendations in the areas in a life care plan are tailored to the expected short-term and long-term needs of the individual. Specific dates and frequencies of the needed services are detailed, as are the costs associated with those services. Additionally, a section of the life care plan addresses potential complications. This section is provided for informational purposes only; as previously noted, the frequency of complications and associated costs cannot be predicted. However, a well-developed and carefully implemented life care plan should proactively minimize the occurrence of complications. If, despite appropriate care and services, a condition is expected to worsen or function is expected to decrease over time, the expected need for increased services and appropriate equipment should be addressed directly within the life care plan. Such expected changes in need are not labeled as complications, because complications (by definition) cannot be anticipated.

Plan Implementation

Ethical, creative, and critical thought processes are used for the development and implementation of life care plans. The application of ethical standards drives decisions and ensures that a high standard of care is maintained. The process of creative thinking is utilized to meet the needs of individuals with catastrophic injuries over time. All possible strategies for prevention of further problems should be considered, whether applied to minimizing the potential for medical complications or to maximizing mobility and independence by ensuring that equipment maintenance is carried out. If new information about effective techniques for prevention of anticipated problems becomes available after the life care plan has been written, the rehabilitation counselor or case manager should revise the plan to incorporate those techniques, as feasible.

Problem solving is important, whether applied as a reaction to an acute event or applied to the theme of prevention as age and disability combine, resulting in decreased function over time. As client needs change over time in ways that may not have been anticipated by the original life care planner, the person coordinating the implementation of that plan should update and revise the plan. Critical thinking is required to prioritize client needs in plan implementation and allocation of available resources. Life care plans should outline client needs that are dictated by the onset of disability; unfortunately, sufficient funding may not always exist to fully address all of the needs identified. One must often not only find creative ways to supplement resource availability, but also work with the client to prioritize service needs identified in the life care plan, carefully identifying relative risks associated with reduction or revision of specific services.

Computers and Life Care Planning

Given the need to keep track of multidimensional information and to present it in an easily understandable manner, most life care planners are attracted to a variety of computer applications. Databases are used to maintain updated information about resources, and word processors and graphics programs are used to present the information in an accessible manner. One integrated "case management system" software program for LCP is LCPStat (Thomas, 1997). This program can be used to build databases of resources, summarize and organize medical records, track client information, and print life care plan tables, for example.

RESEARCH AND RESOURCE SUPPORT

Life care planners and professionals implementing life care plans have a critical need to know and understand medical aspects of specific disabilities and the means by which programs can be set up to prevent the onset of further problems or complications. They need to understand the methodological steps for case management planning and be able to maintain a current grasp of reference material and research literature.

LCP recommendations should be data-based, rather than simple opinions. Planners should collect data from as many sources as possible, obtaining information not only about the individual client and resources for service provision, but also about relevant research studies that have been published related to the needs of similar individuals with disabilities. It is essential that life care planners utilize critical thinking skills to examine relevant literature and its appropriateness for a given case. For example, if a given research article concludes that a particular set of services will be needed by individuals with bilateral above-the-knee amputations around the tenth year following amputation, can the life care planner assume that these services will be needed for her or his client with bilateral above-the-knee amputations? The answer to that question should be, "It depends. . . ." How similar are the characteristics of the sample in the study to the characteristics of this client? For example, are study subjects the same gender, same age, with the same level of physical activity and similar interests? Do they have the same combination of disabilities, acquired in the same manner, as does this individual?

Life care planners need not only critical thinking skills, but also creativity and an ability to organize and maintain complex databases of information. Life care plans should be developed using cost estimates from suppliers who are located in the area where the catastrophically injured individual will be living. Sometimes, locating providers of unusual services in remote locations requires considerable creativity and problem-solving ability. Once such resources are located or developed, it would be foolish for the planner to lose track of those resources. Development and maintenance of an updated set of resources in various local areas is important to life care planners, as well as the people who implement previously developed plans.

Life care plans are projected to life expectancy, and they cannot depend on any one individual, service, or supplier for fulfilling plan recommendations. More than one potential supplier should be identified to fulfill each recommendation. In situations where a family member plans to provide some of the services, the life care plan should also reflect alternative options. It may happen that the family member becomes unable or unwilling at some future point to provide that service. In addition, even if the family member chooses to provide the service, the value of that service (i.e., what it would cost if another person were to be hired to provide it) should be included in the overall cost detailed in the life care plan.

A variety of guides have been published to serve as starting points for factors to consider when developing life care plans for individuals with specific disabilities. Examples include Deutsch and Sawyer's (2000) *A Guide to Rehabilitation*, which is updated annually and provides information about various disabilities. Blackwell, Powers, and Weed (1994); Deutsch, Weed, Kitchen, and Sluis (1989); and Kitchen, Cody, and Deutsch (1989) have addressed LCP with individuals who have had traumatic brain injuries. Issues to consider in life care planning with people who have had spinal cord injuries have been discussed by Blackwell, Weed, and Powers (1994), and Kitchen, Cody, and Morgan (1990). Weed and Sluis (1990) addressed LCP with individuals who have had amputations.

KNOWLEDGE, SKILLS, AND EXPERTISE REQUIRED

Life care planning has become a specialty area requiring not only global application of general case management concepts, but also the development of skills specific to particular disabilities. Life care planners should be trained in the areas of medical aspects of disability, psychological and behavioral aspects of disability, facility and agency placement (i.e., making effective referrals), preventative care techniques, rehabilitation engineering (i.e., equipment related to disability), and vocational aspects of disability.

The Commission on Disability Examiner Certification (CDEC) describes the process of life care plan development as requiring data collection, resource development, and planning strategies in an interdisciplinary rehabilitation environment. The life care planner must be able to document the needs of catastrophically injured individuals and project the costs of needed services, treatment, and equipment over each individual"s life span. Skills and expertise in the areas of research, development, coordination, integration, interpretation, and management of life care plans are required. For certification in this area, the CDEC requires a minimum of 120 clock hours of postgraduate or postspecialty degree training in LCP, an appropriate degree and certification/licensure within the planner's own professional area, and professional experience developing life care plans (CDEC, 1997).

It should be noted that, although the life care planner provides information about the current costs of services and equipment, it is usually an economist who is responsible for projecting those costs over the expected life span, taking into account differing growth trends for different categories of costs. The length of that expected life span is usually estimated by a physician, preferably a physiatrist with expertise and experience treating patients with the individual's specific disabilities. However, life care planners conducting follow-up contacts with their clients can help to gather valuable data to refine life expectancy estimates for such clients in the future.

Life care plans are generally completed by rehabilitation counselors, case managers, rehabilitation psychologists, or rehabilitation nurses. These individuals can effectively use their training as case managers and team leaders in an interdisciplinary approach to rehabilitation and long-term management of disability. In contrast, most physicians tend to be limited in their responsibility to meeting the acute care needs of their patients, instead of bringing together medical, rehabilitation, educational, and family considerations into a unified and systematic approach to goal development (Deutsch & Kitchen, 1994).

Taylor (1996) reviewed the trial outcomes of several court cases in which life care plans were presented. Taylor found that courts favored life care plans "which (1) are prepared by qualified rehabilitation experts, (2) show the real need for the plaintiff to incur the expenses noted in the plan, and (3) demonstrate reasonable costs for future care" (p. 7). These criteria were more important than whether the life care planner was a physician or whether the planner was hired by plaintiff or defense attorneys.

SAMPLE NARRATIVE REPORT

Presented in this section is a sample narrative report that typically accompanies a life care plan. This document summarizes the client's medical history, current functioning and ongoing service needs. Following the report is a brief summary of the comprehensive life care plan information normally provided in a series of detailed tables. An example of actual life care plan tables for such a case can be found in Reid, Deutsch, Kitchen, and Aznavoorian (1999).

> Client: "Stuart Rice"
> Social Security No.: Not Given (along with other identifying information)
> Date of Evaluations: August 13 and September 25, 2000
> Date of Narrative Report: October 21, 2000

Stuart Rice is a 7-year, 11-month-old Caucasian male referred for rehabilitation evaluation by his attorneys, Mr. X and Ms. Y. The purpose of this evaluation is to assess the extent to which Stuart has incurred handicapping conditions secondary to a birth onset of disability. The specific manner in which the resulting handicapping conditions impede his educational development and potential for vocational development, as well as any supportive services he will require throughout his life expectancy, have been considered in the conclusions and appendix attached to this report. In reaching these conclusions, consideration has been given to all of the medical, psychological, and rehabilitation data, along with appropriate test information.

Stuart was seen for evaluation initially in the office of Z and Associates on August 13, 2000, by Ms. P, CDMS, for the purpose of gathering initial background and demographic information. Subsequently, on September 25, 2000, he returned accompanied by his father (John), and a clinical history and child assessment was completed.

Stuart presented as an active, seven-year-old Caucasian male, who was quite talkative and interacted easily and effectively with the evaluators. His father described his vision as 20/200 bilaterally, which is considered legally blind.

Assistive devices employed by Stuart included a slant board device on his desk at school to allow him to see the information more easily. His father indicated that no other specific aids were employed; however, the school did use a white chalkboard for better visualization instead of the standard blackboard. Additional aids had been identified through Stuart's vision consultant, and these will be outlined within the life care plan pages.

Stuart's father gave a history of Stuart being born prematurely at 23 weeks. He noted that Stuart"s birth weight was one pound, three ounces, and at one point Stuart had dropped below the weight of one pound. Stuart was the surviving member of a twin birth.

His father noted that Stuart initially came home on a heart monitor, and subsequently it was "a while before therapy could be initiated." He started a program in Florida; however, John was unsure of the specifics of the program. At age three, Stuart participated in occupational and speech therapy two times per week for one hour each session. He was also involved in the Teaching Lab for about two years and was involved in a home schooling situation with his mother early on. John gained full custody of Stuart in September 1999 by mutual agreement of both parents. Since September 1999, Stuart had been in speech therapy fairly consistently with Ms. S, CCC, until funding problems interfered with the continuation of services. He participated in physical therapy, which was provided through the school system. This therapy continued through the summer, during which he also participated in the Learning Institute two days per week. At the time of the evaluation, Stuart had been in the first grade for two weeks. His father noted that Stuart was having difficulty paying attention and staying on task. He was not particularly hyperactive, but he did have difficulty staying focused. His father noted that the school system wanted to hold him back last year as he was not academically at age level; however, because of his age, he was moved on to the next level.

Chief Complaints

During this portion of the evaluation, John was asked to outline for us Stuart's primary problems. It is important to note that the demographic information and Chief Complaints, Physical Limitations, and Environmental Influences sections of this report are all as a result of client and family report, not based on any physical examination.

John began by explaining that Stuart was "frequently sick with colds and has an immune system deficiency. When he gets sick, it will stay with him for weeks. He has little immune system function to fight it at all. He has poor hand-eye coordination. His fine motor skills are bad— he cannot cut paper on the line; he is clumsy basically. He runs awkwardly, like something is out of rhythm. We took him to a podiatrist who said it was his hips, not his feet, which are causing the problems with the gait. When he runs, he waddles, and he falls down all of the time. The podiatrist says his pelvis rotates more than it should, and it throws off his center of gravity. His pediatrician just says he has multiple dysfunctions from prematurity. He has a high arched palate, thick tongue, and hence has speech problems as well as dental side effects, which the pediatrician says should be evaluated by a dentist. This hasn't been accomplished yet. His mother took him earlier, but she was told by the periodontist that later in life they could place a plate in his mouth to give his tongue something to hit. Ms. S (speech/language pathologist) feels that oral-motor exercises may also help. He has a weak voice; he can't scream. His voice comes out in a breathy whisper. He has significant scarring and has had open-heart surgery due to heart valve malfunctioning and has had a hernia. Because he was so little, his skin kept separating from his legs and other areas when the sheets would come in contact with it. He had a tube taped to his mouth in the hospital, and at one point, when he had a problem, the tube and tape were jerked off and "it just tore the skin right off with it."

Clearly, John had difficulty enumerating the many areas of deficits he sees in Stuart. Stuart did have problems in learning and retaining new information, as well as immediate and delayed memory problems. He was unable to follow serial instructions, and he had to be given one task at a time. According to his father, Stuart was frustrated very easily if he could not do something, and "he just shuts down." He father was convinced that Stuart had a "wandering eye," and this may be the cause of some of the headaches he had about twice a week.

John noted that Stuart was in the hospital for four months. He came home on a heart monitor, and they had an in-house nurse during this time for the first month. Someone was needed to stay awake with Stuart through the night to monitor him. The monitor was discontinued about a month after he was home. Stuart was fed through a tube through his mouth for three months. Upon discharge to home, he was initially fed through a preemie bottle.

John noted that, early on, Stuart's mom found it difficult to deal with the reality of a special needs child. Dad had since then enrolled Stuart in school and was trying to do everything he could to bring stability into Stuart's life. The school system had suggested he be sent to a different school for visual impairments; however, his father had determined that there was only one "special" class that would be offered at this other school, as compared to what he was already receiving. Stuart had enlarged print books and a special board overlay for him to be able to visualize the chalkboard. In trying to bring stability into Stuart's life, Dad was reluctant to switch him to another school at this point in time. Additionally, his school at that time was close to his home.

In continuing, Dad noted that Stuart can chill easily, and his lips will turn blue. He cannot go to the beach on a hot day and enjoy the water, as he gets too cold. His father was trying to "put weight on him," but without much success. Stuart took vitamins but no food supplements. John noted that the pediatrician is not too concerned about Stuart's weight.

In addition to the above, Stuart's learning disabilities and behavioral problems such as not listening and not paying attention are also areas of concern. He was not in special education classes at the time of the evaluation.

John noted that this has been a tremendous strain on both parents. Stuart's mother had been through three tubal pregnancies with artificial insemination and then in vitro fertilization, which produced the twins, of which Stuart is the surviving member.

John was unsure of any future surgery that Stuart may need. He noted that there might be an eye surgery later in life. He also mentioned Stuart's hips being "out," and he was unsure if bracing will help and be used or if surgical intervention will be required.

As part of this evaluation, specific questions relating to developmental delay were asked. Stuart had no seizures at the time, with no history of seizures being present. He had one heart surgery to open a valve in the past. His father was unsure of any other specific surgeries required in the future.

Stuart attended school and was in an aftercare program for two hours each day. He also attended XYZ Learning Institute during the summer to avoid a gap in his educational experience.

Stuart"s daily care needs included a highly structured learning and behavioral environment. This was particularly evident, as some problems in his behavior had been seen in the aftercare program, similar to the problems he had experienced during school, relating to his being rather rough with the other children.

When asked about self-stimulating behaviors, John indicated that Stuart used to stiffen up and make animal sounds and grunts, and at the time of the evaluation he still made the sounds but did not stiffen up as much.

To assess the motor skills area, John was observed during a free play session. His grasp (left and right) was intact but not well coordinated. Vision was part of the issue but coordination was a separate issue. He was able to grasp with his thumb and forefinger and make voluntary, purposeful movements of the upper and lower extremities. He was able to ambulate but did have a gait disturbance that may be orthopedic in origin or it may be neurological.

John reported that Stuart did not regularly dress himself, although he was able to do so. He has had problems, such as when his underwear was inside out and "he has no clue as to how to turn it back." He would cooperate and assist with dressing. He picked up his toys and cleaned up his closet with cueing and prompts. His father noted that when he does this, he insists on lining everything up in a straight line, such as all the shoes exactly placed in line. Regarding personal hygiene chores, he required help and prompting. He seemed to want to brush his teeth, but he was simply unable to coordinate that activity. Stuart could ascend and descend stairs with caution and guidance, but he fell frequently.

In the cognitive area, Stuart was able to follow simple one- or two-step commands. His father noted, "You have to be careful because he doesn't always avoid hazards." For example, if Stuart was playing with a ball and it rolled out into the street, he would run out into the road chasing his ball, without giving thought to traffic. Stuart"s attention to task was very limited, with moderate hyperactivity shown during the evaluation and also near the end of the evaluation. Stuart was observed punching his father and reaching out to squeeze his face and neck with both hands. Stuart appears to think he is playing, but he shows no sense of strength or if he is hurting someone during these activities.

Physical Limitations

John said he was not aware of any loss of tactile sensation that Stuart might experience. Stuart did show a normal range of motion in the upper extremities. He could lift weights that were appropriate for his age and weight. Stuart's prehensile action and grip strength were strong bilaterally. He had no physical restrictions with sitting, but he was constantly out of his seat due to his attention deficits. He had no physical restrictions on standing, restricted only in terms of his attention span. Stuart had an altered gait and stumbled frequently when he tried to run. His podiatrist indicated that Stuart's hips do not rotate properly, and this needs to be evaluated by an orthopedist in the future. He had no physical restrictions with bending or twisting, stooping, squatting, or climbing. His balance was fair, as he was uncoordinated and tended to "wobble." He fatigued easily and displayed no shortness of breath while at rest, but with an activity, he would tend to get out of breath. He had headaches frequently, typically two times per week. He did not take medications for these. As noted earlier, Stuart was considered legally visually impaired. His hearing was intact, as was his sense of humor. When asked if he is able to hear, he responded, "What?"

Stuart did have bowel accidents on occasion, maybe once every couple of months, or maybe more. He noted that if he strains, he might have an accident. He had easy fatigueability and his physical stamina and endurance were not at an age-appropriate level.

Additional Data

Careful consideration was given to a collection of data concerning activities of daily living, social activities, personal habits, socioeconomic status, and state or federal agency involvement in rehabilitation. Although not reported in its entirety within the context of this narrative report, that data remains available within the clinical notes and was utilized in developing rehabilitation conclusions and recommendations. Additionally, a vocational report is available to address the impact this injury will have on Stuart's ability to be placed in the competitive labor market.

Current Medical Care

Stuart was seeing RS, M.D., as his primary care physician. He was not seeing any other specialists at the time of the evaluation.

Stuart had been receiving speech therapy through Ms. S, although those services had been temporarily interrupted due to funding issues;

vision therapy through the school system; and additional speech therapy and occupational therapy as well though the school system. He had also been seen by an educational consultant and occupational therapist. Each of Stuart's treating professionals was contacted with specific questions regarding his long-term care needs. Their recommendations will be outlined within the life care plan.

At the time of the evaluation, Stuart was taking no prescription medication.

Education and Training

Stuart attended first grade at ABC Elementary School in Florida. He was not in special education classes but did have the assistance of a vision teacher.

Behavioral Observations

Stuart was alert and oriented; his stream of thought was clear, however, it was not fully age appropriate. He was somewhat, but not severely, behind in his social maturation. His approach to the evaluation was positive, in line with his age level.

Test Administration

Stuart's school and medical records contained a range of standardized test results and it was not felt necessary at this time to repeat those items. I do feel consideration should be given to completing a neuropsychological workup, but I stress this is for establishing the right structured environment and enhancing educational development. I am not recommending this be done for trial purposes. I chose to administer the Slosson Intelligence Test as a means of gaining insight into his current fund of knowledge and his ability to function over time on a task.

Stuart had to be constantly redirected to this task orientation, but with prompts and reinforcement he was able to complete the effort. His total standard score (IQ) was 103, with a mean age equivalency of 7.3. He fell in the 57th percentile in this measure, which shows his ability to learn and retain information if an effort is made to meet his individual needs.

Medical Summary

Stuart Rice was a seven-year-old, Caucasian male born on 11/26/92. Stuart was delivered three weeks after his twin. The twin was delivered vaginally, and Stuart was delivered by cesarean section. His twin died at birth.

On 8/14/93, Stuart was seen at the Eye Clinic with a history of retinopathy of prematurity, status post cryo treatment. The impression was that Stuart had an excellent result status post cryo treatment; however, he was significantly myopic. A prescription for glasses was made.

On 10/1/93, Stuart was seen at Riverside Children's Hospital for a neurological consultation. Apparently Stuart was born with intraventricular bleeding, and since then he had been hyperactive. He had a short attention span. He had self-stimulating behavior, and he did not sleep well at night. His legs were stiff and he moved constantly. In relation to language, Stuart did not make any sounds. He reached for objects mostly with his left hand, and he was unable to sit on his own. He scooted on the floor, but he was not able to maintain a crawling pattern. The diagnoses were: 1) macrocephaly with cortical atrophy, probably secondary to prematurity; 2) extraocular movement imbalance with bilateral alternating internal strabismus; 3) spastic quadriparesis; 4) pseudobulbar palsy; 5) language disorder, receptive and expressive with practically no speech articulation; 6) rule out gastroesophageal reflux; and 7) behavior disorder, attention deficit disorder, hyperactivity, and irritability.

In a follow-up visit to the Neurology Clinic at Children's Hospital on 10/23/93, a CAT scan showed definite signs with moderate ventriculomegaly and sucal prominence indicating atrophic changes of the cortex and also of the central structures with central and cortical atrophy diffusely distributed. An EEG was within normal limits. Stuart was seen by the speech pathologist, who recommended speech therapy. His speech development was below the three-month level with no evidence of cooing and babbling. Continued physical therapy and occupational therapy were also recommended.

On 4/12/94, Stuart was seen for a neurology re-evaluation at Children's Hospital. Upon examination, he appeared to be very hyperactive and had an attention deficit disorder. He also had self-stimulating behavior. He reached for objects fairly well. His gait was absent, and his sitting balance was very poor. His motor development was approximately six to seven months. At that time, medicine for hyperactivity was not necessary. Continued therapies were recommended.

In a follow-up visit to the Eye Clinic on 11/22/97, there was a slight increase in Stuart's myopic correction.

On 10/28/99, Stuart was seen for an oral motor evaluation at Z and Associates. The impression was dysarthria. Oral motor intervention one time per week with home carry-over was recommended.

In a letter dated 2/13/00 (Vision Center), it was indicated that Stuart met the definition of legal blindness.

On 4/4/00, Stuart was seen for an evaluation by Mr. LM. It was believed that Stuart would benefit from occupational therapy services to rehabilitate his visual motor skills. Stuart had slightly hypotonic muscle tone and problems with bilateral integration, upper body control, graphomotor skills, and fine motor control. He had visual impairment and difficulty with initiation, completion, and planning out motor tasks. He functioned below his age level and capability due to these problems. It was felt that he would benefit from placement in a regular classroom with assistance from a vision teacher and an occupational therapist. A home program follow-through with therapeutic interventions was also recommended.

On 4/4/00, Stuart was seen for a functional vision assessment. Overall, he utilized vision as his main learning modality. His performance was below average in two areas of assessment, which were ocular pursuits and acuity (distance and near). It was indicated that both areas could affect his performance, but with compensation strategies they should not affect his ability to learn. It was believed that Stuart would at least need large print with 18-point text for school. It was suggested that he would be able to succeed in a regular classroom with itinerant services from a teacher of the visually impaired .

Records Reviewed:

Dr. RS: 4/4/00
Ms. S: MS, CCC-SLP: 10/28/99-4/14/00
Mr. LM, M.Ed., OTR/L: 4/4/00-6/17/00
Eye Clinic: 8/14/93-3/19/99
Pediatrics: 11/8/99; 6/93-10/96
Vision Center: 2/13/00

Medical Bills: 9/99-4/00
Children's Hospital: 10/1/93-10/11/94
Primary Care: 9/24/00
Prescription Records: 1999
School Records (in file): 2/00-5/00

Conclusions

Careful consideration has been given to all of the medical, psychosocial, rehabilitation/mental health counseling, and test data contained within this file and my report. There is certainly no question that we are dealing with an individual who has incurred significant handicapping conditions, which will affect his future educational and social development secondary to his premature birth and resulting sequela.

Stuart will need a neuropsychological evaluation to help identify how he learns best; then all of his therapists, family members, and teachers must be trained accordingly. Based on the findings of the neuropsychological evaluation, it is suggested we follow through with a behavioral/developmental psychological evaluation and structure his home, behavioral, and educational environments using consistent cues, prompts, and reinforcers. Additionally, contact will be made with the Bureau of Vision Services to see if any services may be appropriate at this age and as he goes through each developmental stage.

The life care plan outlines all of Stuart's needs secondary to the sequela from his premature birth, which include psychological and educational supports as well as specific aids for independent function and medical follow-up.

After you have had an opportunity to review this narrative report and the attached appendix, please do not hesitate to contact me should you have further questions.

Respectfully submitted,

QRS, Ph.D., C.R.C., C.C.M.
Licensed Mental Health Counselor
TUV & ASSOCIATES, P.A.

SUMMARY OF CASE EXAMPLE LIFE CARE PLAN
INFORMATION

Stuart Rice's life care plan tables were presented in separate sections for each of the following topical areas: Projected Evaluations, Projected Therapeutic Modalities, Education, Orthotics/Prosthetics, Aids for Independent Function, Medications, Home Care/Facility Care, Future Medical Care (Routine), Transportation, and Potential Complications (for information only; no prediction of frequency or occurrence was given). For all but the Potential Complications page, the tables included six columns with the following headings: Item/Service, Age/Year, Frequency/Replacement, Purpose, Cost, and Comments. For each item or service listed in the life care plan tables, a starting date and ending date for that particular need was given, as well as the frequency of the service (how many times per week or year) or frequency of replacement for the item. The purpose of each specific item or service, as well as the cost per unit for each, was provided. Economists and financial planners tend to be most interested in the columns detailing Age/Year (starting and ending dates), Frequency/Replacement, and Costs for each Item/Service. People seeking to understand the individual's disability-related needs, including those individuals responsible for implementing the life care plan, will also find the Purpose and Comments columns to be very helpful.

Stuart's Projected Evaluations page included items such as a Rehabilitation/Long-Term Needs Assessment (to be conducted twice; once was already accomplished prior to the writing of the report, and the other was recommended at age 13); Psychological Evaluation (once every three years until age 18, to help structure behavioral programming and develop protocols); Vocational Evaluation (one exploratory evaluation to be conducted at age 16, and a full evaluation at age 18); Neuropsychological Evaluation (once every three or four years until age 18, to determine best learning methods); Nutritional Evaluation (annually until age 18, then once every two or three years through life expectancy); Functional Vision Evaluation (once every one or two years until age 18, then once every three or four years through life expectancy); Speech/Language Evaluation (annually through age 18); Occupational Therapy Evaluation (annually through age 18); and Physical Therapy Evaluation (annually through age 18).

Stuart's Projected Therapeutic Modalities page included items such as the following: Psychological Counseling, Family Counseling/

Education, Career Guidance and Counseling, Physical Therapy, Occupational Therapy, and Speech Therapy. Note that these therapy areas related clearly to Stuart's needs as described in the narrative, and were tied specifically to the projected evaluations. For each therapy area, details were provided regarding starting and ending dates, frequency, purpose of the therapy, and comments to further explain issues such as how these therapies supplement, rather than overlap, those considered educationally necessary and provided by Stuart"s school system. For some of these areas, it is difficult to predict exactly when a service will be needed, so estimates and appropriate explanations were provided. For example, estimates of the need for future psychological counseling were given based upon anticipated ages for specific developmental milestones. The course of psychological counseling was estimated to require sessions once per week for six months at each of the following ages: 8, 11, 14, 17, and 20. After age 21, a yearly allowance was estimated for supportive intervention, based on four to six times per year, through life expectancy.

The Education page of Stuart's life care plan included Special Education Services (throughout primary and secondary school, listed at no cost because such services are covered under the Individuals with Disability Education Act), Tutoring (two hours per week, 48 weeks per year, continuing through the developmental years), and Vocational School or Two-Year College (starting at age 18 and allowing three years to complete a two-year program).

The Orthotics/Prosthetics page of Stuart's life care plan was brief, including only orthodontic services for correction of a narrow palate.

Stuart's recommended Aids for Independent Function page included a Computer (for visual training, school work, and vocational endeavors; to be replaced once every three or four years, through life expectancy); Service and Upgrades for that computer (annually); Enlarged Print Software (to be upgraded every two or three years); Symbol/Letter Tracking Software (to be changed four times a year, through age 18); Tape Player for Books on Tape (at no cost, funded through the Library of Congress); Miscellaneous Aids for People who are Visually Impaired (including items such as a slant board, large display alarm clock, big button telephone, jumbo playing cards, low vision watch, large print calendar, etc.); Glasses (annually, through life expectancy); and an Alladin Rainbow Personal Reader (replaced once every three or four years, through life expectancy). (*Note:* The Alladin

Reader listed was a one-piece color personal reader that magnified while producing high-contrast images in either black and white or full color. That equipment had an unusually large depth of field, permitting easy reading of three-dimensional objects such as prescription bottles.)

On the Medications page of Stuart's life care plan, there is a note that no prescription medications were utilized at the time of the life care planning evaluation. However, the possibility of using attention-enhancing medications in the future was noted.

The Home Care/Facility Care page, often the most expensive part of a life care plan, was quite brief in Stuart's case. Assuming the success of the interventions detailed elsewhere in the life care plan, the planner predicted that Stuart would be able to live independently, with case management services available for resource intervention. The plan included allowances for two to four hours per month of case management services for the first six months of implementing the life care plan, followed by a reduction to one or two hours per month through age 22 to enable Stuart to transition to independent community living. Thereafter, case management services were planned for four to six hours per year.

Future Medical Care detailed in Stuart's life care plan included routine Neurology (annual), Opthalmology (twice per year to age nine, then annual); and Physical Medicine and Rehabilitation (annual) assessments. A one-time orthodontic evaluation was recommended. Annual Cardiology Evaluation (to assess for heart problems) and Orthopedic Evaluation (to assess for hip rotation) were recommended through life expectancy.

The Transportation page of Stuart's life care plan included an extensive explanation of how the transportation allowance (starting at age 16 and continuing through life expectancy) was calculated. The allowance was set to begin at the time a person typically begins to drive. It is difficult to quantify how much time would be spent in actual driving, but the following provides an example of how an estimate of costs for a driver could be estimated. Using the average of 1,000 miles driven in a month, at 35-45 miles per hour (40 MPH average), this is equal to 25 hours per month of typical driving time. If one privately hires a person to drive, at a rate of $6 to $8 per hour, this would cost approximately $150 to $200 per month, or $1,800 to $2,400 per year. Naturally, a life care planner would need to find out what the actual prevailing hourly rate for drivers in the client's area is before putting together such an estimate. *Note:* Although public transportation may be another option for some clients, it is often unreliable and quite restrictive in terms of availability in many areas of the country. Another possibility would be to consider taxi services; the estimated cost of such services was presented as an option in Stuart's life care plan.

The Potential Complications page of Stuart's life care plan included an explanation that this listing was for informational purposes only; no prediction of the frequency or occurrence of these possibilities was available. Potential complications included Falls/Fractures (secondary to balance/gait problems and visual impairments); Impaired Cognitive Functioning (which could interfere with decision-making capabilities); Respiratory Complications and other frequent illnesses (due to an impaired immune system); and Surgical Intervention (for visual needs or orthopedic surgery). *Note:* If a specific "complication" is expected "more likely than not" to occur, despite proactive preventative efforts, attention would be paid to it within the other pages of the life care plan. For example, if an opthalmologist projected that eye surgery would "probably" be required by the age of 35, that surgery would not show up in the Potential Complications section of the life care plan. Instead, it would be included in a Projected Future Aggressive Medical Care section. Complications, by definition, cannot be accurately predicted.

FUTURE APPLICATIONS OF LIFE CARE PLANNING

A well-developed life care plan could be considered the ultimate facility discharge plan. Some hospitals and rehabilitation facilities providing comprehensive services have found themselves facing complaints from frustrated and disillusioned patients and their families several months after discharge. A carefully developed, understandable life care plan, implemented by a qualified local case manager, could greatly facilitate successful transition from the facility to the home community or alternative living arrangements.

Life care plans can be used by rehabilitation counselors to continue educating their clients and clients' families about what to anticipate in terms of needs associated with disability, as well as to emphasize the importance of measures to prevent predictable complications. The plans can also be used to educate others, such as insurance adjusters and supervisors, about disability-related needs and the cost-effectiveness of preventative measures.

Increasingly, insurance carriers are being called upon to make more effective assessments of the impact of disability and the needs associated with that disability over time to more effectively accomplish financial reserve setting. LCP methodology can be a powerful tool to allow for accurate reserve setting. A well-implemented life care plan also can save the insurance carrier considerable funds through preventing complications and curtailing unnecessary service duplication.

LCP can be an important tool for the development of structured settlements and special needs trusts. Structured settlements have become an increasingly integral part of the litigation and settlement process in catastrophic injury cases. The settlement should be structured in a manner that facilitates implementation of the life care plan, so that funding for services needed at given points in time is available when specified. Requirements for establishing special needs trusts vary from state to state, but they can be a valuable resource for the establishment of funding to pay for disability associated costs while preserving financial eligibility for means-tested services.

Weed (1999) identified additional potential applications of LCP in areas such as mediation, facility based life care planning, divorces, and assisting families with financial and estate planning. He cited an example of how LCP services were obtained by a "soon-to-be" ex-wife who claimed that her husband was attempting to place their child in a facility because it was less expensive than home placement, and because it would therefore reduce his financial burden for child support.

CURRENT DEVELOPMENTS IN
LIFE CARE PLANNING PRACTICE

Recent judicial decisions have influenced the way some life care planners view their professional practice and ability to testify in court. Previously, some life care planners were content to assume that the systematic processes they followed sufficiently addressed the disability related needs of an individual. However, rulings such as *Daubert* (*Daubert v. Merrell Dow*, 1993) and *Kumho* (*Kumho Tire v. Patrick Carmichael*, 1999) have held that for life care planners to testify as expert witnesses, they must demonstrate the scientific reliability and relevance of their processes. Judges have the prerogative to determine whether the scientific basis for each life care planner's testimony is sufficient to qualify that expert to testify. To address legal challenges to the scientific basis of their testimony, life care planners are increasingly attending to follow-up evaluations of their own services, as well as to participation in research to document and assess the reliability of LCP methodology in general. Further information about the *Daubert* and *Kumho* rulings and their impact on life care planning testimony can be found in Field, Garner, and Jayne (2000).

SUMMARY

Life care planning is an important tool for rehabilitation counselors. It is a standardized and comprehensive methodology for analyzing and presenting the framework of services and supports that an individual with a catastrophic disability is likely to require over the course of his or her life. Life care plans are utilized to organize and communicate the multidimensional information that must be considered for effective service provision to maximize quality of life while minimizing complications and service costs. A consistent, empirically based methodology should be used to develop appropriate recommendations based upon the actual needs of the individual. Life care plans should not be used simply as litigation tools; they should serve as "roadmaps" and educational tools for the individual with a disability, his or her family, and service providers. A well-developed and clearly understandable life care plan can become a compelling empowerment tool for people with catastrophic disabilities; increased use of this tool is a positive sign for the profession of rehabilitation counseling.

REFERENCES

Blackwell, T. L., Powers, A. S., & Weed, R. O. (1994). *Life care planning for traumatic brain injury: A resource manual for case managers.* Athens, GA: Elliott & Fitzpatrick.

Blackwell, T. L., Weed, R. O., & Powers, A. S. (1994). *Life care planning for spinal cord injury: A resource manual for case managers.* Athens, GA: Elliott & Fitzpatrick.

Commission on Disability Examiner Certification (CDEC). (1996). *Standards and examination guidelines.* Midlothian, VA: Author.

Daubert v. Merrell Dow, 509 U.S. 579 (1993).

Deutsch, P. M. (1990). *A guide to rehabilitation testimony: The expert"s role as an educator.* Orlando, FL: Paul M. Deutsch Press.

Deutsch, P. M. (1995). Life care planning. In A. E. Dell Orto & R. P. Marinelli (Eds.), *Encyclopedia of disability and rehabilitation,* pp. 436-442. New York: Simon & Schuster Macmillan.

Deutsch, P. M., & Kitchen, J. A. (1994). Life care planning. *Seminars in Hearing, 15*(5), 207 223.

Deutsch, P. M., & Raffa, F. (1982). *Damages in tort actions* (vol. 8-9). New York: Matthew Bender.

Deutsch, P. M., & Sawyer, H. (2000). *A guide to rehabilitation.* White Plains, NY: Ahab Press.

Deutsch, P. M., Weed, R. O., Kitchen, J. A., & Sluis, A. (1989). *Life care planning for the head injured: A step by step guide.* Orlando, FL: Paul M. Deutsch Press.

Field, T., Garner, F., & Jayne, K. (2000). *A resource for rehabilitation consultants on the* Daubert *and* Kumho *rulings.* Athens, GA: Elliott & Fitzpatrick.

Kitchen, J. A., Cody, L. S., & Deutsch, P. M. (1989). *Life care plans for the brain damaged baby: A step by step guide.* Orlando, FL: Paul M. Deutsch Press.

Kitchen, J. A., Cody, L. S., & Morgan, N. G. (1990). *Life care plans for the ventilator dependent patient: A step by step guide.* Orlando, FL: Paul M. Deutsch Press.

Kumho Tire v. Patrick Carmichael. No. 97-1709 (U.S. March 23, 1999).

McCoy, D. (1996). The purpose of a life care plan. *Inside Life Care Planning, 1*(3), 1, 9.

Rehabilitation Training Institute (RTI). (1997). Rehabilitation Training Institute mission. [Online]. Available: http://www.intelicus.ufl.edu/rti.htm

Reid, C., Deutsch, P., Kitchen, J., & Aznavoorian, K. (1999). Life Care Planning. In F. Chan & M. Leahy (Eds.), *Healthcare and disability case management* (pp. 415-453). Lake Zurich, IL: Vocational Consultants Press.

Taylor, J. S. (1996). Neurolaw life: Life care plans in court. *Inside Life Care Planning, 1*(3), 7.

Thomas, R. (1997). LCPStat life care planning software. [Computer program, version 2.0]. Ridgeland, MS: TecSolutions.

Thomas, R., & Kitchen, J. A. (1996). Private hire: The real costs. *Inside Life Care Planning, 1*(3), 1, 3-4.

Weed, R. O. (1995, February). Life care plans as a managed care tool. *Medical Interface,* 111-118.

Weed, R. (Ed). (1999). *Life care planning and case management handbook.* Boca Raton, FL: St. Lucie/CRC Press.

Weed, R. O., & Riddick, S. N. (1992). Life care plans as a case management tool. *The Case Manager, 3*(1), 26-35.

Weed, R. O., & Sluis, A. (1990). *Life care plans for the amputee: A step by step guide.* Orlando, FL: Paul M. Deutsch Press.

Chapter 4

VOCATIONAL ASSESSMENT IN THE AMERICANS WITH DISABILITIES ACT ERA

Lᴀ C. Kᴏᴄʜ ᴀɴᴅ Pʜɪʟʟɪᴘ D. Rᴜᴍʀɪʟʟ

INTRODUCTION

In recent articles, Gilbride and Stensrud (1999) and Mullins, Rumrill, and Roessler (1996) presented the role and functions of rehabilitation professionals as consultants to employers in the Americans with Disabilities Act (ADA) era. They suggested that, for the spirit of the ADA's employment (Title I) provisions to be fully actualized, the rehabilitation profession must broaden its conception of clientele to include employers and community service agencies. In fact, rehabilitation professionals are in great demand to assist the employer and business communities with all aspects of ADA implementation. In a 1993 survey of employers, McMahon, Dancer, and Jaet reported that retaining rehabilitation consultants to implement disability management programs and other ADA-compliance procedures was among respondents' top three management concerns. Gilbride and Stensrud's (1999) model of demand side job development provides a framework for rehabilitation professionals to create employment opportunities for people with disabilities through direct services and technical assistance to employers.

There are undoubtedly "systems change" benefits associated with providing direct services to employers. With effective ADA consultation strategies such as those outlined by Mullins et al. (1996) and Gilbride and Stensrud (1999), rehabilitation professionals can ensure that clients are entering (or re-entering) workplaces that are physically

89

and socially accessible—ones where the letter and spirit of the ADA are both upheld. As this emerging and encouraging trend continues, rehabilitation professionals must 1) keep in mind that the ultimate beneficiaries of the ADA are people with disabilities themselves and 2) view employer consultation as one of several means by which to promote access and opportunity for rehabilitation clients.

The rehabilitation literature is replete with studies of employer responses to the ADA (Bell, 1993; Diksa & Rogers, 1996; Gilbride & Stensrud, 1993; Hergenrader, 1997; McMahon et al., 1993; Scott, 1997; Storey & Certo, 1996; Sumner, 1995), but scant attention has been paid to the need for including ADA information and self-advocacy training in direct services that are provided to people with disabilities (Palmer, 1998; Rumrill, 1994). Given current and future employment trends (e.g., automation, corporate downsizing, the tendency of workers to change career fields, rise in part-time and home-based employment opportunities), it is more important than ever before that rehabilitation clients secure the self-advocacy skills necessary to stay competitive in a constantly changing and unpredictable labor force. Whereas it was once commonly accepted job placement practice for the Vocational Rehabilitation (VR) counselor to find a job for the client and then close his or her case, contemporary concepts of self-determination (Wehman, 1996) and empowerment (Bolton & Brookings, 1996) dictate that counselors work in collaboration with clients to prepare them for long term career development after VR services have been discontinued. In the latter endeavor, primary emphasis is placed on the client's understanding of his or her skills and interests—and how the counselor can provide services that are compatible with the client's stated goals.

The concepts of self-determination and empowerment are especially important themes for future VR practice when viewed in light of current disability legislation. The vast majority of discrimination complaints filed by people with disabilities under the ADA are dismissed as groundless at the first level of administrative review (McMahon & Domer, 1997; Schall, 1998). Even those ADA plaintiffs who make it to trial find an overwhelming majority of jury verdicts coming down in favor of the employer. Indeed, contemporary sentiment among even the most vehement disability advocates is that people with disabilities should enter into litigation only as a last resort—after all nonadversarial conflict resolution strategies have been exhausted. Hence, the purpose of this chapter is to illustrate a model of assessment and planning services that employs the ADA and other relevant legislation as a tool, not a weapon, for consumer empowerment and control of one's career development. The primary theses are that 1) VR services must be compatible with the provisions of federal laws such as the ADA and the Family and Medical Leave Act (FMLA), and 2) information on how to implement those laws at the individual level constitutes an essential VR service.

The chapter begins with an overview of the key employment provisions of the ADA and the FMLA. This section is followed by detailed discussions regarding how the ADA can be used as an assessment and planning tool. Throughout the chapter, the authors emphasize specific instruments and intervention strategies that are compatible with the growing consumer empowerment and self-advocacy orientation of the rehabilitation process.

LEGISLATIVE BASES FOR A SELF-ADVOCACY ORIENTATION IN CLIENT ASSESSMENT AND CASE PLANNING

The ADA of 1990 was designed to eliminate discrimination on the basis of disability in the areas of employment, public services, public accommodations, and telecommunications. In fact, the ADA is the most comprehensive civil rights legislation passed since the Civil Rights Act of 1964. Title I of the ADA requires *covered employers* to provide *reasonable accommodations* that enable *qualified* people with *disabilities* to perform the *essential functions* of the job, unless the accommodation would constitute an *undue hardship* to the employer. In this section, the authors provide definitions of key terms and procedures under Title I of the ADA.

Covered Employers

All public and private employers with 15 or more employees must comply with the provisions set forth in Title I. The federal government, Native American tribes, and tax-exempt private membership clubs are not covered.

Reasonable Accommodations

Reasonable accommodations are modifications to the job or to the work environment that enable *qualified* people with *disabilities* to perform the *essential functions* of their positions. Examples of reasonable accommodations include:

- restructuring of existing facilities
- restructuring of the job
- modification of work schedules
- reassignment to a vacant position
- modification of equipment
- installation of new equipment
- provision of qualified readers and interpreters
- modification of application and examination procedures or training materials
- flexible personal leave policies
- use of supported employment programs.

Reasonable accommodations do not include:

- eliminating an essential job function
- lowering production standards that are applied to all employees (although an employer may have to provide reasonable accommodations to enable an employee with a disability to meet production standards)
- providing personal use items such as prosthetic limbs, wheelchairs, eyeglasses, hearing aids, or similar devices
- excusing a violation of uniformly applied conduct rules that are job-related and consistent with business necessity (e.g., violence, threats of violence, stealing, destruction of property)

Disability

The ADA defines an individual with a disability as a person who 1) has a physical or mental impairment which substantially limits functioning in one or more major life activities, 2) has a record of such impairment, or 3) is regarded as having such an impairment. Major life activities include (but are not limited to) walking, seeing, hearing, speaking, learning, working, and self-care. Individuals who are not protected by the ADA include

1. people with disabilities who pose a direct threat to the health or safety of themselves or others in the workplace;
2. active abusers of illegal substances;
3. employees who use alcohol during work;
4. people who are homosexual, transvestites, bisexual, or transsexual;
5. voyeurs or people who have other sexual disorders;
6. people who have the disorders of kleptomania, compulsive gambling, or pyromania; and
7. people whose medical conditions can be mitigated by assistive technology, medication, or surgery.

Qualified

Under Title I of the ADA, a qualified person with a disability is one who satisfies the primary requirements of the position and who can perform the fundamental duties (essential functions) of the job with or without reasonable accommodations. The employer is not required to give preference to applicants with disabilities or to hire or retain an employee with a disability who does not have the required training, skills, and experience.

Essential Functions

Essential job functions are those primary duties that the person with a disability must be capable of performing, with reasonable accommodations if required. A function is considered essential when: 1) the position exists to perform the function; 2) there are a limited number of other employees available to perform the function, or among whom the function can be distributed; and/or 3) the function is highly specialized, and the person in the position is hired for his or her special expertise and ability to perform the function. Essential functions do not include tasks that are marginal or unnecessary to performing the primary duties of the job (e.g., requiring a driver's license when driving is not required to carry out work-related tasks).

Undue Hardship

An employer is not required to make an accommodation if it would impose an undue hardship on the operation of the business. Undue hardship refers to any accommodation that exceeds the bounds of practicality (e.g., it costs more than alternatives that are equally effective; requires extensive and disruptive renovations; or negatively affects other employees, customers, or the operation of the business). Undue hardships are determined on a case-by-case basis using criteria such as the cost and nature of the accommodation, the overall financial resources of the facility, and the type of operation of the employer.

Other Employment Protections in Title I of the ADA

Although reasonable accommodations are an important part of the ADA, the employment protections available to people with disabilities go far beyond on-the-job accommodations. Under Title I, people with disabilities have the civil right to enjoy the same benefits and privileges of employment as their nondisabled coworkers. This means that personnel decisions (e.g., hiring, promotion, layoff, termination) must be made without respect to the person's disability status. Workers may not be harassed on the basis of their disabilities, and the compensation they receive must be commensurate with their qualifications and productivity irrespective of disability.

Enforcement of the ADA

Title I of the ADA is enforced by the Equal Employment Opportunity Commission (EEOC). Job applicants and employees are required to file claims with the EEOC within 300 days of the alleged violation. If it is determined by the EEOC that discrimination has likely occurred, one of two courses of action is taken—the EEOC may either prosecute or issue the plaintiff a "right to sue" letter. The "right to sue" letter allows the plaintiff to retain an attorney and proceed in federal civil court with a jury trial (McMahon & Domer, 1997). If the employer is found to have discriminated against the applicant or employee, remedies are then prescribed. Examples of such remedies include hiring, reinstatement, court orders to stop discriminatory practices, and punitive and compensatory damages.

Schall (1998) analyzed Title I complaint data collected by the EEOC between July, 1992 and September, 1996. During this period, the most frequently alleged Title I violations were unlawful discharge (51.9% of all complaints), failure to provide reasonable accommodations (28.1%), harassment (12.0%), hiring (9.8%), discipline (7.8%), layoff (4.7%), promotion (3.9%), benefits (3.9%), wages (3.4%), rehire (3.4%), and suspension (2.2%). The EEOC received a total of 72,687 complaints during Schall's retrospective observation period, of which 59,014 were resolved. At the time of Schall's study, the remaining 13,673 complaints had not yet been acted upon by the EEOC. Of the complaints that were resolved, the EEOC closed 39.4 percent for administrative reasons (e.g., EEOC had no statutory jurisdiction; complainant was not located, failed to respond to EEOC communication, refused to accept full relief, or independently resolved the issue with the employer). A near majority (46.9%) of Title I complaints filed with the EEOC were determined to have no reasonable cause. Only 14.2 percent of complaints between 1992 and 1996 were determined to have legal merit. The latter finding underscores the importance of providing accurate information to rehabilitation clients concerning Title I of the ADA. As part of the case planning process, clients need to know what their rights are, but they also need to know the limitations of the ADA's protections. ADA Title I cases that are adjudicated in civil court turn out predominantly (as many as 85%) in the employer's favor (McMahon & Domer, 1997); therefore, before leveling a charge of discrimination, clients must have access to current information about ADA enforcement and remediation procedures.

THE FAMILY AND MEDICAL LEAVE ACT

Another important law with which rehabilitation clients must become familiar in the current era of self-advocacy and consumer empowerment is the Family and Medical Leave Act (FMLA) of 1993. The FMLA has enabled thousands of American employees to retain their jobs while taking unpaid leaves of absence to attend to important family health concerns. The law requires employers in the public and private sectors to hold workers' jobs open and continue paying health insurance premiums while employees take time off to treat and/or recover from illnesses or injuries. It also provides leave for employees who must attend to the health care needs of their family members. A covered employer under the FMLA is one who has 50 or more employees residing within a 75-mile radius of the work location. Employees are eligible for protection if they have at least one year of seniority on the job (defined as at least 1,250 hours worked within the 12 months preceding the requested leave date) and have a serious health condition.

The FMLA defines a *serious health condition* as any illness, injury, impairment, or regimen of treatment that renders one unable to perform any essential function of his or her job. The term *serious health condition* is broader and more inclusive than the ADA's definition of *disability*. This means that a worker could be a person with a serious health condition under the FMLA but not meet the ADA's standard as a person with a disability. Unlike the term *disability*, *serious health condition* pertains to both temporary and permanent conditions. Examples of commonly invoked serious health conditions under the FMLA include pregnancy, birth or adoption of a child, surgery, chemotherapy, and chronic illnesses.

The FMLA requires employers to provide up to 12 weeks of unpaid leave per calendar year for an eligible employee coping with a serious health condition. The 12 weeks need not be taken consecutively, and the employer must allow the worker to return to the same or a similar, equivalent position. Return to work following unpaid leave may be denied only to "key" employees–those earning the highest 10 percent of salaries. This exception applies only when holding open those employees' jobs would create substantial and grievous long-term economic injury to the employer's operations. The employer's burden of proof for this exception is more stringent than for the ADA's defense of undue hardship.

Eligible employees may take time off to attend to their own serious health conditions or to assist in the care and treatment of family members who have serious health conditions. Family members are defined as spouses, children, or parents. For example, a person whose wife has cancer and needs transportation to weekly appointments with her oncologist could request unpaid time off to accompany her to doctor's visits.

In the event that the need for leave is foreseeable (e.g., pregnancy, elective surgery), the employee must give 30 days advance notice. If the need for leave is unforeseeable (e.g., an exacerbation of a chronic illness, accident), employees are required to give "reasonable" notice (undefined in FMLA regulations). Once the employee has filed a request for leave, the employer has two business days to determine the employee's eligibility for the requested time off. Failure to respond within two business days automatically renders the employee eligible for the leave that he or she has requested. Of course, an employer may request that the employee verify his or her serious health condition or the condition of a family member. If requested, the employee must provide verification from a health care provider, with the following conditions:

1. The provider should verify only the need for a medical leave and not disclose the underlying medical condition.
2. The information reported should be job-related (e.g., need for, length of, and timing of the medical leave).
3. Inquiry into the possible future effects of the serious health condition should be avoided.
4. Leave requests should be processed by a designated knowledgeable person so that discussion with the employee's supervisors and coworkers is limited.
5. Supervisors should be notified of facts related to the circumstances of the leave, not about specific aspects of the employee's (or a relative's) serious health condition.
6. Records related to medical leave must be maintained in a separate file from the employee's personnel records.

Although the FMLA pertains only to people with serious health conditions who are employed, rehabilitation professionals will be well served to incorporate FMLA provisions into the assessment and case planning phases of the rehabilitation process. Assessing the client's potential need for future medical leave (especially for those coping with chronic or progressive disabling conditions) can yield useful information in determining appropriate courses of training and/or job placement. Additionally, clients who can incorporate foreseeable medical leave into an overall accommodation planning strategy will be more knowledgeable and effective self-advocates once they enter the world of work.

THE ADA, FMLA, AND CLIENT ASSESSMENT

Regardless of the sector or service delivery setting, the rehabilitation process always begins with a comprehensive appraisal of the client's medical, psychosocial, and vocational status. Rehabilitation professionals apply both standardized and situational measurement techniques to gauge the background and present functioning of the "whole person," all in an effort to determine attainable vocational goals (Rubin & Roessler, 1995). This process is referred to as ecological assessment, which Parker, Szymanski, and Hanley-Maxwell (1989) operationalized as the assessment of the individual, the environment, and the congruence between the individual and the environment.

Because the ADA and FMLA provide important mechanisms for people with disabilities to advocate for and empower themselves, these statutes have a crucial role to play in the ecological assessment process which drives all subsequent rehabilitation services. In this regard, applicable assessment issues include ADA awareness, identification of worksite barriers and the client's accommodation needs, career exploration activities, technology transfer, and the counselor's appraisal of the client's employability.

ADA Awareness

If clients are to successfully advocate for themselves in the workplace, they must be well-versed regarding both their rights and responsibilities as set forth in the ADA. Therefore, rehabilitation professionals are advised to conduct an initial assessment of the client's awareness of the provisions, eligibility standards, grievance policies, and remedies that are promulgated in ADA regulations (Equal Employment Opportunity Commission & Department of Justice, 1991; McMahon & Domer, 1997). An experimental study conducted by Rumrill and Garnette (1997) provides an example of an objective (multiple choice), ten-item quiz that can be used to test clients' knowledge of the ADA's employment provisions. The results of a short ADA quiz could inform the rehabilitation professional about the extent and type of training the client will need to advocate for his or her rights in employment. Then, appropriate consultation and referral services can be identified and provided as part of the service delivery phase of the VR process.

Identification of Worksite Barriers and Accommodation Needs

In addition to assessing the client's awareness of his or her rights under the ADA (and providing the client with information concerning the FMLA), it is important to identify barriers to performing essential job functions and potential job accommodations that will remove or reduce those barriers. This can be accomplished using a variety of ecological assessment tools that empower the client to assume personal control of his or her own career development. Examples of such tools are the job analysis, the Work Experience Survey (WES; Roessler, 1995), and barrier/solution worksheets.

Conducting an in-depth job analysis is, perhaps, the most effective strategy for identifying an employee's essential job functions, worksite barriers, and accommodation needs. The job analysis requires the rehabilitation professional to gather, evaluate, and record accurate information about both the work performed (e.g., essential functions, work materials, items produced, subject matter, services provided, work schedule) in a specific occupation and the worker characteristics (e.g., qualifications, general educational development, aptitudes, temperaments, environmental conditions, physical demands) required of the employee (Blackwell & Weed, 1992). This information is gathered at the worksite using a variety of methods such as questionnaires, work diaries or logs, worker task inventories or checklists, interviews, observations, and observation interviews (Patterson, 1996).

Conducting an in-depth job analysis requires the rehabilitation professional to complete several general steps that culminate in a written report (Patterson, 1996). The first step is to research the industry and occupation to learn about the equipment, materials, and terminology used at the employment site where the analysis will be conducted. This will prepare the rehabilitation professional to communicate appropriately about the specific job with the employer and others involved in the job analysis. Resources such as the Internet, the *Dictionary of Occupational Titles* (United States Department of Labor, 1991), the *Occupational Outlook Handbook* (United States Department of Labor, 1998), and the *Classification of Jobs* (Field & Field, 1992) are often consulted during the introductory phase of the job analysis.

The second step in job analysis is to select a job site at which to conduct the assessment. Patterson (1996) identified several considerations in choosing the site: size of the business, location, purpose of the job analysis, product or service provided, number of representative jobs at the site, and company policies regarding job analyses.

After a job site has been identified, the third step is to contact the establishment. Patterson (1996) noted that it is often more efficient to send a letter or call the top administrator than it is to arrange the analysis through the personnel office.

The fourth step involves meeting with the company representative to "explain the purpose and scope of the proposed job analysis, obtain permission, and gather preliminary information, such as job descriptions (if available), union contracts, and other information on the company that was not part of the [rehabilitation professional's] initial research" (Patterson, 1996, p. 235). At this meeting, the rehabilitation professional needs to 1) find out the time limits for conducting the analysis, the safety rules to be observed, and the appropriate attire that is necessary; and 2) ensure the company representative that he or she will be given a copy of the job analysis to review for accuracy and that confidentiality will be maintained as requested.

After the preliminary meeting with the company representative, the rehabilitation professional should make arrangements to tour the job site to obtain an understanding of how the position being analyzed fits into the "big picture" (Patterson, 1996). The tour can be conducted immediately following the initial meeting or at a later date, depending on the employer's preference.

The sixth step is to conduct the job analysis. In addition to the rehabilitation professional, others (e.g., employee, supervisor, union representative, personnel representative) may be present while the analysis is being conducted. These individuals can answer specific questions about the position being analyzed. The job analysis report can be written in either a narrative or checklist format. Figure 4.I presents a sample job analysis report (Millington, 1997).

Figure 4-I
Sample Job Analysis Report

Company: Lohman's Custom Cabinets
Position: Furniture Assembler
DOT#: 763.684-038
Participants: Belinda Bradford (Analyst)
      Connie Smith-Lohman (Owner)
      Jimmy Webb (Production Manager)
      Brian Cooke (Furniture Assembler)

Company Description

Lohman's Custom Cabinets (LCC) is a third generation family business, established in 1940, to offer: (a) custom kitchen design, manufacture and installation; (b) a private product line of dining room ensembles; and (c) antique furniture finishing and repair. The original LCC location on Parkview Avenue has been turned into a showroom boutique, with antiques and the antique workshop available to patron viewing in the back. Production, warehouse, and shipping are located in the Reardon Industrial Park in Livingston. Connie is the owner of the company and manager of the Parkview Avenue storefront.

Retail and contract business has been steadily increasing for the last three years. There is a 4-week backlog on special orders for dining room ensembles, and a third kitchen installation crew was recently added to the payroll. Connie sees her three major personnel issues as: 1) improving coordination between sales, manufacturing, and installation of product; 2) increasing productivity on the shop floor; and 3) finding, training, and keeping "good" workers.

The furniture assembly position is at the Livingston location. The building houses three production lines dedicated to chair, table, and cabinet assembly in order of complexity. A production manager, 6 supervisors, 36 assemblers, 4 maintenance personnel, 12 material handlers, and a secretary are employed in the plant. Jimmy Webb, production manager, sees his three major personnel issues as: 1) keeping workers after they have been trained, 2) reducing waste, and 3) injury and accident prevention.

Job Description and Essential Functions

Set-up and preparation. Collect and organize all materials, tools and equipment required to fill the production order. Production orders include a job number (for supervisor tracking purposes), catalog numbers that identify which items will be assembled during the shift, a target number of each product to be assembled during the shift, and the names of the workers on the assembly team responsible for meeting the quota. Two workers retrieve "kits" from Central Supply using a forklift. The third worker cleans and sets up the assembly area according to the procedural specifications established for the particular product. Typically this includes: refill glue guns, replace drill bits and post assembly instructions, clean and inspect assembly table and safety equipment.

Once all supplies, materials, tools, and equipment are in place and at optimal function, the kit pieces are inspected for blemishes or defects. Identified defects are remediated if possible, or the piece is replaced.

Essential functions: Transport materials; stock supplies; clean work station; inspect equipment; maintain tools.

Assembly. Furniture is assembled according to established procedure. Some component pieces are pre-assembled at a work bench; larger assembly occurs on the assembly table (an articulated device to which the item is secured and can then be rotated, raised, and lowered pneumatically). Electric hot glue guns and pneumatic power drills are suspended on retractable line above the work stations, and battery-powered drills are stationed at the work benches.

Assemblers work in teams of three in coordinated and sequential activity. Multiple assemblies of the same item are done concurrently, allowing time for the glue to set between stages. All eight stations on the assembly line are used whenever possible. When the furniture is complete, the surface is treated with a finishing oil, applied by hand via a soft cloth, and the item is moved off-station for wrapping and palletizing by the material handlers.

Essential functions: Communicate with coworkers; follow instructions; apply glue to furniture pieces; drill appropriate lead holes for screws; secure furniture pieces with screws; remove unwanted excess metal and wood from pieces; remove furniture from bench and move to material handling stations.

Salary and Benefits

Starting salary for a furniture assembler is $7.50/hr. After 90 days probationary period, the successful worker receives an automatic raise to S8.50/hr. Overtime is paid at time-and-a-half after eighty hours worked in any two week pay period. Employees are paid time-and-a-half for working on holidays. Employees who work overtime on holidays are paid double time. Overtime is mandatory. Average yearly income for assemblers after 5 years (with 250 hrs. overtime) is $33,000.

Employees receive 1 day off paid vacation every two months during the first two years of employment. Paid vacation hours are accrued at one day a month thereafter. The company subsidizes health insurance; dental insurance is extra. The company matches 50% on retirement; workers are vested after 7 years.

Work Hours and Schedule

Assemblers work one of two regular shifts: 7:30 am - 4:00 pm or 4:30 pm - 1:00 am Monday-Friday. Overtime hours are available on Saturdays and Sundays. Assemblers can also earn overtime pay by arriving early for the first shift or by staying late for the second shift.

Qualifications and Training

No particular qualifications are noted. Employees learn techniques on the job during the first week of formal training and develop proficiency and speed during the course of probation (90 days). Fomal on-the-job training is provided by a line supervisor and includes technique, policy orientation, and saftey rules. Informal training is provided by members ofthe work team. Summary evaluation is based on coworker evaluation and production rate statistics. Failure to rate satisfactorily at the conclusion of probation results in dismissal.

General Educational Development

Minimal math skills (addition, subtraction) are required for occasional measuring. An 8th grade reading level is required to carry out written instructions. Writing and spelling are not required.

Aptitudes Required

General	Average
Verbal	Below average
Numerical	Below average
Spatial	Average

Form Perception	Average
Clerical Perception	Below average
Motor Coordination	Average
Finger Dexterity	Below average
Manual Dexterity	Average
Eye-Hand-Foot Coordination	Negligible
Color Discrimination	Negligible

Temperament, Organizational Climate and Culture

The product is high quality, appealing to an upscale home and office market. Workers must be conscientious, observant, and attend to detail. The growth in demand has created a need for speed. Workers must be able to maintain high levels of production over the course of the shift, without a reduction in quality. Consequently, work on the factory floor has become stressful. Higher quotas and longer hours have resulted in more items being rejected, and negative emotions between the manager and supervisors, and between supervisors and workers. Morale is low. New workers are expected to catch on quickly and "carry their weight." Turnover is high among new employees, and recently there has been an increase in absenteeism among more established workers, and a disturbing increase in accidents, though none have resulted in injury yet. Workers in this climate need to be rather "thick-skinned," and be even-tempered when dealing with supervisors.

The job requires teamwork and fast-paced manual assembly. Work requirements are episodic, varied with each furniture order, but roughly equivalent across orders. Workers have developed jargon and physical cues to facilitate cooperative work elements (adjusting large pieces, checking for level, off-loading finished work) which must be learned before the new worker will be able to work in concert with others. Work teams form and remain fairly stable.Good work teams develop strong bonds between workers, and tend to be competitive with other good teams, e.g., production "races" when a shipping deadline is imminent. Workers who don't meet employee expectations for production and cooperation are called "sandbags" if they don't produce and worse if they don't fit in socially, and otherwise harrassed on the job until they rectify their behavior or quit.

Typical Physical Demands

This work is generally described as medium. The heaviest kit component weighs 60 pounds, and requires, by policy, two people to move (appx 30# each). While other pieces may weigh as much as 50 pounds, no one worker is allowed to lift more than 30 pounds by themselves. Carrying of weights up to 30 pounds for 50 yards or more may occur twice per day. Carts, come-alongs, and dollies are used occasionally to push or pull kits or finished products. Weights under 10 pounds are manipulated bi-manually constantly throughout the shift. Most tool use occurs between waist and eye level, though occasionally a worker on the team will be required to crouch or kneel when using a tool. Walking, standing, reaching, and feeling are typically used. No crawling, climbing, balancing, or sitting is required. Shifts are eight hours standard, but often expanded by overtime to 10 or 12 hours.

Environmental Conditions

The building is a corrugated metal structure with offices in the front, shipping in the back, parts and maintenance along the walls, and the production floor in the center of the building. The production floor is textured/no-slip concrete with brightly painted traffic and work areas. Assembly lines have rubber mats at worker stations, and stools available at work benches. The area is well lit with halogen light in the rafters and strategically placed full spectrum spot and flood lights on the assembly line. Air exchange rates surpass OSHA standards, no noxious fumes were noted. Saw dust collects around the work station from drilling and is collected twice daily by the maintenance crew. All work is performed inside, where the temperature (78°F) and humidity (65-70%) are controlled. Noise levels do not precipitate the use of ear plugs. Background noise includes the sound of drills, compressors, fans, and the occasional phone, which can be heard clearly by all assemblers at normal household volume. Normal conversation volume is sufficient for communicating with coworkers. Workers wear jumpsuits, caps, and safety glasses issued by the company. Work boots are preferred footwear.

Another resource for identifying barriers to job performance and potential accommodations is the Work Experience Survey (WES; Roessler, 1995). The WES is a structured interview that identifies career maintenance barriers in the areas of worksite accessibility, job accommodations and modifications, job mastery, and job satisfaction. The WES interview requires 30 to 60 minutes to complete and can be conducted in person or over the telephone. Using the WES, the rehabilitation counselor and client are able to prepare a job accommodation plan that prioritizes on-the-job barriers and lists possible solutions and resources for the removal of those barriers. The validity of the WES has been demonstrated in a number of empirical investigations, with applications ranging from self-advocacy training (Rumrill, 1999; Rumrill & Garnette, 1997) to correlational studies of the factors associated with job tenure among workers with disabilities (Roessler & Rumrill, 1995; 1998; Rumrill, Roessler, Battersby, & Schuyler, 1998). Researchers have also used the WES in case studies of the career development concerns of people with multiple sclerosis (Roessler & Gottcent, 1994), various chronic illnesses (Roessler, Reed, & Brown, 1998), insulin-dependent diabetes mellitus (Rumrill, Schoenfeld, Holman, & Mullins, 1997), visual impairments and blindness (Rumrill, Schuyler, & Battersby, 1997), and breast cancer (Rumrill, Nutter, Hennessey, & Ware, 1998). In each application, the WES has been demonstrated as a reliable and valid tool for assessing workers' situational needs for on-the-job accommodations (Roessler, Rumrill, &

Reed, 1995). Figure 4.II presents a copy of the WES, reprinted here with the permission of the Arkansas Research and Training Center in Vocational Rehabilitation (Roessler, 1995).

Figure 4-II
Work Experience Survey

WORK EXPERIENCE SURVEY (WES)

Section I: Please provide information on your background, disability, and work experience.

Background
1. Age_____   2. Sex_____   3. Race_____   4. Marital status_____

5. Number of years of education_____

6. Highest educational degree completed_____

Disability
7. Disability of record (primary diagnosis)

_____

8. How old were you when you acquired this disability?

_____

9. What caused your disability?

_____

10. Describe how the disability affects your functioning, e.g., decrease in muscle strength, chronic fatigue, limited visual field, poor balance, low stress tolerance. Rank order the entries in terms of their impact, e.g., the first effect listed represents the greatest problem.

   1. _____

   2. _____

   3. _____

   4. _____

   5. _____

Work Experience
11. Your current job title (the one used by your employer)

_____

12. List three essential job functions that you perform regularly, e.g., take telephone messages, operate forklift, feed/care for livestock.

_____

13. Name/address of company where you work.

_____

   Street address:

_____

   City _____ State _____ Zip Code _____

14. Total number of years employed _____

15. Number of months on current job _____

16. Number of hours working per week _____

17. Weekly gross salary _____

Section II. Accessibility: Check any problems you have getting to, from, or around on your job. List any other accessibility problem not included in the list. Describe solutions for your two most important accessibility barriers.

_____ Parking	_____ Bathrooms	_____ Temperature
_____ Public Walks	_____ Water fountains	_____ Ventilation
_____ Passenger loading zones	_____ Public telephone	_____ Hazards
_____ Entrance	_____ Elevators	_____ Identification signs/labels
_____ Stairs/Steps	_____ Lighting	_____ Access to personnel offices
_____ Floors/Floor covering	_____ Warning devices	_____ Access to general use areas
_____ Seating/Tables	_____ Evacuation routes	

List any other accessibility problems:

#1 _____

#2 _____

#3 _____

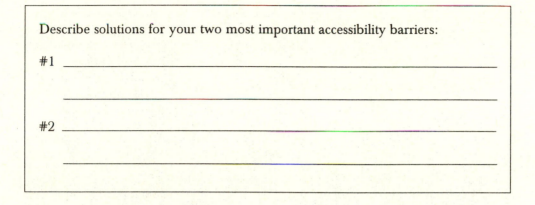

Describe solutions for your two most important accessibility barriers:

#1 _____

_____

#2 _____

_____

Section III. Essential job functions: Check any essential job functions or conditions* that pose problems for you. Describe the two most important job modifications that you need, e.g., modifying existing equipment, adding new technology, or changing the type of work you do.

Physical Abilities
____ Working 8 hours
____ Standing all day
____ Standing part of the time
____ Walking for 8 hours
____ Some kneeling
____ Some stooping
____ Some climbing
____ Much pulling
____ Much pushing
____ Much talking
____ Seeing well
____ Hearing well
____ Handling
____ Raising arms above
  shoulders
____ Using both hands
____ Using both legs
____ Using left hand
____ Using right hand
____ Using left leg
____ Using right leg
____ Lifting over 100 lbs.
____ Lifting 51-100 lbs.
____ Lifting 26-50 lbs.
____ Lifting 11-25 lbs.
____ Lifting 0-10 lbs.

Cognitive Abilities
____ Immediate memory
____ Short-term memory
____ Long-term memory
____ Judgment: safety
____ Judgment: interpersonal
____ Thought processing
____ Reasoning
____ Problem solving
____ Planning
____ Organizing

Task Related Abilities
____ Repetitive work
____ Work pace/sequencing
____ Variety of duties
____ Perform under stress
  deadlines
____ Little feedback on
  performance
____ Read written instructions
____ Able and licensed to drive
____ Attain precise standards/
  limits
____ Follow specific instructions
____ Writing
____ Remembering

Social Abilities
____ Working alone
____ Working around others
____ Working with others
____ Interacting with supervisor
____ Supervising others
____ Working with hostile others

Working Conditions
____ Too hot
____ Too cold
____ Temperature changes
____ Too wet
____ Too humid
____ Slippery surfaces
____ Obstacles in path
____ Dust
____ Fumes
____ Odors
____ Noise
____ Outdoors
____ Sometimes outdoors
____ Always inside

Company Policies
____ Inflexible work schedules
____ No accrual of sick leave

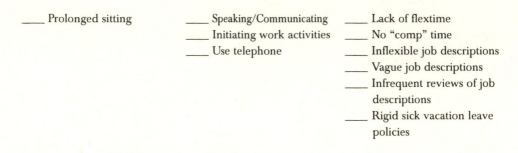

____ Prolonged sitting   ____ Speaking/Communicating   ____ Lack of flextime
                                 ____ Initiating work activities ____ No "comp" time
                                 ____ Use telephone   ____ Inflexible job descriptions
                                                                 ____ Vague job descriptions
                                                                 ____ Infrequent reviews of job
                                                                      descriptions
                                                                 ____ Rigid sick vacation leave
                                                                      policies

---

Describe the two job modifications that would be most helpful to you, e.g., restructuring of the job, modification of work schedules, reassignment to another position, modification of equipment, or provision of readers and interpreters.

#1 _____

#2 _____

_____

---

* Adapted from RehabMatch. Arkansas Research and Training Center

Section IV. Job Mystery: Check any concerns* that affect your success in completing the following tasks. Describe one solution for each of your two most important concern.

1. Getting the job done
   ____ Believing that others think I do a good job.
   ____ Understanding how my job fits into the "big picture," i.e., the meaning of my job.
   ____ Knowing what I need to know to do my job.
   ____ Having what I need to do my job (knowledge, tools, supplies, equipment).

2. Fitting into the workforce
   ____ Scheduling and planning my work ahead of time.
   ____ Working mostly because I like the job.
   ____ Doing a good job.
   ____ Willing to make changes when necessary.

3. Learning the ropes
   ____ Knowing who to go to if I need help.
   ____ Understanding company rules and regulations.
   ____ Knowing my way around work.
   ____ Feeling a "part" of what is going on at work.

4. Getting along with others
____ Eating lunch with friends at work.
____ Having many friends at work.
____ Looking forward to seeing my friends at work.
____ Knowing what is expected of me socially on the job.

5. Getting ahead
____ Having a plan for where I want to be in my job in the future.
____ Understanding what I have to do to get promoted.
____ Knowing what training to complete to improve chances for promotion.
____ Talking with supervisor about what I need to do to get promoted.

6. Planning the next career step
____ Considering what I will do in the future.
____ Knowing what the opportunities are in this company.
____ Wanting to become more specialized in my job.
____ Having a good idea of how to advance in this company.

Describe one solution for each of your two most important job mastery concerns:

#1 _____

#2 _____

---

* Selected items from the Career Mastery Inventory. Used with permission of the author, John O. Crites, Crites Career Consultants, Boulder, Colorado.

Section V. Satisfaction*: Rate your current job on each of the following statements. Describe two ways to make your job more personally satisfying.

In my job ... (check one)	Too Little	About Right	Too Much
I do things that make use of my abilities.	____	____	____
The job gives me a feeling of accomplishment.	____	____	____
I am busy all the time.	____	____	____
I can work alone on the job.	____	____	____
I do something different every day.	____	____	____
My pay compares well with that of other workers.	____	____	____
The job provides for steady employment.	____	____	____
The job has good working conditions.	____	____	____
The job provides an opportunity for advancement.	____	____	____
I get recognition for the work I do.	____	____	____
I tell people what to do.	____	____	____

I am "somebody" in the community.   ____   ____   ____

My co-workers are easy to make friends with.   ____   ____   ____

I can do the work without feeling it is morally wrong.   ____   ____   ____

I can do things for other people.   ____   ____   ____

The company administers its policies fairly.   ____   ____   ____

The boss back up the workers with top management.   ____   ____   ____

My boss trains the workers well.   ____   ____   ____

I try out some of my ideas.   ____   ____   ____

I make decisions on my own.   ____   ____   ____

Describe two ways to make your job more personally satisfying:

#1 _____

_____

#2 _____

_____

---

* Working reinforcers from the Minnesota Theory of Work Adjustment. Dawis, R. & Lofquist, L. (1984). *A psychological theory of work adjustment.* Minneapolis: University of Minnesota.

Section VI. Review Sections II - V of the WES and list the three most significant barriers to success in your work. Describe their solutions and people/resources who can help. Be specific.

Barrier 1:

_____

Solution? _____

_____

Who can help? How can they help? _____

_____

_____

Barrier 2: _____

_____

Solution? _____

_____

Who can help? How can they help?_____

_____

_____

Barrier 3: _____

_____

Solution? _____

_____

Who can help? How can they help?_____

_____

_____

_____

Barrier/solution worksheets serve the same purpose as the job analysis and the WES. These worksheets enable the rehabilitation professional and client to specify the employment goal, list barriers to goal attainment, and identify potential solutions. Ettinger, Conyers, Merz, and Koch (1995) designed an instrument that can be used to break down barriers into manageable components so that potential solutions for each component can be identified (see Figure 4.III). In the first section of the worksheet, the rehabilitation client writes a goal statement (e.g., accept employment with ABC Company as an executive secretary). In the second section, the client describes the overall barrier to goal achievement (e.g., office is not wheelchair accessible). The third section requires the client to break down the barrier into its specific components (e.g., desk is too low for wheelchair to fit under, cannot reach files in top drawer of file cabinet, office space is too narrow to maneuver wheelchair). In the final section, the client, prospective employer, and rehabilitation professional brainstorm and list potential solutions to each barrier (e.g., purchase a new desk, raise the desk on blocks, purchase a two-drawer file cabinet, have coworker retrieve files, switch offices with a coworker, rearrange furniture). They must then decide on the solutions that will be implemented to reduce or remove barriers to the client's goal achievement.

Figure 4.III
Barrier/Solutions Worksheet

Identifying Barriers and Solutions to Goal Achievement

Goal Statement:

_____

_____

Barrier to Goal Achievement:

_____

_____

SPECIFIC COMPONENTS OF THE BARRIER	POTENTIAL SOLUTIONS FOR EACH COMPONENT
1. _____	a. _____ b. _____ c. _____
2. _____	a. _____ b. _____ c. _____
3. _____	a. _____ b. _____ c. _____
4. _____	a. _____ b. _____ c. _____

Adapted from: Hecklinger, F.J. & Black, B.M. (1991). *Training for life: A practical guide to career and life planning* (4th ed.). Dubuque, IA: Kendall/Hunt Publishing Company.

Source: Szymanski, Fernandez, Koch, & Merz (1996).

Career Exploration Activities

Contemporary concepts such as empowerment (Bolton & Brookings, 1996) and self-determination (Wehman, 1996) are predicated on the person's awareness of his or her environment and the resources that are available in that environment to assist in the pursuit of important life goals. With regard to the life goal of career development, a key consideration for clients as they explore new and changing work environments is the availability of legal protections, especially on-the-job accommodations.

Szymanski, Hershenson, Enright, and Ettinger (1996) cautioned rehabilitation professionals not to eliminate career possibilities without considering how job accommodations may resolve perceived barriers. For example, when clients explore their options via interest inventories and other standardized assessments, it is important that they are knowledgeable about reasonable accommodations so that the perceived availability of options is expanded, rather than restricted. Therefore, assessing and then improving clients' abilities to identify appropriate job accommodations should be a preliminary step to career exploration so that they do not unnecessarily eliminate career possibilities. This will ensure that clients approach the assessment of their interests and aptitudes with a "can do" rather than a "can't do" attitude.

Technology Transfer

For those clients who will be engaged in postsecondary educational or vocational training programs, the concept of technology transfer poses important ecological assessment considerations as well. In identifying assistive technology and other accommodation strategies that could help the client in his or her career, the rehabilitation professional will be well served to consider what devices and methods the client uses in his or her everyday life to overcome potential disability-related barriers.

Roessler and Kirk (in press) developed a protocol for evaluating the technology transfer needs of rehabilitation clients. Applied in Roessler and Kirk's initial investigation with a sample of university students with disabilities, technology transfer refers to both assistive (i.e., disability related) and generalized (i.e., used by people without disabilities) devices and strategies that could aid respondents in the transition from their educational or training experiences to the world of work.

The first section of the technology transfer interview addresses demographic and disability issues, including information about whether respondents are employed, in training, or seeking employment. Respondents are also asked whether they have experienced barriers in securing accommodations, both in the classroom and in employment. In the second section of the survey, respondents describe the nature and quality of technology and accommodation services that they have received in their educational or training programs. Specifically, they describe their perceptions of their instructors' and counselors' help with technology needs, their evaluation of different types of accommodations used in training, and the satisfactoriness of information about their rights and responsibilities under the ADA. The interview concludes with questions about respondents' satisfaction and self-efficacy levels regarding specific tasks involved in identifying and implementing on-the job accommodations.

Counselor's Appraisal of the Client's Employability

The assessment strategies described to this point in the chapter focus on the client's perceptions, expectations, and attitudes that relate to contemporary legislation. These are important issues in our field's current era of self-determination and empowerment, but it is also important to keep in mind the powerful role that the counselor's expectations can play in the client's ultimate success. During the initial assessment process and throughout the planning and placement phases of the client's rehabilitation experience, it is helpful for counselors to gauge the client's progress in pursuit of a vocational goal.

Millington's (1998) Employment Expectations Questionnaire (EEQ) provides a psychometrically sound example of a tool for measuring the counselor's confidence in the client's employability. Developed to assess employment-relevant attitudes in the screening and hiring of job applicants, the EEQ contains 45 items that comprise five factor scales: Reliability, Production, Social Coping, Organizational Coping, and Safety (see Figure 4-IV). EEQ items reflect counselors' expectations concerning a client's competence in a particular job.

Each item in the EEQ presents semantically differentiated poles of a specific aspect of job performance (e.g., attendance/absence, trustworthy/untrustworthy, resolve conflict/generate conflict, solve problems/cannot identify problems), along with a seven-point response scale for rating the degree of the client's competence on each dimension. The response scale ranges from +3 (very high) to -3 (very low), with 0 representing minimal and adequate competence.

Millington and his associates have used versions of the EEQ in a number of studies (Millington, Szymanski, & Hanley-Maxwell, 1994; Millington, Reid, & Leierer, 1997; Millington, Szymanski, & Johnston-Rodriguez, 1995), and it has been indicated as a reliable and valid tool for assessing employment-relevant attitudes (i.e., expectations) toward various populations of people with disabilities.

In aggregate, EEQ items formulate a profile of the client's future employability. Areas of strength (perceived by the counselor) can be built upon in the planning and service delivery phases of the rehabilitation process. Perceived deficit areas may be remediated, either through skill training or via reasonable accommodations provided to the client once he or she obtains employment. In those regards, the EEQ profile provides an important "jumping off point" for subsequent counseling interventions. Figure 4-IV presents the items of the EEQ.

Figure 4-IV
The Employment Expectations Questionnaire

Rate applicant competence using the following scale. Zero (0) represents minimal competence required to get the job. Positive ratings suggest levels of competence beyond the minimum: (+3) very high, (+2) moderately high, (+1) somewhat high. Negative ratings suggest levels of competence below the minimum required: (-1) somewhat low, (-2) moderately low. (-3) very low.

Reliability

Attendance	+3	+2	+1	0	-1	-2	-3	Absence
Punctuality	+3	+2	+1	0	-1	-2	-3	Tardiness
Stay on task	+3	+2	+1	0	-1	-2	-3	Wander about
Take legitimate breaks	+3	+2	+1	0	-1	-2	-3	Take unnecessary breaks
Respond promptly	+3	+2	+1	0	-1	-2	-3	Slow to respond
Call when late/absent	+3	+2	+1	0	-1	-2	-3	Avoid calling in
Keep appointments	+3	+2	+1	0	-1	-2	-3	Miss appointments
Work with minimum supervision	+3	+2	+1	0	-1	-2	-3	Require close supervision
Trustworthy	+3	+2	+1	0	-1	-2	-3	Untrustworthy

Production

Know job procedures	+3	+2	+1	0	-1	-2	-3	Ignorant of job procedures
Skilled with tools/machines	+3	+2	+1	0	-1	-2	-3	Unskilled with tools/machines
Possess adequate power	+3	+2	+1	0	-1	-2	-3	Weak
Possess adequate stamina	+3	+2	+1	0	-1	-2	-3	Tires easily
Possess adequate speed	+3	+2	+1	0	-1	-2	-3	Too slow
Maintain production levels	+3	+2	+1	0	-1	-2	-3	Diminished production
Maintain quality standards	+3	+2	+1	0	-1	-2	-3	Poor quality of work
Know job objectives	+3	+2	+1	0	-1	-2	-3	Ignorant of job objectives
Maintain work station	+3	+2	+1	0	-1	-2	-3	Disorganized work station
Work efficiently	+3	+2	+1	0	-1	-2	-3	Waste resources
Work accurately	+3	+2	+1	0	-1	-2	-3	Commit errors

Social Coping

Respond constructively to crticism	+3	+2	+1	0	-1	-2	-3	Respond negatively to criticism
Maintain self-control under stress	+3	+2	+1	0	-1	-2	-3	Lose self-control under stress
Tolerate frustration	+3	+2	+1	0	-1	-2	-3	Act out when frustrated
Accept supervisor authority	+3	+2	+1	0	-1	-2	-3	Challenge authority
Cooperate with coworkers	+3	+2	+1	0	-1	-2	-3	Uncooperative with coworkers
Communicate work needs	+3	+2	+1	0	-1	-2	-3	Lack communication skills
Resolve conflict	+3	+2	+1	0	-1	-2	-3	Generate conflict
Socialize with coworkers	+3	+2	+1	0	-1	-2	-3	Isolated from coworkers
Maintain proper dress/grooming	+3	+2	+1	0	-1	-2	-3	Inappropriate dress/grooming

Organizational Coping

Learn new skills quickly	+3	+2	+1	0	-1	-2	-3	Learning is problematic
Adapt to organizational change	+3	+2	+1	0	-1	-2	-3	Poor adjustment to change
Implement change	+3	+2	+1	0	-1	-2	-3	Cannot plan or execute
Solve problems	+3	+2	+1	0	-1	-2	-3	Cannot identify problems
Innovate	+3	+2	+1	0	-1	-2	-3	Does not generate ideas
Communicate with written documents	+3	+2	+1	0	-1	-2	-3	Cannot read or write
Communicate with numbers	+3	+2	+1	0	-1	-2	-3	Cannot perform math
Teach skills to others	+3	+2	+1	0	-1	-2	-3	Cannot lead or train

Safety

Use equipment/tools as designed +3	+2	+1	0	-1	-2	-3	Misuse of tools/equipment
Follow safety policy and procedure +3	+2	+1	0	-1	-2	-3	Disregard safety policy and procedure
Maximize health and wellness +3	+2	+1	0	-1	-2	-3	Engage in unhealthy habits
Minimize risk +3	+2	+1	0	-1	-2	-3	Danger to self or coworkers
Troubleshoot/prevent injury or accident of job site +3	+2	+1	0	-1	-2	-3	Cannot identify dangerous situations
Protect physical well-being +3	+2	+1	0	-1	-2	-3	Overextend or misuse body
Report incidents or unsafe conditions +3	+2	+1	0	-1	-2	-3	Do not communicate with management/ignore problems
Minimize work loss due to sick/disability days +3	+2	+1	0	-1	-2	-3	Slow return to work following illness or injury

IMPLICATIONS FOR CASE PLANNING

The purpose of assessing client attributes such as ADA awareness, accommodation needs, and technology transfer concerns, is, of course, to identify employment barriers to be reduced or removed through rehabilitation planning. Services to remedy knowledge and skill gaps can then be included, as needed, in the Individualized Plan for Employment (IPE) to 1) increase the client's awareness of the protections afforded by legislative mandates such as Title I of the ADA and the FMLA, 2) communicate worksite accommodation needs to employers, 3) promote collaboration with employers in implementing and evaluating reasonable accommodations, and 4) teach the client how to negotiate with employers and resolve conflicts that may arise in the accommodation planning process.

Increase Rights Awareness

Once the client's awareness of his or her rights and responsibilities as set forth in the ADA and FMLA has been assessed, the rehabilitation professional and client must then develop and carry out a plan for remediating knowledge gaps. Clients must have an accurate understanding of the provisions of Title I of the ADA and the FMLA if they are to effectively assert their rights. They may need specific information about the key provisions of these laws, including definitions and examples of ADA concepts such as *disability, qualified individual, essential functions, reasonable accommodations,* and *undue hardship* and FMLA concepts such as *covered employee, serious health condition, unpaid leave,* and *reasonable notice.* They may also need instruction regarding 1) disability-related questions that can and cannot be asked by employers in the the job application process, 2) how to communicate about their disability status with potential employers (e.g., whether to disclose one's disability status, when and how to disclose, what information should and should not be shared), and 3) how and where to file complaints and pursue remedies if they feel their rights have been violated.

The identification and remediation of knowledge gaps can be accomplished through individual counseling and/or in group sessions (e.g., job club meetings, job-seeking skills training sessions). Information sharing, role plays, and self-assessment activities can be utilized to increase clients' rights awareness. Once clients have an accurate understanding of their rights and responsibilities, they are then ready to learn how to communicate about their accommodation needs with employers.

Request and Implement Accommodations

If clients are to secure meaningful employment once their rehabilitation plans have been completed, they must be equipped with the communication skills necessary to convey their unique strengths to potential employers and to assert their rights to necessary job accommodations. Therefore, the rehabilitation plan may need to include client training in requesting and implementing reasonable accommodations. The ADA's Title I regulations (Equal Employment Opportunity Commission & Department of Justice, 1991) prescribe a collaborative, nonadversarial process involving the applicant or employee and the employer. The steps of this process are as follows:

1. The applicant/employee initiates a request for an accommodation (preferably in written form).
2. The applicant/employee and employer collaborate to identify factors that limit the person's ability to perform the job's essential functions.

3. Using the applicant/employee as a resource, the employer identifies a variety of accommodations that would reduce or remove barriers.
4. The employer assesses the cost-effectiveness of each accommodation to determine which one(s) could be implemented with the least economic hardship.
5. The employer implements an appropriate accommodation, considering the applicant/employee's preferences when two equivalent accommodations have been identified.

As an outgrowth of ADA-compatible assessment and planning strategies, the Accommodations Planning Team (APT) seminar (Rumrill, Roessler, & Cook, 1998) is another example of how rehabilitation professionals can deliver career services that promote self-advocacy, empowerment, and collaboration with employers. The APT is a half-day program designed to prepare rehabilitation clients to seek and secure career-entry employment. Applying multiple emphases on accommodations, self advocacy, job-seeking, resource utilization, the ADA, and the FMLA, the seminar is a large-group program that teams clients with rehabilitation professionals, technology specialists, and employers in their chosen fields. In those teams, clients participate in a series of job-seeking and self-advocacy training activities, all of which are facilitated by technical assistance from rehabilitation professionals and employers. The culminating product of the APT program is a placement and accommodation plan that guides the client's future job search activities. As the client begins to look for jobs that are compatible with his or her interests and aptitudes, he or she is assisted by team members who serve as valuable resources for job leads and other support. Figure 4-V presents an agenda for the APT seminar (Rumrill, Koch, & Reed, 1998).

Figure 4-V
Accommodations Planning Team Seminar Agenda

1:00 p.m.   Interview Skills Training
                  Dressing for success
                  Communication skills
                  Job search etiquette
                  Questions all employers ask
                  Questions about disability and disclosure

2:00 p.m.	Introduction to APT and Simulated Interviews
	Welcome and overview
	Practice interviews - employers/applicants
	Feedback from rehabilitation professionals
2:30 p.m.	Identifying Accommodation Needs
	The Work Experience Survey
	Barriers, solutions, and resources
	A team approach to accommodation planning
3:10 p.m.	The Americans with Disabilities Act (ADA)
	Title I definitions and regulations
	Consumer rights and responsibilities
	Employer obligations
	Disclosure
	Collaborating to implement accommodations
3:30 p.m.	Discussing Accommodations with Your Employer
	The "Win-Win" approach
	Communication: The key to success
	Employer/applicant accommodation discussion
	Feedback from rehabilitation professionals
4:00 p.m.	Placement Planning: Starting Your Career
	Where to look and who can help
	Widening your options
	Follow-up contacts: Be persistent
	A team approach to step-by-step planning
4:30 p.m.	Social Security Work Incentives
	Overview
	Where to get assistance
4:45 p.m.	Reflections on the APT Process
	Applicant's next steps
	Conclusion and program evaluation

Negotiate and Resolve Conflicts

As part of the rehabilitation planning process, it is also critical that clients proactively prepare to deal with employers' potential lack of disability awareness and resistance to accommodating workers with disabilities. Not only is it important to be knowledgeable about one's rights and responsibilities as promulgated by such legislation as the ADA and the FMLA, it is also necessary to be aware of employer concerns and potential misconceptions about hiring and retaining employees with disabilities. Based on the responses of 600 human resource managers, Rutherford, Merrier, and Parry (1993) made the following recommendations regarding how to address disclosure issues and accommodation considerations with prospective employers who may lack disability awareness:

1. Employers only need to know about a person's disability status if a reasonable accommodation is necessary for him or her to perform the functions of the job.
2. Be prepared to recommend necessary accommodations and resources for securing accommodations–don't assume that employers know what accommodations to offer.
3. Let employers know that the costs of accommodations are often quite inexpensive.
4. Employers may feel uncomfortable communicating with a job applicant regarding his or her disability status and accommodation needs–therefore, applicants should be prepared to openly offer assistance to employers in this area.

The rehabilitation professional and client can role play these steps so that the client is prepared to deal with objections when he or she begins the job search process. If the client has used reasonable accommodations in classroom settings or at other job sites, he or she should be encouraged to secure a letter of recommendation from an instructor or past employer describing how the accommodation enabled the client to carry out job functions.

Training in negotiation and conflict resolution will also prepare clients to deal effectively with misconceptions that the employer may have about hiring workers with disabilities and to identify mutually agreeable solutions to problems with implementing accommodations. Roessler, Rumrill, Brown, and Palmer (1999) suggest that job applicants take the following steps to address employer objections to accommodation requests:

1. Specify the nature of the employer's objection. Ask the employer to elaborate on the objection that he or she has to the request. Use questions such as "What are your concerns about this accommodation?" or "What is it about this accommodation that bothers you?"
2. Reflect what you heard the employer say using phrases such as "So you feel that . . ." or "Oh, I see, what you're saying is. . . ."

This allows the employer to further clarify his or her point of view and communicates to the employer that you understand the nature of his or her objections.

3. Focus on common ground and shared interests. The goal here is to consolidate the discussion so that it is seen as a shared difficulty which both parties are interested in resolving. Examples of statements that emphasize mutuality include: "From our conversation, I can tell that we are both genuinely concerned about identifying an appropriate accommodation" and "It appears that we are really after the same thing but coming from it at different angles."

4. Use collaborative statements to identify options for resolving the problem. Examples of collaborative statements include: "So, can we take a couple of minutes and try to come up with some alternatives that will be acceptable to both of us?" and "You know, I'll bet if we did a little brain-storming right now, we could come up with a number of fair solutions."

5. Identify as many alternative solutions to the problem as possible. Communicate your openness to new ideas using statements such as "You know, the accommodation I requested is only one way to address the barrier. I'll bet we can come up with a number of different ways to do this."

6. Keep a written list of all the options that were generated and summarize the options in the order of their generation, without prioritizing. In summarizing, use statements such as "Okay, these are the possible solutions we've come up with so far."

7. Select one or two of the generated options to implement in a manner which affords mutual gain. In the process of selecting options, use statements such as "Of the options we generated, what would be your preference?" or "Perhaps we could try one choice and if it doesn't work out for either of us, we can give the other choice a try. Which one should we start with?"

SUMMARY

As the field of rehabilitation counseling looks ahead to the twenty-first century, the impact of disability law on rehabilitation policy and practice must be closely monitored. By incorporating the ADA, the FMLA, and reasonable accommodations into the ecological assessment process, the rehabilitation professional is able to identify gaps in the client's awareness of his or her legal rights and self-advocacy skills. These gaps can then be targeted for intervention through the use of such tools as the job analysis, the WES, and barrier/solution worksheets.

Key constructs such as civil rights awareness, the client's needs for reasonable accommodations, and counselor appraisals of the client's employability must be considered early, often, and throughout the rehabilitation process. Rehabilitation professionals who prepare clients for the increasing responsibilities that are conferred upon people with disabilities in the ADA era can ensure that vocational rehabilitation services remain responsive to clients' needs, grounded in societal priorities, and compatible with the laws which promote access and opportunity for all Americans.

REFERENCES

Bell, C. (1993). The Americans with Disabilities Act and injured workers: Implications for rehabilitation professionals and the worker's compensation system. *Rehabilitation Psychology, 38*(2), 103-114.

Blackwell, T., & Weed, R. (1992). *Job analysis and the ADA: A step by step guide.* Athens, GA: Elliot & Fitzpatrick.

Bolton, B., & Brookings, J. (1996). Development of a multifaceted definition of empowerment. *Rehabilitation Counseling Bulletin, 39*(4), 256-264.

Diksa, E., & Rogers, E. (1996). Employer concerns about hiring persons with psychiatric disability: Results of the employer attitude questionnaire. *Rehabilitation Counseling Bulletin, 40*(1), 31-44.

Equal Employment Opportunity Commission and Department of Justice. (1991). *Americans with Disabilities Act handbook.* Washington, DC: United States Government Printing Office.

Ettinger, J., Conyers, L., Merz, M. A., & Koch, L. C. (1995). *Strategies and tools for counselors, consumers, and educators* (Working Paper No. 3). Madison, WI: University of Wisconsin, Madison, Rehabilitation Research and Training Center.

Field, T., & Field, J. (1992). *Classification of jobs.* Athens, GA: Elliott & Fitzpatrick.

Gilbride, D. D., & Stensrud, R. (1993). Challenges and opportunities for rehabilitation counselors in the Americans with Disabilities Act era. *Journal of the National Association of Rehabilitation Professionals in the Private Sector, 8*, 67-74.

Gilbride, D. D., & Stensrud, R. (1999). Demand-side job development and system change. *Rehabilitation Counseling Bulletin, 42*(4), 329-342.

Hergenrader, R. (1997). Hands-on disability management on the rise. *National Underwriter 101*(7), 8-10.

McMahon, B. T., Dancer, S., & Jaet, D. N. (1993). Providers of technical assistance and employers: Myths, concerns, and compliance behaviors related to the Americans with Disabilities Act. *Journal of the National Association of Rehabilitation Professionals in the Private Sector, 8,* 53 66.

McMahon, B. T., & Domer, T. M. (1997). Twenty questions surrounding unpaid medical leave: Navigating the Bermuda Triangle of employment law. *Work: A Journal of Prevention, Assessment, and Rehabilitation, 9*(2), 129-145.

Millington, M. (1997). *Sample job analysis report.* New Orleans: Louisiana State University Medical Center.

Millington, M. (1998). *The Employment Expectations Questionnaire.* New Orleans: Louisiana State University Medical Center.

Millington, M., Reid, C., & Leierer, S. (1997). Employment expectations in rehabilitation counseling: Factors of employment selection. *Rehabilitation Counseling Bulletin, 40*(3), 215-229.

Millington, M., Szymanski, E., & Hanley-Maxwell, C. (1994). Effect of the label mental retardation on employer concerns and selection. *Rehabilitation Counseling Bulletin, 38*(1), 27-43.

Millington, M., Szymanski, E., & Johnston-Rodriguez, S. (1995). A contextual-stage model for employment selection. *Journal of Job Placement, 11*(1), 31-36.

Mullins, J. A., Jr., Rumrill, P., Roessler, R. T. (1996). The role of the rehabilitation placement consultant in the Americans with Disabilities Act era. *Work: A Journal of Assessment, Prevention, and Rehabilitation, 6*(1), 3-10.

Palmer, C. D. (1998). Self-advocacy and conflict resolution: Requesting academic accommodations at postsecondary education institutions. Unpublished doctoral dissertation, University of Arkansas, Fayetteville.

Parker, R., Szymanski, E., & Hanley-Maxwell, C. (1989). Ecological assessment in supported employment. *Journal of Applied Rehabilitation Counseling, 20*(3), 26-33.

Patterson, J. B. (1996). Occupational and labor market information and analysis. In E. M. Szymanski & R. M. Parker (Eds.), *Work and disability: Issues in career development and job placement* (pp. 209-254). Austin, TX: Pro-Ed.

Roessler, R. T. (1995). *The Work Experience Survey.* Fayetteville, AR: Arkansas Research and Training Center in Vocational Rehabilitation.

Roessler, R., & Gottcent, J. (1994). The Work Experience Survey: A reasonable accommodation/career development strategy. *Journal of Applied Rehabilitation Counseling, 25*(3), 16-21.

Roessler, R., & Kirk, M. (in press). Improving technology training services in post-secondary education: Perspectives of recent college graduates with disabilities. *Journal of Postsecondary Education and Disability.*

Roessler, R., Reed, C., & Brown, P. (1998). Coping with chronic illness at work: Case studies of five successful employees. *Journal of Vocational Rehabilitation, 10*(3), 261-269.

Roessler, R., & Rumrill, P. (1995). The relationship of perceived worksite barriers to job mastery and job satisfaction for employed people with multiple sclerosis. *Rehabilitation Counseling Bulletin, 39*(1), 2-14.

Roessler, R., & Rumrill, P. (1998). Reducing worksite barriers to enhance job satisfaction: An important postemployment service for workers with chronic illnesses. *Journal of Vocational Rehabilitation, 10*(3), 219-229.

Roessler, R. T., Rumrill, P., Battersby, J. C., & Garnette, M. R. (1996). *Employee's guide to reasonable accommodations.* Hot Springs, AR: Arkansas Research and Training Center in Vocational Rehabilitation.

Roessler, R., Rumrill, P., Brown, P, & Palmer, C. (1999). *Self-advocacy classroom accommodations: Student workbook.* Fayetteville, AR: Arkansas Research and Training Center in Vocational Rehabilitation.

Roessler, R., Rumrill, P., & Reed, C. (1995). *The Work Experience Survey (WES) manual.* Fayetteville, AR: Arkansas Research and Training Center in Vocational Rehabilitation.

Rubin, S., & Roessler, R. (1995). *Foundations of the vocational rehabilitation process* (4th ed.). Austin, TX: Pro-Ed.

Rumrill, P. (1994). The "win-win" approach to Title I of the Americans with Disabilities Act: Preparing college students with disabilities for career entry placements after graduation. *Journal of Postsecondary Education and Disability, 11*(1), 15-19.

Rumrill, P. (1999). Effects of a social competence training program on accommodation request activity, situational self-efficacy, and Americans with Disabilities Act knowledge among employed people with visual impairments and blindness. *Journal of Vocational Rehabilitation, 12*(1), 25-31.

Rumrill, P., & Garnette, M. (1997). Career adjustment via reasonable accommodations: The effects of an employee-empowerment intervention for people with disabilities. *Work, 9*(1), 57-64.

Rumrill. P., Koch, L., & Reed, C. (1998). Career maintenance and multiple sclerosis. *Journal of Job Placement and Development, 14*(1), 11-17.

Rumrill, P., Nutter, D., Hennessey, M., & Ware, M. (1998). Job retention and breast cancer: Employee perspectives and implications for rehabilitation planning. *Work, 10*(3), 251-259.

Rumrill, P., Roessler, R., Battersby, J., & Schuyler, B. (1998). Situational assessment of the accommodation needs of employees who are visually impaired. *Journal of Visual Impairment and Blindness, 92*(1), 42-54.

Rumrill, P., Roessler, R., & Cook, B. (1998). Improving career re-entry outcomes for people with multiple sclerosis: A comparison of two approaches. *Journal of Vocational Rehabilitation, 10*(3), 241-252.

Rumrill, P., Schoenfeld, N., Holman, C., & Mullins, J. (1997). Ecological assessment of the career maintenance needs of employees with diabetes mellitus. *Work, 9*(2), 111-120.

Rumrill, P., Schuyler, B., & Battersby, J. (1997). Profiles of on-the job accommodations needed by professional employees who are blind. *Journal of Visual Impairment and Blindness, 91*(1), 66-76.

Rutherford, L., Merrier, P., & Parry, L. (1993, Fall). To disclose or not disclose: These university professors find the answer in a survey sent to human resource managers. *Careers and the Disabled,* 36-38.

Schall, C. M. (1998). The Americans with Disabilities Act: Are we keeping our promise? An analysis of the effect of the ADA on the employment of persons with disabilities. *Journal of Vocational Rehabilitation, 10*(3), 191-203.

Scott, M. (1997). Small and midsize employers tackle disability. *Employee Benefit Plan Review, 51*(9), 19-22.

Storey, K., & Certo, N. (1996). Natural supports for increasing integration in the workplace for people with disabilities: A review of the literature and guidelines for implementation. *Rehabilitation Counseling Bulletin, 40*(1), 62-77.

Sumner, G. (1995). Project Alliance: A job retention program for employees with chronic illnesses and their employers. New York: National Multiple Sclerosis Society.

Szymanski, E. M., Hershenson, D. B., Enright, M. S., & Ettinger, J. M. (1996). Career development theories, constructs, and research: Implications for people with disabilities. In E. M. Szymanski & R. M. Parker (Eds.), *Work and disability: Issues in career development and job placement* (pp. 79-126). Austin, TX: Pro-Ed.

United States Department of Labor. (1991). *Dictionary of occupational titles.* Washington, DC: United States Government Printing Office.

United States Department of Labor. (1998). *Occupational outlook handbook.* Washington, DC: United States Government Printing Office.

Wehman, P. (1996). *Life beyond the classroom: Transition strategies for youth with disabilities.* Baltimore, MD: Paul H. Brookes.

Chapter 5

PSYCHOSOCIAL CHARACTERISTICS OF THE NEW AMERICAN WORKPLACE: IMPLICATIONS FOR JOB DEVELOPMENT AND PLACEMENT

MARY ANN MERZ, JOHN BRICOUT, LYNN C. KOCH, AND PHILLIP D. RUMRILL

INTRODUCTION

The purpose of this chapter is to take a broad look at the contemporary American workplace, especially the psychosocial characteristics of work in the early twenty-first century. More specifically, we will attempt to apply current principles from vocational and industrial/organizational psychology to the employment experiences of people with disabilities, as well as to the rehabilitation counseling subfield of job development and placement. The chapter begins with an examination of the changing nature of work and its impact on the psychosocial well-being of workers with disabilities. The psychosocial benefits of work are then highlighted to provide a motivational context for the seemingly natural desire of most people to be employed and to succeed in their careers, despite the increasing levels of stress that workers are likely to encounter on the job. Subsequent sections address theoretical models that are available to help social scientists understand the psychosocial work environment, the relationship between the work environment and employee well-being, and psychosocial considerations in job development and placement. Throughout the chapter, the recurring theme is that people with disabilities may be especially vulnerable to job stress and other work related psychosocial difficulties, that the impending changes in the way work is done in the United States are likely to affect them disproportionately in comparison to other workers, and that rehabilitation counselors must be acutely attuned to psychosocial aspects of the work environment if people with disabilities are to play an important role in the new global economy.

WORK IN THE TWENTY-FIRST CENTURY

In the United States, the world of work is being affected by dramatic changes such as increased global competition, the rapid expansion of information technology, the reengineering of business practices, the replacement of large companies with smaller companies that employ fewer workers, the shift from a product orientation to a service and information orientation, and the elimination of "the job" as a fixed bundle of tasks (Cascio, 1995). These changes have translated into demands for greater cognitive flexibility, multitasking, and increased worker decision making (Perry, 1995; Traiforos, 1995). Such demands may place added strain on workers with disabilities, especially those who have cognitive and/or psychiatric limitations, and increase their risk for stress-related disorders (Perry, 1995). Workers with disabilities are often at an increased risk for stress-related disorders for several other reasons: 1) the changing workplace, with its emphasis upon technically sophisticated "knowledge workers" may relegate less-skilled workers with disabilities to low-level, socially isolating, monotonous "pink collar" work with low pay and high turnover (Perry, 1995; Wellman, Salaff, Dimitrova, Garton, Guila, & Haythornwaite, 1996); 2) certain disabling conditions (e.g., epilepsy, diabetes, multiple sclerosis, mental illness) can be exacerbated by unmanaged job stress (Falvo, 1999); and 3) people with disabilities do not always have access to the same social supports that other workers have to assist them in managing on-the-job stress (Gates, 2000).

Traditional approaches to the management of occupational stress, which focus primarily on the individual as the unit of change, may not be appropriate in the contemporary American workplace (Syme, 1991). In fact, empirical evidence has linked stress-related disorders directly to features of the work environment, indicating that modification of the work design may be more effective than attempting to modify individual behavior (Johnson & Johansson, 1991). Furthermore, measures of the work environment as it affects the mental health of individuals with disabilities are very recent (e.g., Kirsh, 2000; Sartawi, Abu-Hilal, & Qaryouti, 1999), so that considerations of psychosocial factors in the work environment are still incipient in vocational rehabilitation.

PSYCHOLOGICAL BENEFITS OF EMPLOYMENT

Although work can have a negative impact on health if risk factors are not adequately managed, employment is the primary institution in American society that serves the individual's needs for psychological well-being (Muchinsky, 2000). The psychological benefits of employment include 1) the imposition of a daily structure or routine upon one's activities, 2) the provision of opportunities for social interaction, 3) the connection of people with goals and purposes, 4) the establishment of personal status and a sense of identity, and 5) the enforcement of physical and mental activity (Jahoda, 1981). Unemployment, on the other hand, deprives people of these benefits by restricting choices, limiting perceived control over one's life, reducing opportunities to use one's skills, constricting variety in daily activities, decreasing social contacts, creating uncertainty about the future, and removing a socially approved role along with the positive self-evaluations that accompany this role (Muchinsky, 2000).

Employment has additional psychosocial benefits for people with disabilities. It plays a crucial role in community reintegration and psychosocial rehabilitation (Bradt, Crilly, & Timvik, 1993; Desisto, Harding, McCormick, Ashikaga, & Brooks, 1999; Krause, 1996; Krause & Anson, 1997; Priebe, Warner, Hubschmid, & Eckle, 1998). Employment has been linked to improved life satisfaction, quality of life, self-esteem, and functional ability for people with various physical and psychiatric disabilities (Bond, Drake, Mueser, & Becker, 1997; McColl, Stirling, Walker, Corey, & Wilkins, 1999; Robinson, 2000; Webb, Wrigley, Yoels, & Fine, 1995). Unfortunately, however, available work roles for people with disabilities are often limited to low-status positions. This limited availability and restriction of work roles is often attributable to a lack of previous work experience, as well as to stigmatization and discrimination in the workplace (Rumrill & Roessler, 1999).

Although rehabilitation counselors are keenly aware of the psychological benefits of work, they may be less cognizant of how work environmental factors can undermine the psychological well-being of clients. In the next section, we introduce two models that attempt to explain the complex interaction between the work environment and employee mental health.

THEORETICAL MODELS OF THE PSYCHOSOCIAL WORK ENVIRONMENT

Conceptual models of the psychosocial work environment and its impact on mental health incorporate the interdisciplinary perspectives of industrial engineering and ergonomics, industrial and organizational psychology, sociology, cognitive science, applied physiology, social work, medicine, social epidemiology, biobehaviorism, clinical psychology and psychiatry, and community and social psychology. Two models that have particular relevance to the experiences of workers with disabilities are the demand/control/support model and the vitamin model.

The Demand/Control/Support Model

Karasek and Theorell's (1990) demand/control/support model proposes that as psychological work demands (e.g., the mental arousal required to carry out job tasks, manage workload, and pace work) increase and decision latitude (e.g., the worker's ability to control work demands) decreases, risk for psychological strain and physical illness increases.

The demand/control/support model categorizes jobs along two dimensions: 1) high-strain/low-strain and 2) active/passive. High-strain jobs are those that are highly demanding but afford the worker a limited amount of decision latitude or control (e.g., servers, nurses' aides, assemblers, firefighters, computer operators, telephone operators, delivery persons, sales clerks) (Karasek & Theorell, 1990). Low-strain jobs are those with low demands and high control (e.g., carpenters, machinists, clerk supervisors, programmers, architects, natural scientists).

Active jobs are those with high demands and high control (e.g., teachers, managers, public officials, engineers) (Karasek & Theorell, 1990). These jobs tend to promote learning and growth up to the point at which too many demands may cause fatigue and other symptoms of strain.

Passive jobs are those with low psychological demands and low decision latitude or control (e.g., janitors, clerical workers, stock and billing clerks). These jobs tend to produce a phenomenon among workers that is similar to learned helplessness in which there is "a gradual atrophying of learned skills and abilities" (Karasek & Theorell, 1990, p.37). Although risk for psychological strain is not elevated, long-term loss of work motivation and productivity may result.

Karasek and Theorell (1990) later expanded their model to include the interaction between the degree of social supports available to the worker and the worker's decision latitude. They identified four worker types as representative of this interaction: 1) participatory leader (high control/high support); 2) cowboy hero (high control/low support); 3) obedient comrade (low control/high support); and 4) isolated prisoner (low control/low support). These theorists also noted that economic conditions and technological advances can alter the demands and decision latitude of a given occupation. For example, the decreased amount of job control experienced by many physicians as a result of managed care initiatives has led to a reclassification of this occupation from the active job category to the high-strain category (Levi, 2000).

The demand/control/support model was recently extended by Mikkelsen, Saksvik, Eriksen, and Ursin (1999) to include learning opportunities that afford the acquisition of skills and knowledge beyond that needed for the person's current job. They proposed that such learning opportunities provide a buffer against the stress which often accompanies the fast changing working conditions and increasing employer expectations that are common in today's economy. In other words, the availability of ample learning opportunities in the workplace has health benefits for employees.

The Vitamin Model

The vitamin model (Warr, 1994) proposes that the effects of the work environment on mental health are similar to the effects of vitamins on physical health. As occurs with vitamin deficiencies, the absence of principal work environmental features such as control, skill use, interpersonal contact, externally generated goals, variety, and environmental clarity can lead to mental health and physical problems. Similarly, moderate levels of these work environmental features can be beneficial, whereas levels that exceed certain thresholds generally do not produce additional benefit, and excessively high levels can even be harmful. Continued increases in other work environmental features (e.g., pay, benefits, physical security, social status) are not expected to have a detrimental effect on physical and mental health (Warr, 1994). Like vitamins C and E, these environmental features produce a constant effect (CE). Components of mental health, which are considered to be relatively stable but susceptible to influence by work environmental factors, include affective well-being, competence, autonomy, aspiration, and integrated functioning.

A recent study of psychosocial work environmental factors and employee well-being has provided partial support for the vitamin model. In a survey of 1,437 Dutch health care workers, De Jonge and Schaufeli (1998) examined the relationships among three job characteristics (i.e., job demands, job autonomy, workplace social support) and three aspects of well-being on the job (i.e., job satisfaction, job-related anxiety, emotional anxiety). On the basis of Warr's model, they hypothesized curvilinear relationships between the three job characteristics and the three aspects of well-being on the job. The results supported this hypothesis, indicating that, with the important caveat that personal factors may moderate the relationship between job characteristics and perceived well-being on the job, the vitamin model may provide a more complete picture of the impact of the work environment on psychological strain than even the extended demand/control/support model.

RELATIONSHIP OF THE WORK ENVIRONMENT TO EMPLOYEE WELL-BEING

Of the many factors addressed in models of the psychosocial work environment, the five that have received the most attention from researchers are control, job demands, uncertainty, conflict, and social support. The potential impact of these factors on employee well-being is discussed in the following paragraphs.

Control

Worker control over job tasks, work pace, and decisions about job-related activities is the factor that has been the most widely studied and that has the greatest consensus among researchers regarding its link to occupational stress and employee health (Hall, 1991; Landy, 1992; Sauter, Hurrell, & Cooper, 1989). Research findings indicate that:

1. Control is a mediator of stress hormone production. Cortisol (which plays a role in the body's immune system) tends to be low in controllable situations (Frankenhaeuser, 1991).
2. Perceived control is not merely a mediator of job stress; also, it has a direct influence on job satisfaction (McLaney & Hurrell, 1988).
3. Employee assessments of job autonomy (i.e., control) are positively correlated with overall job satisfaction (Loher, Noe, Moeller, & Fitzgerald, 1985).
4. Overall job satisfaction, work motivation, and affective well-being improve when work groups are given control over the pace of production, the distribution of tasks among team members, the organization of breaks, and the allocation of overtime (Wall & Clegg, 1981).

Job Demands

The nature of job demands has been linked to levels of stress in workers, especially as these interact with control levels (Karasek & Thoerell, 1990; Sutherland & Cooper, 1993). Job demand factors that have been associated with poor mental health and job dissatisfaction include "narrow, fragmented, invariant, and short-cycle tasks that provide little stimulation, allow little use of skills or expression of creativity, and have little intrinsic meaning for workers" (Sauter et al., 1989, p.1151). Research findings along this line of inquiry provide evidence that:

1. Both repetitive monotony (e.g., assembly line work) and uneventful monotony (e.g., monitoring a control room) can affect physical and mental health. However, repetitive monotony tends to be more hazardous to health than uneventful monotony (Johansson, 1991).

2. White collar workers with intellectually undemanding and routine jobs (e.g., assembly line workers) produce neuroendocrine stress profiles similar to those of assembly line workers (Frankenhaeuser, 1991).

3. The effects of technological change on both work structure (through increased workload and decreased control) and work performance (through technology breakdowns and information overload) can lead to long-term as well as short-term stress (Carayon, 1997).

4. Less-skilled workers are at a greater risk for increased job stress with the introduction of new technology into the work environment, but employee participation can mitigate some of the stressful effects of new technology (Smith, Conway, & Karsh, 1999).

5. Computerized workplaces do not always lead to more monotonous work and may even make work more interesting. However, even in such instances, work stress may increase due to greater cognitive demands and requirements for a faster work pace (Huuhtanen, 1997).

6. Repetitive, machine-paced jobs extend the duration of the stress response and slow the time it takes to unwind when the worker leaves the task (Frankenhaeuser, 1991). This phenomenon is extended for workers who return home to family responsibilities or who go to a second job. It also carries over into leisure time.

7. The view that people compensate for boring jobs with stimulating free time does not hold up empirically. People who have monotonous jobs tend to have leisure activities that require very little planning or effort (Karasek & Theorell, 1990). Interestingly, this does not appear to be an individual preference because leisure activities change when jobs become more interesting (Frankenhaeuser, 1991; Karasek & Theorell, 1990).

8. Uneventful monotony can be harmful as well. However, it is more likely that the effort required to remain alert causes stress, rather than the monotony itself (Huuhtanen, 1997).

9. Uneventful monotony is often found in jobs with high levels of responsibility for the safety of others (e.g., process monitor at a

nuclear power plant). In these situations, problems are often blamed on human error. An alternative explanation was provided by Frankenhaeuser (1991), who has studied the brain's need for stimulation, attention, and biological rhythms. Frankenhaeuser argued that when human beings are expected to perform beyond the limits imposed by basic biological and psychological constraints, the fault lies in the situation. There is nothing wrong with the person who does not cope with such requirements" (p. 55).

Social Support

Social support is defined differently across studies, but it generally relates to the available emotional support and assistance in performing job demands. There are both empirical data and theoretical reasons to propose that social support has a role in reducing strain in the workplace (Johnson & Johansson, 1991; Karasek & Theorell, 1990; Landy, 1992; Van der Dorf, Maes, & Diekstra, 2000). It has been theorized that social support reduces occupational stress by 1) acting as a buffer between stressors and health, 2) meeting basic human physiological needs for companionship and group affiliation, 3) facilitating active coping patterns, and 4) influencing the development of personal identity and adult socialization (Karasek & Theorell, 1990; Johnson, 1991).

Empirical research has linked inadequate social support in the workplace to a variety of illnesses, including coronary heart disease, high cholesterol levels, angina pectoris, and psychological disorders (Johnson, 1991). The amount of on-the-job stress experienced by women and members of minority groups is reduced proportionately in relation to the number of similar members in the organization (Reskin, McBriar, & Kmec, 1999). In relation to his vitamin model, Warr (1994) cited evidence that very low and very high levels of social interaction are harmful to mental health. Interestingly, extremely high levels of social support can be as problematic as the lack of social support because it can impinge upon personal territory and needs for privacy (Warr, 1994).

Several studies have found that supervisor social support mediates job stress (e.g., Moyle, 1995; Stephens & Long, 2000; Van der Dorf et al., 2000). There is also evidence that the benefits of coworker social supports are qualified. For example, in a study of seasonally employed book dealers, Beehr, Jex, Stacy, and Murray (2000) found no evidence of a stress-buffering effect from coworker social support. However, using a very different worker group (i.e., male soldiers in the United States Army), Bliese and Castro (2000) found that work-group support moderated the relationship between work demands and psychological strain. It seems reasonable to infer that the benefits of social support will vary with the degree to which the support is instrumental and meaningful.

Uncertainty

Uncertainty is created by role or job ambiguity (Breaugh & Colihan, 1994) and lack of environmental clarity (Warr, 1994). Factors of uncertainty that have been studied include ambiguity about performance criteria (i.e., how work is to be evaluated), work method (i.e., what procedures are to be followed), and scheduling (i.e., in what order are tasks to be completed; Breaugh & Colihan, 1994). Other facets of uncertainty may be the unpredictability of a coworker's or supervisor's behavior, dependency on other departments to complete work, the constant introduction of new technology to the worker's role, and the financial stability of the organization (Landy, 1992).

In comparison to other work environmental factors, less is known about how uncertainty on the job relates to occupational stress. However, it has been postulated that uncertainty can trigger stress-related disorders because 1) it is an inherently noxious state that humans are motivated to change, and 2) it interferes with goal accomplishment and the ability to perform jobs effectively (Breaugh & Colihan, 1994).

Lack of clarity about the worker's own behavior and about role requirements has been strongly correlated with job-related affective well-being (Warr, 1994). Consistent with the vitamin model, very low clarity has been shown to be unusually harmful, and higher levels of clarity have been found to have a broadly constant effect (Warr, 1994). More recent studies have borne out the importance of role clarity in mitigating the negative effects of work stressors (Bliese & Castro, 2000). As was noted previously in the discussion about threats to job continuity, uncertainty about the future has been studied in terms of anticipated negative events such as unemployment, and it has been associated with lowered affective well-being (McDonough, 2000). Little is known about the effects of uncertainty regarding positive events (e.g., promotions) or family needs (e.g., reliable child care, transportation). Uncertainty is also theorized to interact with other psychosocial work environmental factors such as personal control and use of skills (Landy, 1992).

Conflict

At work, conflicts may arise surrounding issues of task demands (especially when time pressures do not allow for optimal performance) and work roles (e.g., serving client needs versus employer interests). Research in this area has focused extensively on the work-family conflict and how it affects both men and women (Zedeck & Mosier, 1990). In contrast to the commonly held view that family conditions moderate the effect of work on women's well-being, Lennon and Rosenfield (1992) found some support for the view that certain work moderates the effect of demands in the family on women's well-being.

Women in dual career couples report lower levels of coping, greater stress, and more role overload than men, despite the fact that the work conditions associated with life quality are the same for men and women. This finding suggests the influence of differential role expectations and social status for men and women, with women experiencing more role strain and having lower level jobs with less autonomy. Thus, women may be more likely to seek home-based work for family, personal, or stress reduction reasons, whereas men may be concerned about career costs incurred from home-based work (Mokhtarian, Bagley, & Salomon, 1998).

In another study, investigators discovered that emotional well-being in police officers was negatively associated with work-family conflict (Burke, 1993). A study of male administrators of correctional institutions and their spouses found that both husbands and wives agreed on the relative presence of stressors, but there was almost no agreement about their perceived levels of life satisfaction (Burke, 1986). Some evidence exists that the impact of work and family stressors may vary across career stages. For example, stressful events outside the job had an increasing effect on the physical health of United States postal workers during the middle stage of their careers, whereas stressful events on the job had less of an impact (Hurrell, McLaney, & Murphy, 1990).

Families have been reported to function as buffers to workplace stress. Landy (1992) pointed out that organizations should not demand levels of commitment that result in barriers between an individual and his or her non-work emotional support systems. He further stated that "the emotional support of a family unit may be the most widely under-utilized 'treatment' for strain in the organizational environment" (p.137). "Spillover" of work-based stress threatens the ability of families to function as buffers to workplace stress (Standen, Daniels, & Lamond, 1999). However, work-family conflict that compromises well-being, even for home-based teleworkers, is not inevitable (Standen et al., 1999).

PSYCHOSOCIAL CONSIDERATIONS IN JOB DEVELOPMENT AND PLACEMENT

Vocational rehabilitation professionals, especially job development and placement specialists, recognize the huge impact that environmental factors (e.g., coworker attitudes, architectural barriers) can have on the individual's ability to succeed in employment. To assist clients to achieve their individualized career goals, the rehabilitation model places as much emphasis on assessing and changing the environment as it does on assessing and changing the individual. The growing body of literature on the psychosocial effects of work design offers job development and placement professionals some new conceptual frameworks, strategies, and tools to aid in rehabilitation planning.

Individuals differ in terms of what situations they find stressful and how they react to on-the-job stressors (Szymanski, 1999). As part of the career assessment process, it is, therefore, extremely important that vocational rehabilitation professionals help clients identify their vulnerabilities, coping skills, and the environmental risk factors that may trigger negative reactions. Indeed, individual characteristics, such as "positivity" or "negativity" of affect, trait anxiety, and coping resources have been found to influence occupational distress, principally by moderating the impact of work stressors on the strain experienced by workers (e.g., Dollard & Winfield, 1995; Fogarty, Machin, Albion, Sutherland, Lalor, & Revitt, 1999; Moyle, 1995).

One personal attribute that could be assessed by vocational rehabilitation professionals to facilitate career planning and job placement is the individual's sense of coherence (Lustig, Rosenthal, Strauser, & Haynes, 2000). Rather than focusing on negative aspects of the individual's disposition that might exacerbate workplace stress, coherence focuses on attributes that promote health. Coherence speaks to the ". . .belief that the world is comprehensible, manageable, and meaningful" (Lustig et al., 2000, p.135). A sense of coherence gives the individual the motivation and capacity to persist in the face of adversity. An individual with a sense of coherence is also likely to have confidence in his or her problem solving abilities in the workplace. Lustig et al. noted that previous studies have found a negative association between a sense of coherence and trait anxiety, somatic complaints, and perceived stressors. In their own study of college students with disabilities, Lustig et al. found a positive correlation between a sense of coherence and positive adjustment (i.e., psychological well-being). An individual's sense of coherence can be assessed using the 29-item Sense of Coherence Scale (SOCS) or informally through interviews aimed at appraising the client's resiliency and coping resources.

Szymanski (1999) provided a useful list of questions that can be used by rehabilitation professionals to assess the client's sources of stress, the stressors that could be present in the careers that he or she might want to pursue, and his or her coping strategies and resources. Examples of these questions include: "What are my current sources of job and personal stress? What additional job or personal stressors are connected to my future goals? How have I reacted to excess stress in the past? How well do I use social support on or off the job to moderate the effect of stress? How can I anticipate and lessen unhealthy levels of stress?" (p. 289).

In addition to analyzing individual risk factors for job stress, the stress factors in potential work environments must also be evaluated (see Chapter 4). Traditional job analysis approaches emphasize the gathering of information about job tasks and the worker characteristics required to perform those tasks (Patterson, 1996). Cascio (1995) noted the need to update job analysis methods because many occupations no longer consist of a preestablished bundle of tasks. Indeed, many employers today are shifting away from a task-based approach to organizing job duties–toward a process-based approach that cuts across organizational boundaries and job titles. This shift necessitates a job analysis method that focuses on 1) identifying the environmental, social, and contextual dimensions of work; and 2) describing roles rather than jobs. Questions that can be used as a guide for analyzing psychosocial work environmental factors include:

- What are the job demands in relation to the amount of control that the worker has over the demands?
- How much social support is available on the job?
- What degree of uncertainty exists in the work environment?
- Are there conflicting role responsibilities?
- How might the job be modified to reduce stressors?

Another approach to gathering information about the psychosocial work environment is the informational interview. The informational interview is a particularly effective tool for clients who want to acquire detailed and up-to-date information about an occupation of interest from the perspective of an individual employed in that occupation (Koch, 1999). Questions such as those listed above can be incorporated into the interview to find out about the psychosocial work environmental factors present in a given occupation or workplace. In addition, clients can tour the job site and shadow the employee to observe, first-hand, what stressors and employee supports are present on the job.

The number of people with and without disabilities who work primarily at home has almost tripled since 1990, with the total number of American home-based workers currently estimated at 11 million (Rumrill, Fraser, & Anderson, 2000). By the year 2010, labor market analysts project that as much as 40 percent of the American workforce will be telecommuting at least part of the time. Working at home is becoming a normative aspect of employment in the twenty-first century, and an increasingly common employment goal for people with disabilities is telework, or paid work that is conducted away from the office using information and communication technologies such as computers, videophones, and telephones (Hone, Kerrin, & Cox, 1998).

Telework can take place at home or at a centralized location called a "telecenter" containing a number of computer workstations. In either case, telework makes employment more accessible for people with disabilities, both by increasing physical proximity and by reducing the likelihood of stigma (Cassam, 1995; Hesse, 1995; Milpied, 1995). However, there is some concern that members of marginalized groups, such as people with disabilities, might be relegated to the most monotonous, routinized tasks, while being subjected to intense scrutiny and having little autonomy or control (Burris, 1998; Schoeffel, Loveridge, & Davidson, 1993; Wellman et al., 1996). These conditions, together with the increased social isolation, may put teleworkers with disabilities at risk for greater psychological strain unless specific attention is given to relevant issues of job design, work structure, and social support. Rehabilitation professionals should also assist clients to find venues other than the work environment to meet their social and recreational needs (Rumrill et al., 2000).

Assisting clients to manage stress on their current jobs is not enough. In today's rapidly changing world of work, proactive planning for future job stress is a key to job retention and career advancement. Therefore, rehabilitation professionals must equip clients with the skills and resources to deal with future work challenges. The message for vocational rehabilitation professionals is that a future-oriented strategy of career development, like the one proposed by Rumrill and Roessler (1999), may also have stress-reduction and health-enhancement benefits for workers with disabilities. One tool that certainly meets the criteria of being future-oriented is the career portfolio. The career portfolio is a personalized planner that contains work-related information organized in a manner that enables the individual to display his or her unique skills, self-monitor his or her career development, and plan for the future (Koch & Johnston-Rodriguez, 1997). Szymanski (1999) described how the career portfolio can be used to promote planning for resilience by incorporating a section on "stress analysis and strain prevention" (p. 286). Clients can use this section of the portfolio to self-assess their vulnerabilities to stress and identify strategies for minimizing those vulnerabilities.

SUMMARY

The American workplace and corporate culture have undergone dramatic changes in the past twenty years, and the foreseeable future appears to hold equally (if not more) radical transformations in the way work is conceptualized and performed. Among these changes are technological advances, the continued movement into an information-based economy, and the conception of jobs as dynamic sets of expectations and problem solving skills rather than fixed bundles of tasks. These and other new developments provide exciting opportunities for American workers, but they also bring with them considerable stress as workers struggle to meet the changing and heightening demands of their employers.

People with disabilities are perhaps more susceptible to work-related stress than are other worker populations, and their needs regarding the psychosocial work environment must play a prominent role in rehabilitation planning and service delivery. By understanding the theoretical and empirical relationships between the work environment and employee well-being, the specific psychosocial stressors that are likely to affect people with disabilities in the new global economy, and strategies for alleviating or eliminating those stressors during the job development and placement process, rehabilitation professionals can help to ensure that people with disabilities continue to function as valued members of the American workforce in the New Millenium.

REFERENCES

Beehr, T. A., Jex, S. M., Stacy, B. A., & Murray, M. A. (2000). Work stressors and coworker support as predictors of individual strain and job performance. *Journal of Organizational Behavior, 21*(4), 391-405.

Bliese, P. D., & Castro, C. A. (2000). Role clarity, work overload and organizational support: Multilevel evidence of the importance of support. *Work and Stress, 14*(1), 65-73.

Bond, G. R., Drake, R. E., Mueser, K. T., & Becker, D.R. (1997). An update on supported employment for people with severe mental illness. *Psychiatric Services, 48*, 335-346.

Bradt, S., Crilly, J., & Timvik, U. (1993). Computer training for young adult patients with Serious mental illness. *Journal of Rehabilitation, 59*(3), 51 54.

Breaugh, J. A., & Colihan, J. P. (1994). Measuring facets of job ambiguity: Construct validity evidence. *Journal of Applied Psychology, 79,* 191-202.

Burke, R. J. (1986). Occupational and life stress and the family. *International Review of Applied Psychology, 35*(3), 347-369.

Burke, R. J. (1993). Work-family stress, conflict, coping, and burnout in police officers. *Stress Medicine, 9*(3), 171-180.

Burris, B. H. (1998). Computerization of the workplace. *Annual Review of Sociology, 24,* 141-157.

Carayon, P. (1997). Temporal issues of quality of working life and stress in human-computer interaction. *International Journal of Human-Computer Interaction, 9*(4), 325-342.

Cascio, W. F. (1995). Whither industrial and organizational psychology in a changing world of work? *American Psychologist, 50,* 928-939.

Cassam, D. (1995). Telework: Enabling the disabled. *Search, 26*(7), 201-202.

DeJonge, J., & Schaufeli, W. B. (1998). Job characteristics and employee well-being: a test of Warr's vitamin model in health care workers using structural equation modeling. *Journal of Organizational Behavior, 19*(4), 387-407.

Desisto, M., Harding, C. M., McCormick, R. V., Ashikaga, T., & Brooks, G. W. (1999). The Maine and Vermont three-decade studies of serious mental illness: Longitudinal course comparisons. In P. Cohen & C. Slomkowski (Eds.), *Historical and geographical influences on psychopathology* (pp. 331 348). Farmingdale, ME: Lawrence Erlbaum Associates.

Dollard, M. F., & Winfield, A. H. (1995). Trait anxiety, work demand, social support and psychological distress in correctional officers. *Anxiety Stress and Coping, 8*(1), 22-35.

Falvo, D. R. (1999). *Medical and psychosocial aspects of chronic illness and disability* (2nd ed.). Gaithersburg, MD: Aspen Publishers.

Fogarty, G. J., Machin, M. A., Albion, M. J., Sutherland, L. F., Lalor, G. I., & Revitt, S. (1999). Predicting occupational strain and job satisfaction: The role of stress, coping personality, and affective variables. *Journal of Vocational Behavior, 54*(3), 429-452.

Frankenhaeuser, M. (1991). A biopsychosocial approach to work life issues. In J.V. Johnson & G. Johansson (Eds.), *The psychosocial work environment: Work organization, democratization, and health* (pp. 49-60). New York: Baywood.

Gates, L. B. (2000). Workplace accommodations as a social process. *Journal of Occupational Rehabilitation, 10*(1), 85-98.

Hall, E. M. (1991). Gender, work control, and stress: A theoretical discussion and an empirical test. In J.V. Johnson & G. Johansson (Eds.), *The psychosocial work environment: Work organization, democratization, and health* (pp. 89-108). New York: Baywood.

Hesse, B. W. (1995). Using telework to accommodate the needs of employees with disabilities. *Journal of Organizational Computing and Electronic Commerce, 6*(4), 327-343.

Hone, K. S., Kerrin, M., & Cox, T. (1998). CORDiT: A multi-dimensional model for evaluating the psychological impact of teleworking. *European Psychologist, 3*(3), 227-237.

Hurrell, J. J., McLaney, M. A., & Murphy, L. R. (1990). The middle years: Career stage differences. *Prevention in Human Services, 8*(1), 179-203.

Huuhtanen, P. (1997). Toward a multilevel model in longitudinal studies on computerization in offices. *International Journal of Human-Computer Interaction, 9*(4), 383-405.

Jahoda, M. (1981). Work, employment, and unemployment: Values, theories, and approaches in social research. *American Psychologist, 36*, 184-191.

Johansson, G. (1991). Job demands and stress reactions in repetitive and uneventful monotony at work. In J. V. Johnson, & G. Johansson (Eds.), *The psychosocial work environment: Work organization, democratization, and health* (pp. 61-72). New York: Baywood.

Johnson, J. V. (1991). Collective control: Strategies for survival in the workplace. In J. V. Johnson, & G. Johansson (Eds.), *The psychosocial work environment: Work organization, democratization, and health* (pp. 121 132). New York: Baywood.

Johnson, J. V., & Johansson, G. (1991). *The psychosocial work environment: Work organization, democratization, and health.* New York: Baywood.

Karasek, R. & Theorell, T. (1990). *Healthy work: Stress, productivity, and the reconstruction of working life.* New York: Basic Books.

Kirsh, B. (2000). Organizational culture, climate and person-environment fit: Relationships with employment outcomes for mental health consumers. *Work: A Journal of Prevention, Assessment, and Rehabilitation, 14*, 109-122.

Koch, L. C. (1999). Career development interventions for transition-age youths with disabilities. *Work: A Journal of Prevention, Assessment, and Rehabilitation, 13*, 3-11.

Koch, L. C., & Johnston-Rodriguez, S. (1997). The career portfolio: A vocational rehabilitation tool for assessment, planning, and placement. *Journal of Job Placement and Development, 13*(1), 19-22.

Krause, J. (1996). Employment after spinal cord injury: Transition and life adjustment. *Rehabilitation Counseling Bulletin, 39*(4), 244-255.

Krause, J., & Anson, C. A. (1997). Adjustment after spinal cord injury: Relationship to participation in employment or educational activities. *Rehabilitation Counseling Bulletin, 40*(3), 202-214.

Landy, F. J. (1992). Work design and stress. In G. P. Keita & S. L. Sauter (Eds.), *Work and well-being: An agenda for the 1990's* (pp. 119-158). Washington, DC: American Psychological Asociation.

Lennon, M. C., & Rosenfield, S. (1992). Women and mental health: The interaction of job and family conditions. *Journal of Health and Social Behavior, 33*(4), 316-327.

Levi, L. (2000). Stressors at the workplace: Theoretical models. *Occupational Medicine, 15*(1), 69-105.

Loher, B. T., Noe, R. A., Moeller, N. L., & Fitzgerald, M. P. (1985). A meta analysis of the relation of job characteristics to job satisfaction. *Journal of Applied Psychology, 70,* 280-289.

Lustig, D. C., Rosenthal, D. A., Strauser, D. R., & Haynes, K. (2000). The relationship between sense of coherence and adjustment in persons with disabilities. *Rehabilitation Counseling Bulletin, 43*(3), 134-141.

McColl, M. A., Stirling, P., Walker, J., Corey, P., & Wilkins, R. (1999). Expectations of independence and life satisfaction among ageing spinal cord injury adults. *Disability and Rehabilitation, 21*(5-6), 231-240.

McDonough, P. (2000). Job insecurity and health. *International Journal of Health Services, 30*(3), 453-476.

McLaney, M. A., & Hurrell, J. J. (1988). Control, stress, and job satisfaction in Canadian nurses. *Work and Stress, 2*(3), 217-224.

Mikkelsen, A., Saksvik, P. O., Eriksen, H. R., & Ursin, H. (1999). The impact of learning opportunities and decision authority on occupational health. *Work & Stress, 13*(1), 20-31.

Milpied, M. (1995). Telework for people with disabilities: Opportunities, stakes and limits. *European Journal of Teleworking, 2*(1), 243-246.

Mokhtarian, P. L., Bagley, M. N., & Salomon, I. (1998). The impact of gender, occupation, and the presence of children on telecommuting motivations and constraints. *Journal of the American Society for Information Science, 49*(12), 1115-1134.

Moyle, P. (1995). The role of negative affectivity in the stress process: Tests of alternative models. *Journal of Organizational Behavior, 16*(6), 647-668.

Muchinsky, P. M. (2000). *Psychology applied to work* (6th ed.). Belmont, CA: Wadsworth/Thomson Learning.

Patterson, J. B. (1996). Occupational and labor market information and analysis. In E. M. Szymanski & R. M. Parker (Eds.), *Work and disability: Issues and strategies in career development and job placement* (pp. 209-254). Austin, TX: Pro-Ed.

Perry, D. A. (1995). The information age: What it means for business and vocational rehabilitation. Switzer Monograph, (18th ed., *Vocational rehabilitation: Preparing for the 21st century,* 24-36.

Priebe, S., Warner, R., Hubschmid, T., & Eckle, I. (1998). Employment, attitudes toward work, and the quality of life among people with schizophrenia in three countries. *Schizophrenia Bulletin, 24*(3), 469-477.

Prusti, S., & Branholm, I. B. (2000). Occupational roles and life satisfaction in psychiatric outpatients with vocational disabilities. *Work, 14*(2), 145 149.

Reskin, B. F., McBrier, D. B., & Kmec, J. A. (1999). The determinants and consequences of workplace sex and race composition. *Annual Review of Sociology, 25,* 335-361.

Robinson, J. E. (2000). Access to employment for people with disabilities: Findings of a consumer-led project. *Disability and Rehabilitation, 22*(5), 246-253.

Rumrill, P., Fraser, R., & Anderson, J. (2000). New directions in home based employment for people with disabilities. *Journal of Vocational Rehabilitation, 14,* 3-4.

Rumrill, P., & Roessler, R. (1999). New directions in vocational rehabilitation: A career development perspective on closure. *Journal of Rehabilitation, 65*(1), 26-30.

Sartawi, A. A. M., Abu-Hilal, M. M., & Qaryouti, I. (1999). The causal relationship between the efficacy of training programs and the work environment for workers with disabilities. *International Journal of Disability, Development & Education, 46*(1), 109-115.

Sauter, S., Hurrell, J. J., & Cooper, C. L. (1989). *Job control and worker health.* New York: Wiley.

Schoeffel, P., Loveridge, A., & Davidson, C. (1993). Telework: Issues for New Zealand. *Prometheus, 11*(1), 45-60.

Smith, M. J., Conway, F. T., & Karsh, B. T. (1999). Occupational stress in human interaction. *Industrial Health, 37,* 157-173.

Standen, P., Daniels, K., & Lamond, D. (1999). The home as a workplace: Work-family interaction and psychological well-being in telework. *Journal of Occupational Health, 4*(4), 368-381.

Stephens, C. & Long, N. (2000). Communication with police supervisors and peers as buffers of work-related traumatic stress. *Journal of Organizational Behavior, 21*(4), 407-424.

Sutherland, V. J., & Cooper, C. L. (1993). Identifying distress among general practitioners: Predictors of psychological ill-health and job dissatisfaction. *Social Science and Medicine, 37*(5), 575-581.

Syme, S. L. (1991). Social epidemiology and the work environment. In J. V. Johnson, & G. Johansson (Eds.), *The psychosocial work environment: Work organization, democratization, and health* (pp. 21-32). New York: Baywood.

Szymanski, E. M. (1999). Disability, job stress, the changing nature of careers, and the career resilience portfolio. *Rehabilitation Counseling Bulletin, 42,* 279-289.

Traiforos, A. (1995). Vocational rehabilitation: Preparing for the 21st Century - a labor perspective. Switzer Monograph, 18th ed., *Vocational rehabilitation: preparing for the twenty-first century,* 37-42.

Van der Dorf, M., & Maes, S. (1999). The job demand-control-support model and psychological well-being: A review of 20 years of empirical research. *Work & Stress, 13*(2), 87-114.

Van der Dorf, M., Maes, S., & Diekstra, R. (2000). An examination of the job demand-control-support model with various occupational strain indicators. *Anxiety Stress and Coping, 13*(2), 165-185.

Wall, T. D., & Clegg, C. W. (1981). A longitudinal field study of group work redesign. *Journal of Occupational Behavior, 2,* 31-49.

Warr, P. B. (1994). A conceptual framework for the study of mental health. *Work and Stress, 8*(2), 84-97.

Webb, C. R., Wrigley, M., Yoels, W., & Fine, P. R. (1995). Explaining quality of life for persons with traumatic brain injuries two years after injury. *Archives of Physical Medicine and Rehabilitation, 76*(12), 1113-1119.

Wellman, B., Salaff, J., Dimitrova, D., Garton, L., Guila, M., & Haythornwaite, C. (1996). Computer networks as social networks: Collaborative work, telework, and virtual community. *Annual Review of Sociology, 22*, 213-238.

Zedeck, S., & Mosier, K. L. (1990). Work in the family and employing organization. *American Psychologist, 45*, 240-251.

Chapter 6

POST-EMPLOYMENT SERVICES IN VOCATIONAL REHABILITATION: PICKING UP WHERE JOB PLACEMENT LEAVES OFF

PHILLIP RUMRILL AND LYNN KOCH

INTRODUCTION

The purpose of this chapter is to 1) make a case for increased emphasis on postemployment services in the state-federal vocational rehabilitation (VR) program and 2) present specific recommendations to guide VR counselors in helping clients maintain employment. Career development theory, VR regulations, and the disappointing employment outcomes reported by former VR clients all point to the need for improved services once people with disabilities have been placed on jobs. Yet, pressures to remove clients from caseloads due to fiscal constraints continue to make it difficult for rehabilitation professionals to provide the postemployment supports that employed VR clients need.

We begin this chapter with a rationale for providing more comprehensive postemployment services, framed in theoretical, regulatory, outcome, and needs-based terms. Then, we suggest reforms in the VR system that would enable counselors to more effectively meet the long-term career development needs of people with disabilities. Finally, we describe specific intervention strategies that have the potential to enhance VR clients' prospects for ongoing career success after VR services have been discontinued. By broadening the scope of rehabilitation services to more adequately reflect the needs of people with disabilities, our aim is to highlight the importance of postemployment services in today's competitive global marketplace.

RATIONALES FOR IMPROVED POSTEMPLOYMENT SERVICES IN VR

Several issues related to the state-federal VR program point to the need for an increased emphasis on postemployment services. These include contemporary career development theories, regulations of the Rehabilitation Act, postrehabilitation outcomes reported by VR clients, and the expressed needs of people with disabilities for these services.

A Career Orientation for Vocational Rehabilitation Services

In any discussion of the future of VR services in the United States, employment in competitive, integrated work settings is invariably described as the ultimate goal of the rehabilitation process. More specifically, rehabilitationists generally agree that long-term career success for people with disabilities is the objective that should guide case planning and service delivery (Hershenson & Szymanski, 1999). Hershenson (1996) and Rubin and Roessler (1995) noted that the essence of the VR counselor's role is to assist people with disabilities in seeking, securing, and maintaining employment, but actualizing this broad commitment to employment assistance will require the VR process to shift its focus in client services from the concept of occupational choice to the concept of career development. Occupational choice refers to choosing a job at a single point in time, whereas career development refers to a lifelong process of preparing to choose, choosing, and continuing to choose (Szymanski & Hershenson, 1998). Career development and the related service of career counseling are prominent themes in contemporary articles which have called for reforms in the way VR services are delivered (Fraser, 1999; Merz & Harvey, 1998; Rumrill & Roessler, 1999; Strauser, Waldrop, & Ketz, 1999; Szymanski, 1999; Szymanski & Hershenson, 1998). However, in current practice, VR services are limited primarily to helping people seek and secure employment, activities that are more reflective of the concept of occupational choice than of the concept of career development (Roessler & Rumrill, 1995a; Rumrill & Koch, 1998).

Hershenson (1996) pinpointed work adjustment, a process that begins once the person has secured employment, as a phase of career development that is different for people with disabilities than it is for nondisabled people. He noted that, for people with disabilities, the availability of rehabilitation services during the early stages of their jobs is a critical factor in their ability to adjust to and maintain employment. Unfortunately, as can be inferred from the disappointing job retention outcomes reported by former VR clients (described later in this chapter), work adjustment services in the current VR program appear to be insufficient as a means of helping workers establish and maintain successful careers.

Strauser et al. (1999) applied existing theories of work personality to Hershenson's (1996) theory of work adjustment. They noted that many VR clients who are in the initial stages of their careers have not yet fully developed their work personalities. Accordingly, the authors recommended intensive career counseling during the postemployment phase of the rehabilitation process as a means of helping workers with disabilities to formulate long-range career goals that are compatible with personal characteristics such as interests, skills, and aptitudes.

In his theory of career adjustment, Crites (1976) proposed that longevity on the job is primarily determined by the worker's ability to overcome thwarting conditions, or barriers, to career success. Common career adjustment barriers reported by workers with disabilities include inaccessible work sites, negative attitudes of coworkers, changes in health status, unavailability of reasonable accommodations, and employer discrimination. Because career development is viewed as both a process (of ongoing choice and planning) and an outcome (of successful employment in satisfying jobs; Osipow & Fitzgerald, 1996; Szymanski, Hershenson, Enright, & Ettinger, 1996), the career-oriented VR counselor must more effectively assist clients in overcoming work-related barriers than is presently the case in the VR program. Another basis for strengthening the career orientation of the VR process can be found in the second edition of the *Guide for Occupational Exploration* (Harrington & O'Shea, 1984). The authors present a self-directed strategy for using information about one's interests, work values, and preferred daily activities in career planning.

Harrington and O'Shea asserted that an appropriate occupational choice, by definition, takes into consideration the long-term career relevance of that job. Questions like "Would I like this kind of work well enough to do it for a career?" and "What are my chances of getting higher-level jobs in this field?" are essential considerations in the planning, placement, and work adjustment (i.e., postemployment) phases of the rehabilitation process if clients are to parlay their occupational choices into future career success (Rumrill & Roessler, 1999).

In 1991, members of the National Leadership Summit Meeting advanced the concept of "personal careers" as an important consideration in improving VR services (Rumrill & Roessler, 1999; Washington Public Affairs Center, 1991, p. 8). Rumrill and Roessler (1999, p. 27) operationalized the term "personal careers" using the following statements which they selected from the Summit Meeting report:

1. A career implies a lifelong process of personal futures planning that is based on the individual's choice to participate.
2. A personal futures plan is based on self-determination principles and self-satisfaction. It is oriented to a personal vision of the future.
3. Career choice is based on informed decision making and work experiences.
4. A career allows for job changes, flexibility, success, failure, with no minimum or maximum hours of work.
5. A career provides access to quality technology to improve learning, performance, communication, independence, and interdependence.

Bringing theory together with practice, Super's (1980) Life-Career Rainbow Stage model of career development provides a framework for the specific tasks that need to be addressed in postemployment VR services. Encompassing adolescent and adult development, Super's model consists of five stages: growth, exploration, establishment, maintenance, and decline. Across those stages, Super presented career development as a lifelong, fluid process marked by critical life changes –changes in priorities, in resources, in motivation, and in ability to perform career related tasks (Super, Savickas, & Super, 1996). From a VR perspective, these life changes are likely to result in changing needs for services and assistance over time. The stages of exploration, establishment, and maintenance are especially relevant to the provision of postemployment VR services.

Exploration

Tasks of the exploration stage include crystallizing, specifying, and implementing a vocational choice (Super et al., 1996). The end result of a successful exploration, that is, implementation of a vocational choice, involves selecting and securing a good job, one that is compatible with the person's long-term career goals. Successful completion of the exploration stage requires the person to examine and compare job options using qualitative criteria. These criteria could include compatibility of the job with the person's interests, aptitudes, and training; the job's potential to meet the person's needs regarding earnings and fringe benefits; and the opportunities for promotion and advancement. If clients do not complete exploration tasks satisfactorily, they may become fixed in secondary labor market positions with little future. Thus, the resulting career path for people with disabilities resembles a ladder tipped on its side, marked by lateral occupational changes from one entry-level job to another (Roessler & Bolton, 1985; Rumrill & Roessler, 1999).

Establishment

The establishment stage includes the critical tasks of stabilization, consolidation, and advancement in one's position. These three steps are essential in the career development process for people with (and without) disabilities. Dix and Savickas (1995) specified six developmental tasks involved in establishing one's career: adapting to the organizational structure, achieving a satisfactory level of position performance, relating well to coworkers, maintaining productive work habits, advancing on the job, and making future career plans. Because many VR clients in the early stages of career establishment have limited work histories, they are likely to require extensive supports to complete these and other work adjustment tasks (Parker, Szymanski, & Hanley-Maxwell, 1989).

Maintenance

Tasks of Super's (1980) maintenance stage require coping successfully with on-the-job stressors (Crites, 1976) so that the person not only retains but also advances in his or her job (Super et al., 1996). On-the-job stressors are both positive, such as opportunities for training and self-development, and negative, such as employer discrimination, physical barriers in the workplace, instances of poor job/person matches, and interpersonal conflicts with one's supervisor or coworkers (Roessler, 1989). As in the establishment stage, extended postemployment follow-up services from VR counselors would likely increase the probability of workers achieving positive career maintenance outcomes, which currently is not the case for the majority of VR clients. Not only do these services make sense from a theoretical perspective, they are compatible with VR regulations.

A Regulatory Rationale

Career development theory provides a framework for implementing improved post-employment services in VR, and there are two mechanisms in the regulations governing the VR process which allow counselors to provide services and supports for clients who have been placed on jobs. First, the Rehabilitation Services Administration requires VR counselors to wait at least 90 days after a client has acquired employment before closing his or her case in Status 26 (successfully rehabilitated). Second, even after the client's case has been closed, the counselor has the prerogative to re-open the case in Status 32 (Post-Employment Services). Brabham, Mandeville, and Koch (1998) described Status 32 as follows:

> Cases of clients served in this status must have been previously closed rehabilitated in Status 26. Cases are placed in this status to provide simple, short-term services for the purpose of maintaining, regaining, or advancing a client's employment. There is no arbitrary time limit imposed on the provision of post-employment services. The anticipated need for post-employment services must be assessed upon the formulation of the Individualized Written Rehabilitation Plan (IWRP, now known as the Individualized Plan for Employment) and prior to case closure in Status 26 (p. 52).

Indeed, the regulatory mechanism for postemployment services in VR is in place. However, in practice, VR services tend to diminish rapidly in both scope and intensity as soon as the client starts a job. For example, in an in-depth qualitative study of 14 exemplary VR counselors in Arkansas, Mullins (1995) found that the period between initial job placement and case closure (i.e., work adjustment [Hershenson, 1996] and career establishment [Super, 1980]) constituted one of the least active phases of the rehabilitation process from a service provision standpoint. As for postemployment services under Status 32, Roessler and Rumrill (1995a) pointed out that pressure to remove clients from caseloads due to shrinking fiscal resources often precludes VR counselors from providing the career maintenance services that clients need. In fact, Pumpian, Fisher, Certo, and Smally (1997) reported that less than one percent of the Rehabilitation Services Administration's annual budget is expended on post-employment services for VR clients.

An Outcome-Based Rationale

Despite theoretical and regulatory support for the provision of postemployment VR services, the lack of these services is reflected in the poor postrehabilitation employment outcomes that have been reported by former clients for many years. For example, Roessler and Bolton (1985) documented a "lateral movement phenomenon" in their follow-up survey of 57 former VR clients with various disabilities. Respondents' career patterns consisted primarily of transfers from one entry-level job to another, often interspersed with extended periods of unemployment. Neubert, Tilson, and Ianacone (1989) also substantiated the difficulties that people with disabilities encounter in holding jobs following initial placement. Their study of 66 people with disabilities who had completed a postsecondary transition program revealed an encouraging 68 percent employment rate at a one-year follow-up. However, 36 percent of those participants who were employed had not been continuously employed for the entire one-year period. Moreover, participants' occupational changes during the follow-up period were consistent with Roessler and Bolton's (1985) lateral pattern.

Perhaps the strongest case in favor of improved postemployment services for people with disabilities lies in data reported by Gibbs

(1990). In a follow-up survey of 2,536 former VR clients whose cases had been closed as successfully rehabilitated, Gibbs found initial periods of employment of less than three months among more than 25 percent of respondents. One year after case closure, only 51 percent were still employed. During Gibbs's 54-month observation period, 84.4 percent of these successful rehabilitants experienced some interruption of employment, and many were not re-employed during the course of the longitudinal study.

Similarly disappointing long-term outcomes of the VR process have been reported by the United States General Accounting Office (1993). Two years after "successful" case closure, rehabilitants' mean income drops below the income that they reported at the time of enrollment in the VR program (United States General Accounting Office, 1993). Following successful rehabilitants for an eight-year period reveals that two-thirds of these former clients (whose cases were closed because they had obtained competitive employment) have experienced an interruption in employment lasting at least one year (United States General Accounting Office, 1993). If the ultimate purpose of the VR program is to prepare clients for long-term career success (Hershenson, 1996; Rumrill & Roessler, 1999; Strauser et al., 1999; Szymanski, 1999; Washington Public Affairs Center, 1991), the seemingly short-term impact of VR services appears to be incompatible with that mission. Follow-up postemployment services that focus on work adjustment and career maintenance are needed to improve these bleak postrehabilitation outcomes.

A Needs-Based Rationale

Recent research indicates that people with disabilities recognize the potential importance of VR postemployment services to their initial work adjustment and ultimate career success. Rumrill, Roessler, and Koch (1999) reported that a random sample of 227 people with multiple sclerosis expressed high levels of interest in such career maintenance assistance as assistive technology training, consultation regarding health and long-term disability insurance, and information about requesting on the-job accommodations from employers. Similarly, in a needs assessment survey of 35 employed rehabilitants who are blind (Rumrill, Roessler, Battersby, & Schuyler, 1998), one of the respondents' top priorities was to identify and implement reasonable accommodations in the workplace that would enable them to keep their jobs. Specifically, these workers cited the VR system as an important resource with respect to assistive technology, self-advocacy training, planning for promotion and advancement, and transportation.

In intensive interviews with a small sample of recent college graduates with disabilities, Roessler and Rumrill (1995b) found that even well trained, successfully employed rehabilitants had major concerns about their prospects for continued career success. As they address Super's (1980) establishment and maintenance stages (i.e., attempt to hold good jobs), people with disabilities face postemployment concerns such as the cost of assistive devices (Rumrill, 1999; Scherer, 1990); the implications of changing jobs within the same company (Habeck, 1999; Shrey & LaCerte, 1997; Sumner, 1995); and access to fringe benefits, fair treatment and pay, and long-term support networks (Roessler & Schriner, 1991; Roessler & Rumrill, 1995b). In a job retention study involving more than 300 workers with chronic illnesses, Sumner (1995) identified communication problems with employers, the need for extended medical leave, and a perceived lack of promotion and advancement opportunities as prominent career maintenance barriers that could be addressed in VR postemployment services.

Understanding disability-related employment laws such as the Americans with Disabilities Act (ADA) and the Family and Medical Leave Act (FMLA) is another area of postemployment support in which people with disabilities have expressed service needs (McMahon & Domer, 1997; Palmer, 1998). Discrimination, negative attitudes, and stereotypes can also present ongoing counseling issues after the client has been placed in a job, especially for people whose disabling conditions are highly stigmatizing (e.g., psychiatric disabilities, HIV/AIDS; Fabian, 1999; McReynolds, 1998; Merz & Harvey, 1998). Coworkers and supervisors may have misconceptions about specific disabilities that affect how the worker with a disability is treated on the job (Hagner, Fesko, Cadigan, Kiernan, & Butterworth, 1996) –and the worker could benefit from counseling to assist him or her in coping with (and possibly changing) those responses. For example, Millington, Szymanski, and Hanley-Maxwell (1994) found that the label of mental retardation adversely affects employers' expectations, even when documentation of the worker's ability to succeed on the job is provided. In that regard, postemployment services from the VR counselor could help the worker to educate the employer about his or her abilities to do the job, or the counselor could provide supported employment services during the initial work period to alleviate the employer's concerns about the worker's job performance. People with a wide range of physical and psychiatric disabilities have also reported needs for services to help them in overcoming negative coworker attitudes (McReynolds, 1998; Merz & Harvey, 1998), barriers related to the accessibility of the worksite (Allaire, 1998; Krause, 1996; LaRocca, 1995), and problems in securing medical leave (Rumrill, Nutter, Hennessey, & Ware, 1998). To assist rehabilitants in overcoming disability-related barriers (and redressing employer discrimination), VR counselors should be prepared to provide conflict resolution and/or self advocacy training in a postemployment venue (Palmer, 1998).

RECOMMENDED POLICY REFORMS TO PROMOTE POSTEMPLOYMENT SERVICES

Outcomes reported by former VR clients indicate that regulatory support for postemployment services has not yet translated into the work adjustment and career maintenance interventions that employed people with disabilities need. The option to re-open clients' cases in Status 32 for postemployment services is certainly encouraging, but it appears that this service category needs to be utilized more frequently by VR counselors. Also, the 90-day time frame between initial job placement and Status 26 case closure is simply too short for the client to engage in important work adjustment tasks–those that would be expected of any worker and those that are necessitated by his or her disability.

Rumrill and Roessler (1999) proposed two changes in VR regulations that could enhance clients' prospects for postemployment success. First, they recommended that guidelines for the rehabilitation planning process include criteria reflective of the tasks delineated in Super's (1980) exploration stage. They recommended that the client and counselor identify multiple, career-oriented employment options and compare those options systematically using qualitative criteria that reflect the developmental aspects of career choices. These criteria could include wage/salary levels; number of hours worked per week; level and type of fringe benefits; potential for cross-training and advancement; and compatibility with the person's education, training, and work personality. They also suggested applying those same criteria to case closure (i.e., career establishment) determinations, as a means of rewarding counselors for the quality, as well as quantity, of their placement outcomes. Not only would this measure strengthen the career development orientation of the VR process, it would also reduce the likelihood of a poor job-person match and subsequent service recidivism; clients would keep their jobs longer and be less apt to require additional services to achieve alternate employment goals.

Rumrill and Roessler's (1999) second recommendation involved expanding the current 90-day time frame between initial job placement and Status 26 case closure. During this critical stage of work adjustment and career establishment, counselors are encouraged to assist clients in removing or reducing job-related barriers that have the potential to thwart the worker's career development (Crites, 1976). Many of these work adjustment barriers can be minimized by reasonable accommodations under Title I of the ADA. Other barriers, such as socialization difficulties with coworkers or problems associated with responding to supervisors' expectations, may result from the person not having fully developed his or her work personality (Strauser et al., 1999). Regular contact with the VR counselor during this important phase could assist clients in clarifying their work values, temperaments, and reinforcer needs—all of which are important factors in the crystallization of a future-minded career choice.

POSTEMPLOYMENT SERVICE STRATEGIES TO ADDRESS THE CAREER DEVELOPMENT ORIENTATION OF THE VR PROCESS

Regulatory changes regarding postemployment services will help improve the disappointing career outcomes reported by former VR clients only if they are implemented at the individual, counselor-client level. Rumrill and Koch (1998) outlined a range of postemployment services which could be provided by career maintenance specialists— trained rehabilitation professionals who focus on providing services designed to aid employed clients in taking control of their career success. Interventions that could become the purview of career maintenance specialists include case management related to work supports, consultation with employers, job analysis and accommodation planning, information concerning disability legislation such as the ADA and the FMLA, career maintenance clubs, career portfolios, and career advancement counseling.

Case Management Related to Work Supports

One way to conceptualize postemployment services in VR is to think of them as work supports, not just for people with the most severe disabilities (e.g., supported employment) but for any VR client who needs on-the-job assistance. The primary functions of the rehabilitation professional in this expanded work supports capacity include:

1. identifying barriers to job retention and needed on-the-job supports;
2. developing a job retention plan to eliminate or reduce barriers to career maintenance;
3. linking clients to other resources in the community and at the job site that can provide natural supports (Trach, Beatty, & Sheldon, 1998);
4. implementing and coordinating services identified on the job retention plan;
5. monitoring service delivery by maintaining a regular schedule of contact with the client, the employer, and other service providers; and
6. conducting a review of the client's status to ascertain whether adjustments to the plan are needed (Hodge & Draine, 1993; Parker, Szymanski, & Hanley-Maxwell, 1989; Reed & Rumrill, 1997).

In carrying out the work supports case management functions delineated in the preceding paragraph, the rehabilitation professional must develop successful employer relationships, a commitment to client choice, interagency cooperation, natural supports at the job site, and behaviorally-based criteria for client and program evaluation. He or she must also collaborate with professionals from a variety of other disciplines (e.g., job developers, job coaches, special educators, school counselors, psychologists, medical specialists, occupational therapists, speech pathologists, physical therapists, rehabilitation engineers; Gardner & Chapman, 1993; Szymanski, Hanley-Maxwell, & Parker, 1990). The employee, his or her family members, and the employer are actively involved in the interdisciplinary process, as well. In the next section, we talk more specifically about the employer's role in providing postemployment work supports for people with disabilities.

Consultation with Employers

Employers have been described as the "missing link" between successful job placement and long-term career success for rehabilitation clients (Roessler & Rumrill, 1995a), and the need to recruit members of the business community to assist with the design and delivery of postemployment interventions has been identified in numerous publications (Bissonnette, 1994; Habeck, 1999; Millington & Strauser, 1998; Rumrill & Koch, 1997). Bissonnette (1994) suggested that if VR counselors are to directly involve employers in the rehabilitation process, they must "cultivate an equal exchange of resources" that empowers both parties to "give and receive rather than to wield and take" (p. 93). In a similar vein, Rumrill (1996) proposed a "reciprocal benefit model" (p. 177) whereby employers are included as intervention specialists in job placement and retention programs, and VR counselors reciprocate by providing technical assistance and consultation regarding the ADA and disability management. This model serves the needs of both the employer who must hire and retain qualified workers in a manner that complies with federal civil rights mandates and the VR counselor who must assist clients to obtain and retain good jobs.

As members of the rehabilitation partnership, employers provide "real world" perspectives on the labor market, direct referrals to job opportunities, and professional networking opportunities that can be very important to the client's ability to retain employment and advance in his or her career (Rumrill & Koch, 1997). VR counselors can gain input from members of the local business community by establishing employer advisory boards that meet on a regular basis. Employers also can be called upon to mentor clients and provide training on job retention skills. In return, VR counselors can assist employers with such activities as recruiting qualified applicants with disabilities, developing nondiscriminatory hiring and promotion policies, educating managers about the provisions of Title I of the ADA, and promoting disability awareness among all employees (McMahon, Dancer, & Jaet, 1993). In the next section, we describe postemployment interventions that require partnerships with employers to identify and implement reasonable accommodations.

Job Analysis and Accommodation Planning

Because of the constantly changing American economy and the changing nature of work, the need to conduct job analyses and plan for worksite accommodations is not limited to the job placement phase of rehabilitation planning. Changes can occur at any point after the client's initial adjustment to a job that may necessitate these specific post-employment services. The introduction of new technology at the job site, increasing demands on the employee, staff turnover, and the initiation of new strategies for performing job tasks may require the rehabilitation professional to conduct a job analysis and/or to implement new accommodations if the employee is to continue to perform successfully in his or her position.

In Chapter 4, we listed the steps involved in conducting a job analysis and provided a sample job analysis report. We also described other tools (e.g., the Work Experience Survey, Employment Expectations Questionnaire, Barrier/Solution Worksheet) that can be used in assessment and planning to identify one's accommodation needs. These same tools can be used to assist the client with retaining employment. As is the case in assessment and planning, their purpose as postemployment interventions is to identify job accommodations needed for the client to effectively perform his or her job. Then, once worksite barriers and needs are identified, the client can work collaboratively with his or her employer to implement reasonable accommodations at the job site.

Roessler and Rumrill (1995a) proposed a "Three I" model of postemployment services, in which rehabilitation professionals aid people with disabilities in *identifying* their needs for on-the-job accommodations; *initiating* requests that their employers review their accommodation needs; and *implementing*, with employer assistance, cost effective accommodation strategies to reduce career development barriers. Palmer (1998) demonstrated a self-advocacy and conflict resolution intervention that could aid employed rehabilitation clients greatly in the implementation of Three I work adjustment strategies. His training focused on the conversational, cognitive, and behavioral skills that are required to navigate the accommodation process, using provisions of the ADA and the FMLA as an impetus for preparing people with disabilities to be their own "best experts" in matters of job retention. Palmer's intervention is consistent with ADA Title I regulations and emphasizes collaborative, nonadversarial decision making which brings employer and employee together as equal-strength partners in the worker's employment success.

Perhaps the best example of a comprehensive postemployment intervention that addresses clients' worksite accommodation needs is Project Alliance, a service of the National Multiple Sclerosis Society for workers with chronic illnesses (Sumner, 1995). Along with other job retention strategies such as needs assessments and self-advocacy training for employees, Project Alliance adds a "dual clientele" focus that views the employer as an important partner in the worker's success. The rationale for this emphasis is that employees and employers alike benefit when experienced, productive employees stay on the job. Furthermore, according to Sumner, employee turnover (not reasonable accommodations or workers' compensation premiums) is the most costly personnel expense for employers.

During its initial three-year demonstration, Project Alliance served more than 300 employed people with chronic illnesses and their employers at 14 sites nationwide. In fact, Rumrill (1996) reported that more than 85% of the participants in Project Alliance were still employed with the same employer after one year. The primary objectives of Project Alliance were to

1. engage the employee and employer in the process of examining current issues related to job performance;
2. gather information about the person's position (e.g., physical and cognitive requirements, essential and marginal functions, support systems);

3. identify barriers to successful job performance;
4. provide assistance to the employee and the employer in improving communication and in moving toward satisfactory resolution of the work-related issues;
5. assist the employer and employee in understanding the provisions of Title I of the ADA and how voluntary compliance can benefit all concerned; and
6. identify needs of the employee and employer with respect to reasonable accommodations that could aid the employee in satisfactorily performing job tasks (Sumner, 1995).

The rehabilitation professional's role in the Project Alliance intervention was to conduct an on-site job analysis and synthesize the analysis into a report that was presented to both the employee and the employer. Then, the rehabilitation professional followed up with the employee and employer for the next several weeks to assist in the implementation of reasonable accommodations and in consultation with recommended community resources. These are precisely the kinds of services that could be provided more systematically in VR if the time frame between job placement and case closure were expanded.

Information on Disability Legislation

One of the most valuable postemployment services that VR counselors can offer clients is training regarding the scope (and limitations) of their rights and responsibilities under federal laws such as the ADA and the FMLA (see Chapter 4). Direct consultation and referral services should be utilized to provide up-to-date information on the provisions, eligibility standards, grievance procedures, and remedies that are promulgated in the regulations governing those laws.

Chapter 5 includes a comprehensive overview of the ADA and the FMLA, but VR counselors need a more thorough understanding of these laws to meet the expressed postemployment needs of their clients. McMahon and Domer (1997) presented a detailed, side-by-side analysis of the ADA, FMLA, and state workers compensation statutes. The authors highlighted where these laws overlap, as well as areas in which they contradict each other. By understanding such key provisions of these laws as unpaid leave, reasonable accommodations, and return to work procedures, VR counselors can assist clients in interpreting these often complicated legal protections which can aid workers with disabilities in maintaining employment.

Career Maintenance Clubs

Expanding on the job club approach (Azrin & Besalel, 1980; Azrin, Flores, & Kaplan, 1977), the career maintenance club employs a small group format to address the postemployment concerns of workers with disabilities. It is an intensive behavioral counseling program based on the view of career maintenance as requiring work adjustment skills, knowledge of one's employment rights and responsibilities, awareness of community resources, family and community support, communication skills, accommodation planning abilities, self-advocacy skills, and promotion planning skills (Koch & Rumrill, in press).

Career maintenance clubs can be ongoing or time-limited, but ongoing meetings that allow participants to join and disengage from the group as needed are likely to be most helpful (Koch & Rumrill, in press). Peer support, individual goal setting, and resource networking are important components of club meetings. Meetings should be somewhat informal, but time should be set aside to teach and practice specific skills as well as to engage in client-driven discussions.

Topics that can be addressed in club meetings include initial adjustment to a new job, employer expectations, appropriate work habits, problem solving, lifestyle changes resulting from employment, reactions of family members to clients' employed status, effects of working on social security benefits, budgeting, appropriate socialization in the workplace, transportation, coworker attitudes, employment rights and responsibilities, and reasonable accommodations (Rumrill & Koch, 1998; Wolffe, 1997). Many of the postemployment interventions reviewed in this chapter can be incorporated into the career maintenance club.

Ideally, the career maintenance club is organized and facilitated by a rehabilitation professional with training in group process. General guidelines for setting up a career maintenance club include:

1. Gather and review information about establishing career-oriented group interventions that is applicable to designing the career maintenance club.
2. Develop a brief career maintenance club description that outlines the general structure, program goals, and targeted population.
3. Arrange a meeting with administrators, supervisors, and other rehabilitation professionals to describe the proposed career maintenance club, obtain input and support, and identify possible referrals.
4. Describe the specific objectives of the career maintenance club and develop a general outline of content to be covered at each session.
5. Schedule regular career maintenance club meetings and determine where the meetings will be held.
6. Recruit group participants from other rehabilitation professionals and secure an initial commitment from clients who are interested in attending club meetings.
7. Hold meetings on a regular basis (weekly or bi-weekly).
8. Evaluate the effectiveness of the career maintenance club with systematic research   studies and open-ended questionnaires that ask participants to identify those aspects of the meetings that were the most and least helpful.
9. Revise the career maintenance club format as needed to improve its effectiveness.

As a postemployment intervention, the career maintenance club incorporates powerful group dynamics into a mechanism for VR clients to examine their prospects for long-term job retention. It serves the added purpose of identifying additional VR services that employed clients will need to meet their career objectives. In that regard, career maintenance clubs constitute a potentially valuable postemployment service that is compatible with both career development theory and VR regulations.

Career Portfolios

The career portfolio is a collection of samples that demonstrate the client's work-related competencies, achievements, and aspirations

(Koch & Johnston-Rodriguez, 1997; Szymanski, 1999). As a postemployment intervention, the career portfolio serves the purpose of 1) storing and organizing information to enhance educational and career-related experiences and 2) self-monitoring the competencies needed to stay current in today's diversified and unpredictable employment arena (Koch, Schultz, & Cusick, 1998; Szymanski, 1999).

The contents and process of developing a career portfolio are highly individualized. In general, however, the samples included in the career portfolio represent the knowledge and skill domains of 1) career exploration and planning (e.g., vocational interest checklists, career decision-making worksheets); 2) training and education (e.g., diplomas, certificates, academic transcripts); 3) vocational skills (e.g., vocational evaluation reports, current resume, work samples, transferrable skills worksheets, employer evaluations, letters of recommendation); and 4) ongoing professional development (statement of future career goals, plan for achieving future goals, continuing education certificates). Samples that are included in the career portfolio reflect strengths (rather than weaknesses) and are updated as the client gains new knowledge and skills (Koch & Johnston-Rodriguez, 1997).

The role of the rehabilitation professional in the portfolio development process is to offer guidance and instruction to the client as needed, but the client assumes primary responsibility for determining the actual contents and structure of his or her portfolio. The steps involved in assembling the career portfolio typically require the client to:

1. Develop a list of all possible samples.
2. Narrow the list to include only those samples that best reflect his or her current attributes.
3. Make a list of samples that he or she would like to acquire through future learning and career-related experiences.
3. Collect the samples.
4. Organize the samples into separate piles according to skill or knowledge domain.
5. Assign categorical labels to each grouping of samples.
6. Arrange samples into career portfolio.
7. Update samples as new knowledge, skills, and experiences are acquired.
8. Keep a file or box of samples that are removed or replaced as a means of monitoring his or her professional development (Koch & Johnston Rodriguez, 1997).

The career portfolio has multiple uses as a postemployment intervention. Because it provides tangible evidence of one's continuing professional development and promotability, it enhances the client's career confidence. It also can be used to self-monitor one's needs for further training and to effectively communicate one's skills to future employers. The client can continue to use the career portfolio throughout his or her work life to manage future career challenges and opportunities. In that regard, it empowers the individual to assume personal control of the career development process, rather than relying on professionals to do this.

Career Advancement Counseling

Although many rehabilitation professionals work in settings where the objective of services is to help clients secure a single job, it is important that issues regarding career advancement be addressed if job retention is to occur (Habeck, 1999; Strauser et al., 1999). The specific job that is identified as the employment goal should be viewed as only one step on the career development ladder (Szymanski, Fernandez, Koch, & Merz, 1996) rather than the final and ultimate outcome of VR services. Accordingly, the VR counselor and client should explore how future career opportunities can be cultivated after the person's case file has been closed. This orientation is also compatible with Rumrill and Roessler's (1999) recommendation that VR case planning include qualitative assessments of the long-term career potential of the client's stated vocational goal.

Even within the context of time-limited services, the VR counselor can engage the client in career advancement planning activities. As the termination of services draws near, the rehabilitation professional and client can explore career advancement issues such as changing labor market trends and pursuant implications for career planning, future career goals, other life goals, utilizing transferable skills to achieve future goals, plans for continuing education, and personal and community resources for confronting future career challenges (Rumrill & Koch, 1998).

Because employment in the twenty-first century will require continuous updating of one's knowledge and skills to stay current with changing work trends, Schoffield (1996) recommended that all workers assemble a personal development plan (PDP). A PDP is a "clear and succinct summary of the individual's personal learning needs and an action plan to meet them" (Schoffield, 1996, p. 36). As a postemployment service, the rehabilitation professional can provide the client with individualized guidance in developing a PDP that specifies his or her short-term and long-term career advancement objectives, steps that will be taken to accomplish those objectives, a time frame for completion of each step, and the resources that will be utilized to achieve career goals. The PDP could then be incorporated into the client's career portfolio and used as a "jumping off point" for the career advancement counseling services recommended by Rumrill and Koch (1998) and Strauser et al. (1999).

SUMMARY

Career development theory and outcome studies conducted with former clients point to a strong need for improved postemployment services in the vocational rehabilitation program. Although VR regulations do allow counselors to provide services that could assist rehabilitants in the initial stages of work adjustment, the practical fact remains that there is simply not enough time or resources in the present configuration of the VR program to serve clients once they have been placed in their jobs.

We believe that the unavailability of effective job retention services in the VR program is more a matter of priority than it is a resource issue. We urge VR policy makers, practitioners, and consumers to examine more deeply the implications of discontinuing rehabilitation services too abruptly (90 days, in many cases) after the person has obtained employment. Case files are often closed before the employed client has been given enough time to go through the important work adjustment and career establishment tasks that have been identified by leading career theorists, and workers with disabilities need more assistance than is currently available if they are to parlay successful rehabilitation into long-term career success.

The VR counselor can improve clients' prospects for long-term employment success by adopting career-oriented, qualitative criteria in the formulation of the clients' career goals. Also within the scope of current VR regulations is the provision of such important postemployment services as case management, employer consultation, career advancement counseling, career portfolios, and career maintenance clubs. At a broader, regulatory level, the VR system must extend the current 90 day time frame between job placement and case closure. These changes in practice and policy could enable the VR system to more effectively respond to the long-term career development needs of people with disabilities. In so doing, rehabilitation professionals can continue what has been a long and distinguished tradition of timely, responsive, and outcome-oriented client services.

REFERENCES

Allaire, S. (1998). Vocational rehabilitation for persons with rheumatoid arthritis. *Journal of Vocational Rehabilitation, 10*(3), 253-260.

Azrin, N., & Besalel, V. (1980). *Job club counselor's manual: A behavioral approach to vocational counseling.* Austin, TX: Pro-Ed.

Azrin, N., Flores, T., & Kaplan, S. (1977). Job finding club: A group assisted program of obtaining employment. *Behavior Research and Therapy, 13,* 17 27.

Bissonnette, D. (1994). *Beyond traditional job development: The art of creating opportunity.* Chatsworth, CA: Milt Wright & Associates, Inc.

Brabham, R., Mandeville, K., & Koch, L. (1998). The state-federal vocational rehabilitation program. In R. Parker & E. Szymanski (Eds.), *Rehabilitation counseling: Basics and beyond* (3rd Ed.; pp. 41-70). Austin, TX: Pro-Ed.

Crites, J. (1976). A comprehensive model of career development in early adulthood. *Journal of Vocational Behavior, 9,* 105-118.

Dix, J., & Savickas, M. (1995). Establishing a career: Developmental tasks and coping responses. *Journal of Vocational Behavior, 47,* 93-107.

Fabian, E. (1999). Rethinking work: The example of consumers with serious mental health disorders. *Rehabilitation Counseling Bulletin, 42*(4), 302 316.

Fraser, R. T. (1999). Rehabilitation counselor placement-related attributes in the present economy: A project with industry perspective. *Rehabilitation Counseling Bulletin, 42*(4), 343-353.

Gardner, J. F., & Chapman, M. S. (1993). *Developing staff competencies for supporting people with developmental disabilities* (2nd ed.). Baltimore, MD: Paul H. Brookes Publishing Company.

Gibbs, W. (1990). Alternative measures to evaluate the impact of vocational rehabilitation services. *Rehabilitation Counseling Bulletin, 34*(1), 33-43.

Habeck, R. V. (1999). Job retention through disability management. *Rehabilitation Counseling Bulletin, 42*(4), 317-328.

Hagner, D., Fesko, S., Cadigan, M., Kiernan, W., & Butterworth, J. (1996). Securing employment: Job search and employer negotiation strategies in rehabilitation. In

E. Szymanski & R. Parker (Eds.), *Work and disability: Issues and strategies in career development and job placement* (pp. 309 340). Austin, TX: Pro-Ed.

Harrington, T., & O'Shea, A. (1984). *Guide for occupational exploration* (2nd ed.). Circle Pines, MN: American Guidance Association and National Forum Foundation.

Hershenson, D. (1996). A systems reformulation of a developmental model of work adjustment. *Rehabilitation Counseling Bulletin, 40*(1), 2-10.

Hershenson, D. B., & Szymanski, E. M. (1999). Vocational and career development in rehabilitation. *Rehabilitation Education, 13*(2), 105-112.

Hodge, M., & Draine, J. (1993). Development of support through case management services. In R.W. Flexer, & P. L. Solomon (Eds.), *Psychiatric rehabilitation in practice* (pp. 155-169). Boston: Andover Medical Publishers.

Koch, L., & Johnston-Rodriguez, S. (1997). The career portfolio: A vocational rehabilitation tool for assessment, planning, and placement. *Journal of Job Placement, 13*(1), 19-22.

Koch, L., & Rumrill, P. (in press). The career maintenance club: Improving rehabilitants' prospects for long-term employment success. *Journal of Job Placement.*

Koch, L., Schultz, D., & Cusick, J. (1998). Encouraging rehabilitation counseling students to develop a portfolio as a career development tool. *Rehabilitation Education, 12*(3), 261-267.

Krause, J. (1996). Employment after spinal cord injury: Transition and life adjustment. *Rehabilitation Counseling Bulletin, 39*(4), 244-255.

LaRocca, N. (1995). *Employment and multiple sclerosis: Current status and recommendations for services.* New York: National Multiple Sclerosis Society.

McMahon, B., Dancer, S., & Jaet, D. (1993). Providers of technical assistance and employers: Myths, concerns, and compliance behaviors related to the Americans with Disabilities Act. *Journal of the National Association of Rehabilitation Professionals in the Private Sector, 8*, 53 66.

McMahon, B., & Domer, T. (1997). Twenty questions surrounding unpaid medical leave: Navigating the Bermuda Triangle of employment law. *Work: A Journal of Prevention, Assessment, and Rehabilitation, 9*(2), 129-145.

McReynolds, C. (1998). Human immunodeficiency virus (HIV): The psychological and physiological effects of HIV in employment settings. Unpublished doctoral dissertation, University of Wisconsin-Madison.

Merz, M., & Harvey, R. (1998). Career development theory as a framework for assessment and planning in clubhouse-based transitional employment programs for people with psychiatric disabilities. *Work: A Journal of Prevention, Assessment, and Rehabilitation, 10*(3), 219-233.

Millington, M., & Strauser, D. (1998). Planning strategies in disability management. *Work: A Journal of Prevention, Assessment, and Rehabilitation, 10*(3), 261-270.

Millington, M., Szymanski, E., & Hanley-Maxwell, C. (1994). Effect of the label of mental retardation on employment concerns and selection. *Rehabilitation Counseling Bulletin, 38*(1), 27-43.

Mullins, J. (1995). A qualitative analysis of rehabilitation counseling for people with the most severe disabilities. Unpublished doctoral dissertation, University of Arkansas, Fayetteville.

Neubert, D. A., Tilson, G. P., & Ianacone, R. N. (1989). Postsecondary transition needs and employment patterns of individuals with mild disabilities. *Exceptional Children, 55*(6), 494-500.

Osipow, S., & Fitzgerald, L. (1996). *Theories of career development* (4th ed.). Boston: Allyn and Bacon.

Palmer, C. D. (1998). Self-advocacy and conflict resolution: Requesting academic accommodations at postsecondary education institutions. Unpublished doctoral dissertation, University of Arkansas, Fayetteville.

Parker, R., Szymanski, E., & Hanley-Maxwell, C. (1989). Ecological assessment in supported employment. *Journal of Applied Rehabilitation Counseling, 20*(3), 26-33.

Pumpian, L., Fisher, D., Certo, N., & Smally, K. (1997). Changing jobs: An essential part of career development. *Mental Retardation, 35*(1), 39-48.

Reed, C., & Rumrill, P. (1997). Supported employment: Principles and practices for interdisciplinary collaboration. *Work: A Journal of Prevention, Assessment, and Rehabilitation, 9*(3), 237-244.

Roessler, R. (1989). Motivational factors influencing return to work. *Journal of Applied Rehabilitation Counseling, 20*(1), 14-17.

Roessler, R. T., & Bolton, B. (1985). Employment patterns of former vocational rehabilitation clients and implications for rehabilitation practice. *Rehabilitation Counseling Bulletin, 28*, 179-187.

Roessler, R. T., & Rumrill, P. D., Jr. (1995a). Promoting reasonable accommodations: An essential post-employment service. *Journal of Applied Rehabilitation Counseling, 26*(4), 3-7.

Roessler, R. T., & Rumrill P. D., Jr. (1995b). The work experience survey: A strutured interview approach to worksite accommodation planning. *Journal of Job Placement, 11*(1), 15-19.

Roessler, R., & Schriner, K. (1991). Implications of selected employment concerns for disability policy and rehabilitation practice. *Rehabilitation Counseling Bulletin, 35*(1), 52-67.

Rubin, S. E., & Roessler, R. T. (1995). *Foundations of the vocational rehabilitation process* (4th ed.). Austin, TX: Pro-Ed.

Rumrill, P. (1996). *Employment issues and multiple sclerosis.* New York: Demos.

Rumrill, P. (1999). Effects of a social competence training program on accommodation request activity, situational self-efficacy, and Americans with Disabilities Act knowledge among employed people with visual impairments and blindness. *Journal of Vocational Rehabilitation, 12*(1), 25-31.

Rumrill, P., & Koch, L. (1997). Job placement revisited: Employers as interdependent members of a working alliance. *Journal of Job Placement, 13*(1), 26-29.

Rumrill, P., & Koch, L. (1998). The career maintenance specialist: Broadening the scope of successful rehabilitation. *Journal of Rehabilitation Administration, 22*(2), 111-122.

Rumrill, P., Nutter, D., Hennessey, M., & Ware, M. (1998). Job retention and breast cancer: Employee perspectives and implications for rehabilitation planning. *Work: A Journal of Prevention, Assessment, and Rehabilitation 10*(3), 251-259.

Rumrill, P., & Roessler, R. (1999). New directions in vocational rehabilitation: A career development perspective on closure. *Journal of Rehabilitation, 65*(1), 26-30.

Rumrill, P., Roessler, R., Battersby, J., & Schuyler, B. (1998). Situational assessment of the accommodation needs of employees who are visually impaired. *Journal of Visual Impairment and Blindness, 92*(1), 42-54.

Rumrill, P., Roessler, R., & Koch, L. (1999). Surveying the employment concerns of people with multiple sclerosis: A participatory action research approach. *Journal of Vocational Rehabilitation, 12*(2), 75-82.

Scherer, M. (1990). Assistive device utilization and quality of life in adults with spinal cord injuries or cerebral palsy two years later. *Journal of Applied Rehabilitation Counseling, 21*(4), 6-44.

Schoffield, P. (1996). Managers without portfolio. *Accountancy, 117*(230), 34-38.

Strauser, D., Waldrop, D., & Ketz, K. (1999). Reconceptualizing the work personality. *Rehabilitation Counseling Bulletin, 42*(4), 290-301.

Sumner, G. (1995). *Project Alliance: A job retention program for people with chronic illnesses and their employers.* New York: National Multiple Sclerosis Society.

Super, D. (1980). The relative importance of work: Models and measures for meaningful data. *The Counseling Psychologist, 10*(4), 95-103.

Super, D., Savickas, M., & Super, C. (1996). The life-span, life-space approach to careers. In D. Brown, L. Brooks, & Associates (Eds.), *Career choice and development* (3rd ed., pp. 121-178). San Francisco: Jossey Bass.

Szymanski, E. (1999). Disability, job stress, the changing nature of careers, and the career resilience portfolio. *Rehabilitation Counseling Bulletin, 42*(4), 279-289.

Szymanski, E., Hanley-Maxwell, C., & Parker, R. (1990). Transdisciplinary service delivery. In F. R. Rusch (Ed.), *Supported employment: Models, methods, and issues* (pp. 199-214). Sycamore, IL: Sycamore Publishing Company.

Szymanski, E., & Hershenson, D. (1998). Career development of people with disabilities: An ecological model. In R. Parker & E. Szymanski (Eds.), *Rehabilitation counseling: Basics and beyond* (3rd ed., pp. 327-378). Austin, TX: Pro-Ed.

Szymanski, E., Hershenson, D., Enright, M, & Ettinger, J. (1996). Career development theories, constructs, and research: Implications for people with disabilities. In E. Szymanski & R. Parker (Eds.), *Work and disability: Issues and strategies in career development and job placement.* (pp. 79 126). Austin, TX: Pro-Ed.

Szymanski, E., Fernandez, D., Koch, L., & Merz, M. (1996). *Career development: Planning for placement* (Training materials). Madison, WI: University of Wisconsin-Madison, Rehabilitation Research and Training Center on Career Development and Advancement.

Trach, J., Beatty, S., & Sheldon, D. (1998). Employers' and service providers' perspectives regarding natural supports in the work environment. *Rehabilitation Counseling Bulletin, 41*(4), 293-312.

United States General Accounting Office. (1993). *Vocational rehabilitation: Evidence for federal program's effectiveness is mixed.* Washington, DC: Author.

Washington Public Affairs Center. (1991). *National leadership summit meeting report.* Washington DC: Author.

Wolffe, K. (1997). *Career counseling for people with disabilities: A practical guide to finding employment.* Austin, TX: Pro-Ed.

Chapter 7

TRENDS AND ISSUES IN PROPRIETARY REHABILITATION

PATRICK L. DUNN

INTRODUCTION

Proprietary rehabilitation (also called *private-for-profit rehabilitation* or *insurance rehabilitation*) is concerned with providing services for individuals with disabilities that are compensible under any of a number of insurance systems. Proprietary rehabilitation has evolved from changes in the public vocational rehabilitation (VR) program, particularly from mandates to serve persons with more severe disabilities, and it has developed into a system distinct from the traditional state-federal program.

The first section of this chapter details the distinctiveness of proprietary rehabilitation from the state-federal VR program in relation to content and process of the two systems, with an emphasis placed upon defining key concepts in proprietary rehabilitation. In the second section of the chapter, emerging challenges to proprietary rehabilitation are discussed. These issues include impending changes in the standard occupational information upon which much of the vocational component of proprietary rehabilitation services are built, disability management as an emerging trend in industry, and the impact of the move to managed health care upon proprietary rehabilitation. The chapter concludes with a review of research concerning the fiscal efficacy of proprietary rehabilitation, which the author believes is a critical element in the continued growth of this sector of rehabilitation services.

PROPRIETARY REHABILITATION AND THE STATE-FEDERAL VOCATIONAL REHABILITATION PROGRAM: COMPARISONS AND CONTRASTS

In the early history of the rehabilitation programs, persons with work-related injuries were the primary focus of these efforts. The Smith-Fess Act of 1920 was the impetus for the creation of the state-federal VR program, and it originally targeted persons injured in industrial accidents as a primary population for service provision. Over time, the scope of populations served was extended to persons with physical disabilities, visual impairments, and cognitive disabilities (Weed & Field, 1986). Each progressive amendment to the mandates of the state-federal VR program expanded the range of services, encompassing a greater number of disability populations.

Current History

The enactment of the Rehabilitation Act of 1973 served as a watershed event in the practice of rehabilitation counseling. This act mandated the state-federal VR system to prioritize services toward individuals with the most significant (severe) disabilities. Significant disabilities are characterized by extreme functional limitation in the ability to sustain employment or other activities of daily living. Most industrial injuries, while often depriving the individual of the ability to return to his or her usual and customary work activity, are less disabling and, thus, not considered to be severe. With the passage of the 1973 legislation, the presence of injured workers in the state federal VR system became a rare occurrence (Siefker, 1992).

The de-emphasis of public rehabilitation on serving persons with work-related injuries coincided with (and many experts believe prompted) a renewed call for rehabilitation as part of the workers compensation insurance system. On the eve of the passage of the Rehabilitation Act of 1973, the 1972 National Commission on State Workers Compensation Laws encouraged states to create mechanisms for the rehabilitation of injured workers within their workers compensation bureaus (Growick, 1991). Since that time, most states have at least experimented with the notion of rehabilitation for injured workers by creating some type of provision within workers compensation statutes (United States Chamber of Commerce, 1991).

The void created in rehabilitation services for industrially injured workers was gradually filled by what have become known as private-for-profit or proprietary rehabilitation agencies. The need for such agencies was evident in their phenomenal growth during the 1970s and the 1980s. Berkeley Planning Associates (1987) estimated that proprietary rehabilitation doubled in size every other year until 1982. The companies that constitute the proprietary sector of rehabilitation vary greatly in size and scope, from small companies with a localized market to large, national corporations (Siefker, 1992). Some rehabilitation professionals in the proprietary sector serve as independent contractors, providing various services to larger companies or functioning as one person businesses.

Even though the expansion of the private sector has created a demand for competent and properly prepared practitioners, graduates may enter the profession with only a basic understanding of rehabilitation's private sector, or with mistaken notions about the policies and procedures of proprietary rehabilitation. In this chapter, the foundations of proprietary rehabilitation will be discussed, and its structure and goals will be contrasted with the public program.

Insurance and Workers Compensation: A Primer

Proprietary rehabilitation receives most referrals for services through contact with insurance companies. The principle of insurance is based upon the concepts of loss (i.e., the reduced value of property or other assets) and risk (i.e., the likelihood that a loss will occur) (Rasch, 1985). Individuals and organizations wishing to protect themselves from potential losses (referred to as the insured) may purchase insurance by paying premiums based upon the risk that a loss will take place. The company providing the insurance (referred to as the insurance carrier) will attempt to predict the likelihood of a loss by studying various statistical and historical trends associated with the item being insured and the party purchasing the insurance. Because insurance companies insure large numbers of persons, a pool of funds is established through the payment of premiums. This allows the company to have funds available if any particular insured party sustains a catastrophic loss (Gann & Moreland, 1992). Most individuals are familiar with insurance for automobiles, homes, health care, or other

common items. The most common form of insurance involved in proprietary rehabilitation is referred to as *workers' compensation*, which,
although bearing many similarities to other forms of casualty insurance, is different in many ways.

It is necessary to understand the history of workers' compensation
to fully appreciate the peculiarities of the system. The origins of workers' compensation laws are a product of the industrialization of the
United States in the late nineteenth and early twentieth centuries.
During these times, workers sustaining injuries on the job had only
one recourse: traditional tort law, in which one entity files suit against
another for redress of injury. Most injured workers received very little
compensation for their injuries due to three principles of common law
that employers could use in their defense. These principles were:

1. *Assumption of Risk.* This principle indicates that workers who chose
   to work for an employer should have been aware of hazards in
   the work environment. Having chosen employment in the conditions present at the workplace, the worker could assume that
   injury was likely to occur.
2. *The Fellow Servant Doctrine.* If an employee performed some action
   or was negligent in some way which resulted in another employee becoming injured (e.g, spilling oil on a floor), the employer
   could claim exemption from fault.
3. *Contributory Negligence.* If the employee could be shown to have
   been responsible for bringing about an unsafe condition, liability
   to the employer could be reduced or eliminated (Obermann,
   1965).

Because of the lack of consequences for employers whose workers
sustained on-the-job injuries, there was little improvement in working
conditions and little motivation to protect workers' health and safety
during America's early industrial years. Because of this situation,
workers were more likely to sustain injuries and, with little or no compensation, their livelihood and that of their dependents became the
province of social welfare and charity agencies (Gann & Moreland,
1992). As the incidence of work-related injuries increased, the social
cost of the new industrial reality became oppressive.

workers' compensation was conceived as a means to alleviate these
concerns. workers' compensation was designed as a "no-fault" system

of insurance; that is, when a worker sustains an injury, benefits are paid regardless of whether the worker, a fellow worker, or the employer caused the injury. Employers pay for the costs of the workers' compensation system through premiums (based upon the concepts of loss and risk), and employees receive medical treatment for the injury and a limited income maintenance payment until they are able to return to work. In return, the injured worker forfeits the prerogative of filing suit against the employer. Because workers' compensation statutes are the only course of redress for the injury, the workers' compensation system is referred to as an *exclusive remedy doctrine* (Decarlo & Minkowitz, 1989).

Many early workers' compensation laws were invalidated by the courts on the grounds that they violated both the employer's and the employee's constitutional right to due process. The first state workers' compensation statute to pass the court's muster was that of Wisconsin (1911), and within ten years 45 states and the federal government had established viable workers' compensation laws. Today, all 50 states have established workers' compensation laws, the last state to do so having been Mississippi, in 1948 (Gann & Moreland, 1992).

workers' compensation premiums paid by employers are based upon the amount of risk of injury that is present in the work environment. The best way to predict the likelihood that workers will become injured is to examine the quantity, frequency, and severity of previous injuries occurring in an employer's workforce. To reduce this level of risk (and thereby, the workers' compensation premium), it is in the employer's interest to pay attention to safety concerns and make necessary improvements. This is one of the key rationales behind the exclusive remedy doctrine of workers' compensation. Likewise, it is in the employer's interest for the injured worker to return to employment as soon as possible, and it is often toward that end that rehabilitation services will be extended to the injured worker.

Another form of insurance in which the proprietary rehabilitation system is often involved is long term disability. Long-term disability insurance is purchased by workers or their employers as an economic safeguard against illnesses or injuries which will prevent performance of work for a period of more than six months. In the case of long-term disability, the cause of illness or injury does not originate in the workplace. Most policies are structured so that the insured party may receive compensation for a period of time (typically up to two years) during which they are unable to perform the occupation *in which they had been employed at the time of the disability.* After this period of time has elapsed, the payment of disability compensation will continue if the insured is deemed to be unable to perform *any type of work.* It is customary for professionals in proprietary rehabilitation to become involved in long-term disability claims at this stage, usually under contract by the insurance carrier, to aid the claimant in obtaining employment. If a claimant becomes employed, this relieves the insurance carrier of some or all of the responsibility for compensating the claimant (Gann & Moreland, 1992).

Although workers' compensation and long-term disability are the two most common types of insurance in proprietary rehabilitation referrals, other types of insurance may occasionally be involved, such as product liability or automobile and casualty. The common thread connecting each type of insurance is that there may be a loss of vocational capacity for an individual which rehabilitation services may be able to restore.

The Structure of Proprietary and Public Rehabilitation Systems

Most professionals involved in the rehabilitation of persons with disabilities have at least some familiarity with the structure and function of the public VR program. Familiarity with the structure and function of proprietary rehabilitation is not as widely spread, even among rehabilitation counselors themselves.

The traditional source of rehabilitation services in the United States has been the state federal VR program. It has been so named as a result of joint funding, with the federal government providing matching funds to states to provide the operating budget of the program. There is a federal administration to oversee each state"s VR program at a broad policy level, whereas actual delivery of services is largely left to the states (Rubin & Roessler, 1995; Wright, 1980). At the federal level, the rehabilitation program is under the auspices of the Rehabilitation Services Administration (RSA), which is a section of the Office of Special Education and Rehabilitative Services (OSERS). OSERS is an office of the Department of Education. A commissioner who supervises ten regions each consisting of a number of states, heads RSA; each region also has its own commissioner. Aside from its administrative duties, RSA oversees federally funded rehabilitation research, special grant programs, continuing education programs, and other activities that are of national consequence.

At the state level, there is an agency known as the "Bureau of Vocational Rehabilitation" (or similar title), which is headed by its own administrator and which is part of each state's government services. The administrative headquarters of the agency are usually located in the state's capitol city. Under the auspices of the state headquarters are a number of satellite offices in which counselors work, thereby allowing them to serve persons with rehabilitation needs in close proximity to their home communities (Wright, 1980). Persons with disabilities who are served by the state VR system may be referred by a number of sources, including self-referral. If they meet certain criteria concerning eligibility, they receive services to assist them with securing suitable employment.

The structure of the proprietary rehabilitation system cannot be as easily described as the state-federal VR system. There is no national system for private sector rehabilitation services, and the structure of proprietary rehabilitation varies significantly from state to state. Because injured workers are such a large part of the proprietary rehabilitation caseload, and because each state has its own system of workers' compensation, any overview of the structure of proprietary rehabilitation must be general in nature, and any description is subject to many exceptions depending upon the state in question.

Perhaps the greatest distinction among state workers' compensation systems divides *voluntary* and *mandatory* rehabilitation states. Many persons believe that voluntary and mandatory rehabilitation systems distinguish between injured workers having the opportunity or option to participate in rehabilitation versus being compelled or coerced into participation. This is not the case. Voluntary and mandatory rehabilitation systems refer to employers making rehabilitation available to employees as a benefit under workers' compensation. In mandatory states, any claimant who asks for rehabilitation services receives them at the expense of the employer or the workers' compensation insurance carrier. In voluntary rehabilitation states, employers may choose which, if any, injured workers will be offered rehabilitation services.

Another distinction is the type of workers' compensation insurance available to employers. In some states, there is a monopolistic workers' compensation fund, to which all employers must contribute. This fund operates much like an insurance company, setting premiums based upon the principles of loss and risk, and paying compensation to injured workers. In other states, private companies provide workers' compensation coverage to employers in accordance with state workers' compensation laws. Employers purchase policies and pay premiums to the company, much as they would for any other type of business insurance.

In all states there is one exception to these insurance systems. Companies that meet certain stipulations have the opportunity to *self-insure*, that is, provide compensation to injured workers directly through their own coffers. In most cases, these companies must demonstrate that they possess adequate resources to pay potential claims, and be able to hold these funds in a separate account called a reserve. The company that self-insures must also have the resources to comply with state workers' compensation statutes that address claim processes, payment of compensation, and other administrative issues. Self-insurance is a privilege for employers, and violation of the statutes can result in revocation of self-insured status by the state. Because of the funds that must be committed and the vigilance that must be paid to claim matters, most self-insured employers are large companies with vast human and financial resources.

Another distinction in workers' compensation is the administration of claims. Depending on the structure of the state workers' compensation system, claims may be filed and tracked through either the company, the state workers' compensation board, or by a third party administrator (TPA). Each claim is handled by a claims representative, who determines the veracity of the claim; tracks the claim from injury to final resolution; and makes decisions concerning payment of bills, allowance of services, and payment of compensation in accordance with state workers' compensation statutes. It is the claims representative who will often make the decisions pertinent to the course of rehabilitation, such as whether rehabilitation will be offered, what proprietary company will provide the services, and which types of services will be included in the rehabilitation plan.

The TPA merits additional comment. TPAs are companies that provide human resource management to employers on a fee-for-service basis. The TPA may deal with any one of a number of benefits issues for companies aside from workers' compensation, including payroll, retirement, unemployment compensation, leave time, and other concerns. It is important for the rehabilitation counselor in proprietary rehabilitation to understand that a particular claims adjuster at a particular TPA may be performing a variety of duties that are not related to workers' compensation.

Finally, the discussion of the structure of the proprietary rehabilitation system comes to the proprietary company itself. There is a vast variance in the structure of these companies and the services that they provide. Companies may range from a sole private contractor to small businesses to large companies that are national in scope. Most companies are independent and seek referrals through marketing, just as any business would attempt to locate customers and sell its product or service. Some insurance companies, however, have in-house rehabilitation units serving injured workers with claims against the company. These rehabilitation units can be vast enterprises in and of themselves (Siefker, 1992).

Proprietary companies maintain their existence through the receipt of fees for services. Claims adjusters are under no obligation to provide referrals for services to any particular proprietary company. Therefore, reputation for quality, a businesslike appearance and manner, and maintenance of good personal and professional relationships with insurance companies, TPAs and their representatives are critical for proprietary companies and those who work for them. Competition for referrals may be extreme.

Rehabilitation Philosophy

Within the state-federal VR system, the rehabilitation process follows a well-standardized course. Individuals with disabilities enter the system through an application for services, followed by determination of eligibility, rehabilitation planning, delivery of services, and job placement and follow-up services. Eligibility is determined through 1) the presence of a physical or mental disability that presents a significant barrier to employment (with priority given to individuals with the most significant disabilities), and 2) the assumption that the person with a disability could benefit from rehabilitation services (Rubin & Roessler, 1995). Documentation of the criteria related to these issues is accomplished through a review of records or, if necessary, evaluation by medical and human service professionals. This sometimes involves an extensive vocational evaluation (Corthell & De Groot, 1987).

When an individual has been found eligible for services, a rehabilitation plan is completed. This plan includes a vocational goal (usually the occupation which the individual will pursue upon completion of services), together with the rights and responsibilities of the individual and the agency. The plan indicates the services that will be delivered to assist the individual in achieving his or her vocational goal, time-lines for services, and service costs. The philosophy that guides rehabilitation planning is often referred to as maximization of potential (Rubin & Roessler, 1995; Wright, 1980).

Within proprietary rehabilitation, individuals enter the system because they have sustained an injury or illness that prevents them from performing the occupation which they held at the onset of the medical condition. If the injury is sustained in the course of employment, it is a concern of the state workers' compensation system; if sustained outside of the work environment (such as a heart attack or non-work-related automobile accident), it may be a concern of the long-term disability insurance carrier. Individuals served in the proprietary system typically present with less severe injuries and illnesses that impose fewer functional limitations to a smaller scope of life activities when compared to consumers of state-federal VR services. In addition, practically all persons served through proprietary rehabilitation will possess a history of employment, with vocational skills and knowledge that have allowed them to locate and maintain employment in the past. The vocational development of the individual has likely been interrupted as a result of injury or illness. This means that services provided to facilitate a return to employment do not need to be as extensive, time-consuming, or expensive, and can build upon the injured worker's past experience and knowledge of the world of work. Services focus upon the identification of a new outlet for those talents and interests that the individual has developed during the course of his or her career, and are intended to return the injured worker to employment as quickly as possible.

Workers' Compensation Claims, Benefits, and Proprietary Rehabilitation Services

Workers' compensation comprises the larger number of claims in proprietary rehabilitation. Individuals who sustain injuries on the job must file a claim, or a formal request for compensation as the result of an injury. Minor injuries that result in little lost time from employment are referred to as *medical only* claims; that is, the only costs incurred by the workers' compensation carrier involve medical treatment. If the injury is severe enough to render the individual unable to work beyond a period of time (usually one or two weeks, depending upon state statutes), the worker is eligible for compensation of lost wages. The worker is then considered to have a *lost time* claim. While lost-time claims represent a smaller proportion of work-related injuries, they account for a much larger proportion of costs than medical-only claims. This is due to the necessity for continuing medical treatment as well as the payment of wage-replacement benefits during the time the worker is not working and recovering from the injury.

Workers' compensation in lost-time claims usually involves a progression of various types of disability benefits. The type of compensation received by an injured worker is classified as either partial or total, and temporary or permanent. When the worker is initially injured and unable to work during treatment or convalescence, he or she is eligible for *temporary total disability* (TTD) benefits. TTD is granted on the basis of the treating physician's determination that the worker may not resume employment for a certain period of time. When this period has passed, an extension may be granted on the recommendation of the treating physician according to the individual's medical status. The injured worker would then continue to receive compensation, until a plateau is deemed to have been reached beyond which the injured worker will not be expected to make additional physical recovery. This plateau is sometimes referred to as *maximum medical improvement* (MMI) or *maximum medical recovery* (MMR). When this point has been reached, the individual will no longer receive TTD benefits, as any residual effects (i.e., disability) from the injury are no longer temporary, but permanent in nature.

During this period of the workers' compensation process, rehabilitation has traditionally been limited to monitoring the claim status as well as consultation by rehabilitation professionals (traditionally, nurse case managers) with health care professionals as to the courses of action that might be taken to speed recovery. The course of the claim may become adversarial between the insurance carrier and the injured worker as the period of TTD lengthens. State statutes allow for insurance carriers to request an independent medical examination (IME) after the claimant has remained in TTD status beyond a certain peri-od of time (e.g., six months). The workers' compensation governing body will appoint an impartial physician to examine the claimant and the pertinent facts of the case, and make a determination of the indi-vidual's medical status and potential for additional medical recovery. Based upon the results of this examination, TTD compensation may be stopped, despite recommendations by the claimant's treating physi-cian to the contrary.

MMI indicates that an individual has recovered to the fullest extent medically possible; however, it does not imply that the individual will have regained the physical capacity necessary to return to his or her previous occupation. If the injured worker is not capable of returning to work after TTD is stopped, he or she will usually be eligible for *tem-porary partial disability* (TPD) compensation. The implication here is that the worker remains unable to perform his or her previous work, but should be capable of performing other types of employment. Because the search for new employment may be lengthy, TPD com-pensation sustains the worker through this job search. The worker may also receive TPD compensation after accepting employment in a new occupation if the new job pays a lower salary than the former occupa-tion. This type of TPD is usually based upon a percentage of the dis-crepancy between the old and new salaries and is paid as a supple-ment to the new wages. Unlike TTD, which has an arbitrary length, TPD is usually paid to the claimant for a predetermined period.

Traditionally, vocational rehabilitation professionals become involved with the injured worker when MMI has been achieved. While many persons are indeed capable of resuming their pre-injury occupations, others will have residual functional limitations that are significant enough to prevent return to employment. The knowledge, training, and experience of the rehabilitation counselor are critical in determining which vocational alternatives are available to the claimant.

The goal of vocational rehabilitation in workers' compensation is to return the worker to employment as soon as possible at a wage as sim-ilar as possible to that he or she earned in the previous occupation. To achieve this goal, the following hierarchy is considered:

1. Return to work, same job, same employer
2. Return to work, different job, same employer

3. Return to work, same job, different employer
4. Return to work, different job, different employer (Welch, 1979)

The return-to-work hierarchy serves a number of purposes for both the injured worker and the workers' compensation insurance carrier. The consideration of alternatives with the previous employer allows the most appropriate occupations and work environments for a particular claimant to be considered first. The same or similar work in the same or similar environment will require the least adjustment on the part of the injured worker, and therefore will increase chances for successful reintegration into employment. If this cannot be achieved, occupations within the local labor market in general are the next consideration, with an emphasis on occupations that require similar skills and that are located in similar work environments. The emphasis upon past work and use of learned vocational skills in this way leads to timely resolution of the insurance claim. Extensive retraining programs are a relatively rare consideration, because they tend to increase the length of time that the claim is active, are costly, and require extensive job placement services upon completion of training.

The rehabilitation professional uses a wide variety of skills and techniques to assist the injured worker through the return-to-work hierarchy. Analysis of jobs to determine their appropriateness to the workers' functional abilities and skills is probably the most pertinent of these tools. Assisting the injured worker in job-seeking skills training is another critical element of the proprietary rehabilitation counselor's function, as the worker may be searching for employment for the first time in many years, and these skills may have eroded over time. Finally, the rehabilitation counselor must be able to communicate with the injured worker, the employer, the claims adjuster, the physician, and others involved in the claims and rehabilitation process to ensure that actions taken are appropriate and that potential alternatives for employment are not inappropriately dismissed.

There are two other forms of workers' compensation benefits that deserve mention. *Permanent partial disability* (PPD) is usually a lump-sum award that is based upon the loss of use in body function resulting from an injury, and is determined in one of two ways. First, the injury may be scheduled. Scheduled injuries relate to the loss or total loss of use of a particular body part, with each body part being assigned a set monetary award. Secondly, in situations where no actual loss of a body part or its total function is involved, a physician will make a determination (based upon standardized guidelines) for the percentage of body function impaired or lost as a result of the injury. Interestingly, any claim, whether it is lost-time or medical-only, may be eligible for PPD consideration. The issue of PPD is strictly medical in nature, and the proprietary rehabilitation counselor usually does not become involved in this type of compensation.

The other type of permanent disability compensation, *Permanent total disability* (PTD), may actively involve the vocational rehabilitation professional. As the term implies, PTD means inability of the worker to ever perform any type of gainful employment. Decisions about the veracity of PTD claims usually involve a combination of medical, psychological, vocational, and socioeconomic factors. Because such awards continue over the duration of the life of the injured worker, they are a major concern for insurance carriers. The rehabilitation counselor often becomes involved in the resolution of PTD issues as a vocational expert—an individual who provides an opinion of the vocational potential of the claimant for the claimant, the employer, or for the adjudicating body that will determine the veracity of the claim. The opinion of the vocational expert can be subjected to rebuttal by the opposing side in the action, and experts themselves may be called to testify in depositions or in a courtroom. Therefore, the vocational expert must be experienced, knowledgeable in vocational theory and information, familiar with the claimant and his or her history, and proficient in both written and verbal communication.

Rehabilitation for claimants under long-term disability insurance, the other major source of referrals for vocational services in the private sector, will follow a course similar to that present with workers' compensation claimants. In many cases, however, rehabilitation may be delayed for two years or more after the injury. Often in long-term disability cases, return to the original job has been ruled out during the first two years of disability. The rehabilitation counselor uses many of the same tools, such as transferable skills analysis and review of labor market information, to assist the claimant in identifying vocational alternatives compatible with his or her residual functional capacities. In addition, litigation issues, including the need for a vocational expert, may have a bearing upon the long-term disability rehabilitation referral.

Proprietary rehabilitation has developed over the last three decades so that it now encompasses a profession with its own definitive structure, process and purpose that is vastly different from the traditional state-federal VR program. Although there are clear differences in the systems, both systems and the rehabilitationists who work within them share many similarities in regard to training and certification, professionalization, and the ultimate goal of assisting persons with disabilities (regardless of their cause or origin) in attaining vocational adjustment.

CHANGE WITHIN PROPRIETARY REHABILITATION: NEW DIRECTIONS FOR THE TWENTY-FIRST CENTURY

As the twenty-first century begins, proprietary rehabilitation faces a number of challenges. Most of these challenges come from changes in the perception and management of workforce injuries, yet other issues will impact directly upon the practices and procedures used by rehabilitation counselors in the private sector. The following section identifies some of the critical issues for proprietary rehabilitation as the new millennium commences.

Emerging Issue I: Changes in Occupational Information

In the previous sections of this chapter, the rehabilitation process in proprietary settings was discussed, with emphasis placed upon the return-to-work hierarchy and its critical influence upon vocational decision making. This hierarchy emphasizes vocational alternatives that are more similar in relation to the work environments and work activities in which an injured worker has previously engaged. The process by which the similarity of work environments and work activities are examined is called *transferable skills analysis*, and the information gained from such a procedure is usually critical in return-to-work planning.

The investigation of transferable skills is essential not only to the goal of swift return to work in the most appropriate job for the injured worker, but it also has strong grounding within vocational adjustment theory. Dawis, England, and Loftquist (1964) described the process by which workers adjust to work environments in the Minnesota Theory of Work Adjustment (MTWA). The MTWA indicates that individuals have differing needs that must be met by participation in work. These needs may be intrinsic (e.g., interest in the work performed, compatibility with coworkers) as well as extrinsic (e.g., salary and benefits). Conversely, the MTWA holds that 1) a work environment will demand that the worker be capable of meeting the expectations demanded of the work that is required, and 2) the worker must have adequate work behaviors and attitudes for the place of employment. The extent to which the worker"s needs are met by the work environment is referred to as *job satisfaction*, while the ability of the worker to meet the demands of the work environment is referred to as *satisfactoriness*. If both job satisfaction and satisfactoriness exist between the worker and the job, the result is *tenure*, or continued employment.

The return-to-work hierarchy, by prioritizing vocational alternatives that are most congruent with those which the worker has performed in the past and which are in similar work environments, allows for identification of vocational alternatives in which the worker may be capable of attaining tenure. The investigation of the similarity of occupations, therefore, is a critical component of the assessment of transferable skills.

To measure occupational similarity, it is necessary to investigate the dimensions of work. Traditionally, the state of the art of this concept has involved the use of the *Dictionary of Occupational Titles* (DOT) (United States Department of Labor, 1991a). Occupations in the DOT are defined according to a number of occupational categories through job analysis, and various characteristics of jobs and the workers who perform them are available for review.

The dimensions of work are defined in the *Revised Handbook for Analyzing Jobs* (United States Department of Labor, 1991b) and consist of two domains: *Worker traits*, or capacities for performing work which are brought to the work environment by the worker, and *work characteristics*, which define the activities and outcomes of work that is performed by the worker in the occupation. Worker traits include such dimensions as aptitudes, interests, academic abilities, training and education, temperaments, and physical capacities and environmental tolerances. The two most critical work characteristics in the consideration of transferable skills are the work field, which can be thought of as the general type of activity performed by the worker in a particular job, and materials, products, subject matter, and services (MPSMS), or the product or service produced as a result of the worker"s labor.

Transferable skills analysis investigates the worker"s demonstrated capacities for the various worker traits through a three-step process. First, the occupations that the worker has performed in the past are identified according to DOT definitions and codes. Secondly, the worker traits required for workers in these occupations are identified, and a profile is developed that indicates the worker"s demonstrated capacities in previous employment. Finally, the profile is adjusted according to changes brought about by the injury or illness; typically, it is the physical capacity or environmental tolerances of the worker that must be considered in the adjustment of the profile. Psychometric testing may also be used to adjust certain portions of the profile. Tests specifically intended for use with the DOT database (e.g., the General Aptitude Test Battery) are particularly important indicators of when and how the worker trait profile can be adjusted.

The adjusted profile is then compared to other occupations in the DOT database that have worker trait requirements within injured workers' residual worker trait capacities. The matching of worker trait profiles does not, however, indicate transferability of work skills from one job to another without consideration of the characteristics of the job being considered as a placement alternative. Work skills are learned behaviors, whereas worker traits reflect capacities for the worker to learn or develop skills. To identify the skills of a job, and whether the worker can actually perform that job, the work field and MPSMS must be considered. Work field and MPSMS are indicated by three-digit codes, and the transferable skills analysis software will search first for worker-trait-appropriate occupations within same or similar work field and MPSMS categories. Jobs with unrelated work field and MPSMS categories are identified secondarily. By focusing upon occupations that require similar worker activities to produce similar products, vocational alternatives requiring less adjustment (either in the form of environment or skill acquisition) can be identified and emphasized to assist the worker in returning to work. This allows for a greater chance of the worker being successful in his or her occupation, as well as for returning the worker to employment more quickly with as little time-consuming skill remediation (i.e., retraining).

The procedure of performing transferable skills analysis in this format was first proposed by Fine (1957) and subsequently refined by

Field and Weed (1989) in the development of the Vocational Diagnosis and Assessment of Residual Employability (VDARE). Manual methods of performing transferable skills analysis with the DOT database, especially the VDARE, were standard until the mid to late 1980s, when the microcomputer became commonplace and software was developed that allowed the user to construct the worker trait profile and perform the search much more quickly and efficiently than through manual methods. There are now several commercially available software packages dedicated to performing transferable skills analysis (Brown, McDaniel, Couch, & McClannahan, 1994).

The occupational information database has centered upon the DOT since the great depression (Smith, 1991), and although significant changes in its structure have taken place over the years, the basic format for presenting functional information pertinent to rehabilitation counseling has remained stable since the 1950s. The information found in the DOT has served the rehabilitation profession well through the years. However, significant changes will come in the new millennium for which rehabilitation counselors must prepare. The United States Department of Labor will replace the venerable DOT with the Occupational Information Network (O-Net; United States Department of Labor, 1998) in the first years of the new century. The O-Net will form the basis for the Department of Labor's occupational database in the future, and studies to validate this new occupational information system are currently in progress.

There are several advantages to the O-Net as compared to the DOT. The new system may be accessed through the Internet or CD-ROM, which will allow quicker updating and more widespread access by users than the current DOT database. The DOT is typically accessed through several bulky volumes and was updated only infrequently (the most recent version was published in 1991; before that, the most recent update was in 1978). The Department of Labor will be able to present updates and additions to occupational information much more quickly than had been possible in the past, which has been a weakness of the previous system. Also, because the O-Net is conceived as an online system, cross-walking to other databases (e.g., labor market statistics or educational information) will be accomplished much more easily than with the DOT.

The number of worker traits and the scaling of traits will increase significantly with the O-Net, necessitating changes in how vocational counselors view of the world of work. This will become particularly critical for proprietary rehabilitation counselors who must convert to the O-Net and use this information to analyze skill transferability. In fact, there seem to be several factors impacting upon transferability that must be resolved:

1. Because the component factors of work and their scaling have changed, the ability to cross-walk between psychometric tests and worker traits must be reconsidered. Tests such as the General Aptitude Test Battery that were directly relevant to the DOT appear to have little direct relationship to the O-Net. Rehabilitation professionals will need to consider which tests bear relationships to which worker traits.

2. The increase in the number of traits to consider in job selection could impact greatly upon the transferable skills analysis process. Because matches of traits may need to occur on many more levels than was necessary in the DOT, this could reduce the number of matching occupations that a transferable skills analysis will produce.

3. Physical demand characteristics do not appear to be stringent enough for use in rehabilitation counseling, where the consideration of physical capacities is paramount in vocational planning. The concrete, specific scales for strength and other physical factors of occupations, which were a valuable part of the DOT, appear to be confused and clouded in O-Net definitions. If the O-Net is to become a useful tool in rehabilitation counseling, the Department of Labor must resolve this issue.

4. The classification of jobs according to work field and MPSMS categories, which has formed the basis for transferable skills analysis since the 1950s, appears to have been abandoned in the O Net. While cross-walks to various other occupational classifications are provided in the O-Net, there is no mention of these two classifications. If indeed occupations are no longer to be classified according to work fields and MPSMS, new guidelines for the consideration of transferable skills between occupations must be determined.

5. Job analysis techniques used in rehabilitation have been based upon the criteria used to develop the DOT database, as indicated in publications such as the *Revised Handbook for Analyzing Jobs* (U.S. Department of Labor, 1991b). No companion publication to

the O-Net relating to job analysis procedures has yet appeared. If rehabilitation counselors are to use the new technology and nomenclature in their analysis of occupations, the Department of Labor must provide some insight into methods for doing so.

Emerging Issue II: Disability Management in the Workplace

Occupational injury is costly, both for employers and employees. In the early 1990s, the cost of workplace injury was increasing at an alarming rate; in 1990, estimated costs per workers' compensation case had escalated to nearly $20,000, and workers' compensation premiums had risen by 23 percent during the 1980s and early 1990s. Among the reasons for these spiraling costs was a poor rate of successful rehabilitation among injured workers, with approximately one quarter of injured workers failing to return to gainful employment after the provision of rehabilitation services (Niemeyer, 1998). Although many of the reasons cited for the increase in costs have been tied to more costly health care practices, the lack of responsiveness of the system to the needs of the injured worker has also been cited. Traditionally, the injured worker has been viewed as the source of failure of rehabilitation services. However, more recently the insufficiency in the structure of the system surrounding the injured worker has received greater scrutiny (LeClair & Mitchell, 1992).

The injured worker may be faced with a sudden set of challenges from external entities that can compromise not only the physical process of healing from the injury but also his or her socioeconomic and psychological security and well-being. The injured worker may have had very little education as to the means by which compensation and medical payment will be provided, and he or she can become lost in the multitude of forms and procedures necessary in the workers' compensation environment. Meanwhile, responsibilities must be met, and improper procedures translate to delays in compensation.

Aside from problems that can arise from poor knowledge of claims practices, the impact of workplace injury and illness upon the injured worker"s social and family roles can be significant. The injured worker becomes separated from the workplace, where work meant not only economic security but also opportunities for enhancing self-efficacy and social interaction. As the period of disability lengthens, the family structure of the worker with a disability may change significantly as spouse and children assume new roles within the family system.

Faced with these burdens, the injured worker may feel it necessary to seek legal assistance with the claim, thereby causing the management of the injury to become more litigious and adversarial in nature. The injured worker may suffer anxiety over the loss of security, and self-esteem may decrease as feelings of helplessness over the actions of the employer, the workers' compensation system, and the medical community mount. All these factors increase the likelihood that the injured worker will begin to consider himself or herself incapable of ever working in any capacity again. Rehabilitation, which is often delayed until healing has been completed, may be of little use in changing the effects of the system after this mindset has become cemented with the injured worker. In an effort to take control of the process of occupational disability and prevent the detachment of the injured employee from his or her identity as a worker, many employers have taken the initiative to create disability management programs for employees who become disabled.

Disability management attempts to minimize the effect of impairments arising from disability on a worker's capacity to function in a work setting (Shrey, 1995). Disability management programs manage the interaction between the worker and workplace so that productivity may be maximized while costs associated with disability are reduced. Disability management may consist of various proactive services to prevent occupational disability (both work and non-work-related), but it also may include reactive programs to assist injured workers in becoming reintegrated into the world of work. Examples of proactive disability management programming include wellness programs, safety awareness, and injury/illness prevention. Reactive programs include employee assistance programs, outplacement, transitional work programs, and work hardening (Sawisch, 1989).

Early return-to-work programs are perhaps of greatest concern to the proprietary rehabilitation counselor. These programs attempt to bring the injured worker to the workplace as soon as possible after an injury has occurred and may involve a variety of techniques (e.g., job modification, job restructuring). When more extensive modifications are necessary to return the worker to the workplace, a *transitional work program* may be considered for the injured worker. The transitional work program, which is usually limited to a two- to three-month period, attempts to match the worker"s current physical capacities with the physical requirements of occupational duties that are present in the workplace (not necessarily the injured worker"s previous position). As injured workers gain strength and endurance, the amount of time spent on the job during the day is increased and duties may be changed in accordance with increased physical capacities. The ultimate goal is the eventual restoration of the injured worker in the previous position, with or without reasonable accommodations. Transitional work programs differ from dubious light-duty programs because they are 1) time limited and 2) often place the light-duty employee in a precarious position in relation to collective bargaining agreements (which can allow the worker to be "bumped" from the light-duty job by workers with greater seniority; Shrey, 1998).

Rehabilitation in the workplace may require a variety of services such as job analysis, physical capacity testing, physical reconditioning (done in the workplace when possible), job modification and ergonomic considerations, and modified work assignments (King, 1998). Most of these services can be provided by properly trained and experienced rehabilitation counselors, and many proprietary rehabilitation companies have capitalized on these business opportunities by branching into disability management. In addition, as disability management programs and early return-to-work become more common, there will be an increasing need for trained and knowledgeable individuals to serve as on-site case managers within industry so that programs can be properly coordinated (Shrey, 1998). Rehabilitation counselors, particularly those with experience in the management of work-related disability, will be ideal candidates for these positions.

Emerging Issue III: Managed Care

The health care industry in the United States has undergone significant change in the last twenty years. Beginning with initiatives to control costs and monitor the quality of care within federal health care programs, the concept of managed care has entered the vocabularies of all those involved in the treatment of medical concerns. Vocational rehabilitation (and especially proprietary rehabilitation) is included within the group of affected professions.

Managed care models emerged from efforts to curb costs in the federal Medicare program. During the 1980s, Medicare developed a means of containing costs through determining average expenditures to be expected for various medical diagnoses. Hospitals were reimbursed on the basis of average costs, rather than for the total costs of treating the medical problem. Hospitals responded by eliminating costly and unnecessary services to ensure profitability. The Medicare program, in turn, realized significant savings and other state and federal health care agencies followed suit, as did private health insurance carriers (Taylor & Taylor, 1994).

Managed care organizations (MCO's) consist primarily of two types of organizations. The first, the *health maintenance organization* (HMO), uses a procedure called capitation to contain health care costs. With capitation, health care providers reap financial benefits through the limitation of more expensive medical treatment. The other type of MCO is *preferred provider organization* (PPO). The PPO consists of a network of medical specialists who have agreed to the PPO"s guidelines concerning fees for services and criteria for referral to specific types of medical specialty services, particularly the more expensive procedures (Beck, 1998).

The MCO has become a common phenomenon for nearly every person in the United States holding medical insurance benefits. More recently, many state workers' compensation systems have been implementing managed care plans to address the upward trend in the cost of workplace injury and medical care costs. For the proprietary rehabilitation counselor, it is the emergence of the MCO within workers' compensation that is of the gravest concern.

There are a number of issues which proprietary rehabilitation companies and the professionals who staff them must take into consideration. Because MCOs control a great share of the referral power within health care services, proprietary rehabilitation companies must change to meet the needs of the health care environment. Among these needed changes are clear definitions of services and how they can assist in the goals of the MCO; the ability to demonstrate that properly trained, experienced, and credentialed professionals will provide requested services; and the ability of the proprietary company to establish itself as a service provider within the various HMO and PPO structures (Beck, 1998).

THE FUTURE OF PROPRIETARY REHABILITATION:
ESTABLISHING EFFICACY

This chapter has described the environment of proprietary rehabilitation through identification of common practices and procedures together with a comparison to practices and procedures common in the state-federal VR program. Proprietary rehabilitation has become an established institution in the spectrum of health care and social service provision, and it has been able to adjust to changes in the environment in which it operates. This chapter has identified three principal challenges that will likely change the face of proprietary rehabilitation in the early years of the next millennium: changes in occupational information, the emergence of disability management, and the emergence of managed care.

There remains one unanswered question in this review: Why provide rehabilitation services to injured workers at all? Insurance systems such as workers' compensation were intended to provide indemnity and medical payments to the injured worker based upon the extent and duration of his or her inability to work and the need for medical attention. These systems were not intended to provide vocational rehabilitation, and the meshing of these goals has sometimes proven cumbersome (Berkowitz & Berkowitz, 1991). Many rehabilitationists would contend that vocational rehabilitation is the "right" thing to do–that the restoration of gainful employment should be paramount in issues of occupational disability–yet the insurance system provides other remedies for the loss of earnings sustained by an ill or injured worker. Why should employers or insurance entities wish to provide rehabilitation services in insurance cases?

The answer from a financial point of view is that vocational rehabilitation services are considered to be cost-effective when instilled into an insurance claim. Yet past research has shown that vocational rehabilitation is often ineffective (Niemeyer, 1998), and ineffective rehabilitation services add to case costs without providing case resolution.

Vocational rehabilitation services in the proprietary sector are based upon certain procedures and theories that are intended to resolve claims quickly in a cost-effective manner. New paradigms for rehabilitation (e.g., disability management, early return-to-work programs) are likewise based upon the premise that appropriate services will resolve claims more quickly and at a lowered cost to employers and insurers. Now, managed care has emerged as a factor to consider in proprietary rehabilitation. Managed care has been created in an effort to measure the necessity of health care services and to ensure their quality, with cost-effectiveness as a primary indicator of the success of a particular service.

Vocational rehabilitation must respond to the greater emphasis on economics by establishing its fiscal efficacy in the era of the managed care organization. Remarkably, the body of research into proprietary rehabilitation contains little in the way of specific research pointing to the cost-effectiveness of vocational rehabilitation services provided to insurance rehabilitation claimants. The tradition of cost-benefit analysis in rehabilitation has belonged to those who study the state-federal VR program.

The methodology of cost-benefits analysis is usually the realm of the economist, not the rehabilitation researcher. To perform the analysis, it is necessary to develop operational definitions of costs and benefits, and determine from which individual or entity's perspective (i.e., whose costs and whose benefits) these definitions should be derived. In addition, consideration must be made of capital that could have been gained by investing the funding of the rehabilitation program into other investments; this is usually referred to as the *discount rate*. In the state-federal program, costs have usually been defined as case service costs borne by taxpayers, benefits as increases in lifetime earnings of consumers, and a discount rate involving the current or projected rate of inflation over the course of the lifetime of consumers.

There have been a number of studies conducted to measure the cost effectiveness of rehabilitation in the state-federal system. The first large-scale studies of the program were conducted by Conley (1965; 1969), in which the cost benefit ratio was estimated at 3.3:1 to 10.9:1, depending upon any of a number of different methods of calculation. Bellante (1972) and Worrall (1978) confirmed the cost-effectiveness of the state-federal VR program by performing additional studies with similar methodologies. Many studies smaller in scope have also been published through the years which have provided a solid foundation for a conclusion that the state-federal VR program is indeed a worthwhile investment of taxpayer dollars.

During the early to mid 1990s, there were a number of papers published indicating a need for increased research activity concerning the efficacy of proprietary rehabilitation. Berkowitz (1990) indicated that although methodologies could be developed to conduct controlled studies of the benefits and costs of proprietary rehabilitation, studies performed by impartial third parties are practically nonexistent. Weed and Lewis (1994) prepared a review of many of the cost-benefit studies of rehabilitation in both the public and proprietary arenas and concluded that rehabilitation is indeed cost-effective. However, these conclusions were drawn primarily from a review of research conducted in the public sector with only one major study cited involving proprietary rehabilitation.

Since the mid 1990s, little has been accomplished in the way of research into this vital question. The shift in proprietary rehabilitation toward managed care and proactive disability management is based largely upon a rationale of reduced costs realized through greater numbers of injured workers returning to work more swiftly. Demonstration of this premise may be accomplished through efficacy studies, and the emergence of managed care should make available data that were previously difficult to obtain. In the meantime, research into the costs and benefits of proprietary rehabilitation remains one of the more underaddressed topics in the field of rehabilitation. The results of controlled studies in this area will, when eventually conducted, determine future changes in the structure of rehabilitation services for individuals with compensible injuries.

SUMMARY

This chapter has reviewed proprietary rehabilitation by comparing and contrasting it with the public VR program and giving a thorough description of insurance and claim practices upon which the proprietary rehabilitation process has been developed. The rationale for the differences in philosophy and practice between the two programs was provided. An understanding of these differences forms the basis for the development of skills in proprietary rehabilitation. The changes and emerging issues discussed in the latter part of the chapter are concepts with which both the experienced and the novice proprietary rehabilitation professional should become familiar in order to maintain professional effectiveness.

Proprietary rehabilitation has grown from nonexistence to a major force in the vocational restoration of individuals with disabilities in the United States over the last thirty years. While the two sectors share common grounding in many rehabilitation principles, the distinctiveness of proprietary rehabilitation from public rehabilitation can be seen in such areas as philosophy, service provision, and populations served. Proprietary rehabilitation continues to expand, and many beginning rehabilitation counselors may find themselves employed in this arena. Because it has traditionally been the mission of rehabilitation counselor education programs to prepare individuals for entry into the public program, many of the distinctive practices of proprietary rehabilitation may not be adequately addressed within rehabilitation curriculum. Rehabilitation educators should make efforts to include information about the proprietary sector in courses covering such topics as rehabilitation foundations, case management, vocational assessment, and job placement. In addition, rehabilitation counseling students anticipating employment in the proprietary sector should become familiar with insurance practice and state workers' compensation laws and practices. Sources for information include attorneys, labor unions, state workers' compensation boards, insurance companies, and professionals currently employed in proprietary rehabilitation.

New ways of defining work and new procedures relating to disability management and managed care have translated to new ways of thinking about the rehabilitation of injured workers. However, the concept of timely reintegration of the worker to the workplace has not changed. Rather, it has been validated by the development of these procedures, which enhance the timeliness of rehabilitation intervention. The changes and challenges to procedures within the proprietary system that have emerged over the last decade will continue to have an impact as the new millennium begins. These changes will likely lead to newer and more innovative services and practices in proprietary rehabilitation as more is learned about the effectiveness of services. Students, rehabilitation practitioners, and academicians will need to stay informed of these changes and their impact so that they may continue to be prepared to meet the needs of these persons with disabilities in the years to come.

REFERENCES

Beck, R. J. (1998). Case management and managed care. In R. T. Roessler & S. E. Rubin (Eds.), *Case management and rehabilitation counseling: Procedures and techniques* (2nd ed.; pp. 255-276). Austin, TX: Pro-Ed.

Bellante, D. M. (1972). A multivariate analysis of a vocational rehabilitation program. *Journal of Human Resources, 7*, 226-241.

Berkeley Planning Associates. (1987). *Private sector rehabilitation: Lessons and options for public policy.* Oakland, CA: Author.

Berkowitz, M. (1990). Should rehabilitation be mandatory in workers' compensation programs? *Journal of Disability Policy Studies, 1*(1), 63-72.

Berkowitz, M. & Berkowitz, E. D. (1991). Rehabilitation in the work injury program. *Rehabilitation Counseling Bulletin, 34*(3), 182-196.

Brown, C., McDaniel, R., Couch, R., & McClannahan, M. (1994). *Vocational evaluation systems and software: A consumer's guide.* Menomonie, WI: Materials Development Center.

Conley, R. W. (1965). *The economics of vocational rehabilitation.* Baltimore, MD: Johns Hopkins Press.

Conley, R. W. (1969). A benefit-cost analysis of the vocational rehabilitation program. *Journal of Human Resources, 4*, 226-252.

Corthell, D. W., & DeGroot, J. (1987). *Proprietary rehabilitation: A better understanding.* Menomonie, WI: Stout Vocational Rehabilitation Institute.

Dawis, R. V., England, G. W., & Loftquist, L. H. (1964). A theory of work adjustment. *Minnesota Studies in Vocational Rehabilitation,* Number 15. Minneapolis: University of Minnesota, Industrial Relations Center.

Decarlo, D., & Minkowitz, M. (1989). *Workers' compensation insurance and law practice.* Horsham, PA: LRP Publications.

Fine, S. A. (1957). A reexamination of "transferability of skills." Part II. *Monthly Labor Review, 80*(8), 938-948.

Field, T. F., & Weed, R. O. (1989). *Transferable work skills.* Athens, GA: Elliott & Fitzpatrick.

Gann, C., & Moreland, T. (1992). Introduction to insurance and workers' compensation. In J. M. Siefker (Ed.), *Vocational evaluation in private sector rehabilitation* (pp. 67-98). Menomonie, WI: Materials Development Center.

Growick, B. S. (1991). On rehabilitating injured workers in America today. *Forum, 5* (5), 11-18.

King, P. M. (1998). Work hardening and work conditioning. In P. M. King (Ed.), *Sourcebook of occupational rehabilitation* (pp. 257-273). New York: Plenum Press.

LeClair, S., & Mitchell, K. (1992). *Rehabilitation in industry: Staff mentoring and development program resource manual.* Worthington, OH: National Industrial Rehabilitation Corporation.

Niemeyer, L. O. (1998). Health care reform. In P. M. King (Ed.), *Sourcebook of occupational rehabilitation* (pp. 69-81). New York: Plenium Press.

Obermann, C. E. (1965). *A history of vocational rehabilitation in America.* Minneapolis, MN: T. S. Dennison.

Rasch, J. D. (1985). *Rehabilitation of workers' compensation and other insurance claimants.* Springfield, IL: Charles C. Thomas.

Rubin, S. E., & Roessler, R. T. (1995). *Foundations of the vocational rehabilitation process* (4th ed.). Austin, TX: Pro-Ed.

Sawisch, L. P. (1989). Workers compensation: Strategies for lowering cost and reducing worker suffering. In E. M. Welsh (Ed.), *Creating a context for disability management.* Fort Washington, PA: LRP Publications.

Shrey, D. (1995). Worksite disability management and industrial rehabilitation. In D. Shrey & M. Lacerte (Eds.), *Principles and practices of disability management in industry* (pp. 3-53). Winter Park, FL: GR Press.

Shrey, D. (1998). Effective disability management programs. In P. M. King (Ed.), *Sourcebook of occupational rehabilitation* (pp. 389-409). New York: Plenium Press.

Siefker, J. M. (1992). What is the difference between public and private sector rehabilitation? In J. M. Siefker (Ed.), *Vocational evaluation in private sector rehabilitation* (pp. 1-30). Menomonie, WI: Materials Development Center.

Smith, B. E. (1991). *Evolution of job analysis and the dictionary of occupational titles (DOT) in the U.S. Employment Service: Historical perspective of the occupational analysis research program and overview of current methodologies.* Paper presented at the annual meeting of the International Personnel Management Association, Assessment Council, Chicago, IL. (ERIC Document 341 828).

Taylor, R., & Taylor, S. (1994). *The AUPHA manual of health services organizations.* Gaithersburg, MD: Aspen.

United States Chamber of Commerce. (1991). *Analysis of state workers' compensation laws.* Washington, DC: Author.

United States Department of Labor. (1991a). *Dictionary of occupational titles* (4th ed., revised). Washington, DC: U.S. Government Printing Office.

United States Department of Labor. (1991b). *The revised handbook for analyzing jobs.* Indianapolis, IN: JIST Works.

United States Department of Labor .(1998). *The Occupational Information Network (O-Net)* (On line). Available: http://www.doleta.gov/programs/onet

Weed, R. O., & Field, T. F. (1986). The differences and similarities between public and private sector rehabilitation: A literature review. *Journal of Applied Rehabilitation Counseling, 17*(1), 11-16.

Weed, R. O., & Lewis, S. H. (1994). Workers' compensation rehabilitation and case management are cost-effective: True or false? *Journal of Rehabilitation Administration, 18*(4), 217-224.

Welch, G. T. (1979). The relationship of rehabilitation with industry. *Journal of Rehabilitation, 45*(3), 24-25.

Worrall, J. D. (1978). A benefit-cost analysis of the vocational rehabilitation program. *Journal of Human Resources, 22*(3), 285-297.

Wright, G. N. (1980). *Total rehabilitation.* Boston: Little, Brown & Company.

INDEX

203

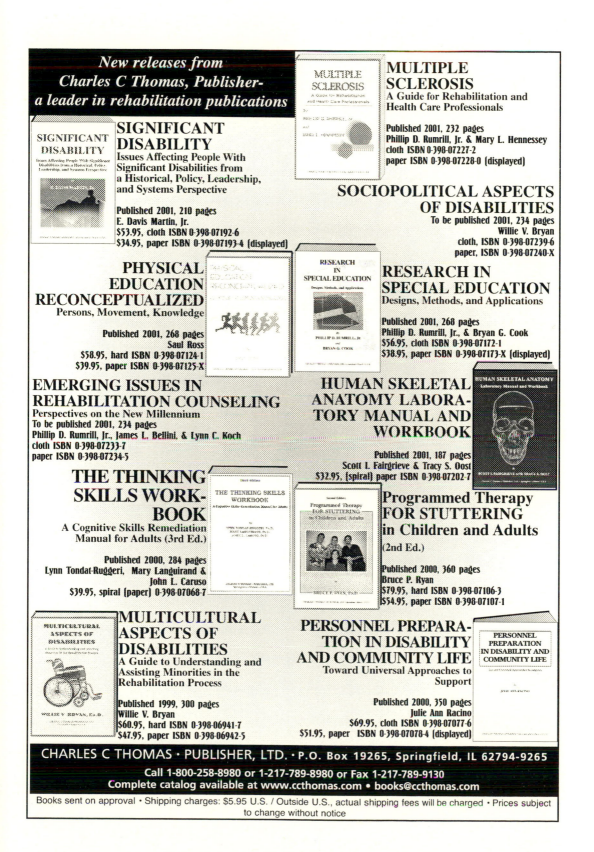

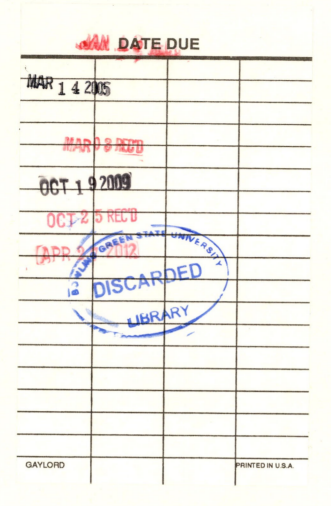